PERSONAL NAMES
AND NAMING

RECENT TITLES IN
BIBLIOGRAPHIES AND INDEXES IN ANTHROPOLOGY

Hispanic First Names: A Comprehensive Dictionary of 250 Years of
Mexican-American Usage
Richard D. Woods, compiler

Ecce Homo: An Annotated Bibliographic History of Physical Anthropology
Frank Spencer, compiler

PERSONAL NAMES AND NAMING

An Annotated Bibliography

Compiled by
Edwin D. Lawson

Bibliographies and Indexes in Anthropology, Number 3

GREENWOOD PRESS
New York • Westport, Connecticut • London

LIBRARY OF CONGRESS CATALOGING-IN-PUBLICATION DATA

Lawson, Edwin D., 1923-
  Personal names and naming.

  (Bibliographies and indexes in anthropology,
ISSN 0742-6844 ; no. 3)
  Includes index.
  1. Names, Personal—Bibliography. I. Title.
II. Series.
Z6824.L39 1987 [CS2305]   016.9294   86-31789
ISBN 0-313-23817-0 (lib. bdg. : alk. paper)

Library of Congress Catalog Card Number: 86-31789
ISBN: 0-313-23817-0
ISSN: 0742-6844

First published in 1987

Greenwood Press, Inc.
88 Post Road West, Westport, Connecticut 06881

Printed in the United States of America

The paper used in this book complies with the
Permanent Paper Standard issued by the National
Information Standards Organization (Z39.48-1984).

10 9 8 7 6 5 4 3 2 1

To ELSDON C. SMITH

CONTENTS

PREFACE

Onomastics is the area of study concerned with the content and process of all types of naming. Among its major concerns, along with literary names and placenames, is the subject of personal names. Personal names are the labels or tags that we use in identifying people or groups of people. We use first names, middle names, surnames, many types of nickname, and even numbers as names!

The reader of this volume will see that the subject of personal names involves many disciplines, from art (nicknames of famous artists) to zoology (use of animal names as first names, nicknames, and surnames). Not only is there a wide range in the disciplines that name study touches upon, but there are also wide cultural, ethnic, and geographical variations in how names are selected and bestowed.

To address these and other concerns Elsdon C. Smith published in 1952 his Personal Names: A Bibliography, a volume which contains over thirty-four hundred entries. The impact of this bibliography and Smith's numerous other published works, along with his contributions as a founder and first president of the American Name Society greatly stimulated scholarly work on the study of names. In the over thirty years since the publication of Smith's original bibliography, a tremendous number of books and articles on personal names has been published. However, while bibliographies by Smith have appeared in Names, and others appear annually in Onoma, there has been a need for an updated bibliography of personal names in a single volume.

Scope and Coverage

What I have tried to do is to supplement the earlier bibliography of Smith. Not included are items already in Smith, some of which have been reprinted since 1952 by Gale Research and other publishers. In general, if an item was unavailable through Inter-Library Loan or was very expensive to borrow, it also was not used.

Regrettably, non-English research contributions were not included unless an English translation was available. There are thousands of valuable contributions in other languages, but due to space and language limitations it was not possible to include them. For further information, the interested reader should consult <u>Onoma</u>, which has bibliographic material from all over the world. Somewhat related to this is my regret that format limitations excluded accent and diacritical marks in entries in the main section.

In order to build the bibliography of twelve hundred items numerous sources were consulted, including <u>Names</u>, <u>Onoma</u>, <u>Onomastica</u>, <u>Onomastica Canadiana</u>. The following abstract indexes were also used: <u>ERIC</u>, <u>MLA International Bibliography</u>, <u>Psychological Abstracts</u>, <u>Religion Index</u>, <u>Social Sciences Citation Index</u>, and <u>Sociological Abstracts</u>. It might be mentioned that at least two hundred additional items which seemed to be appropriate by title turned out upon inspection not be be suitable. About fifty books or articles were unavailable either because no library was willing to loan them or the cost for photocopying was judged prohibitive.

Arrangement

The entries are grouped alphabetically in the forty-eight subject categories as shown in the Table of Contents. Within each subject category, the items are listed alphabetically by author. The category for an item was chosen on the basis of what appeared to be the most salient feature relating to onomastics. However, since most entries have more than one possible category, cross-references are provided in the Subject Index.

Entries

The entries for book include the author, date, title, edition used, location and name of publisher, total pages or specific pages related to topic, annotation, and number of references.

For journals, the author, date, title of article, name of journal, volume, pages, annotation, and number of references are included.

Acknowledgements

Appreciation is expressed to the following libraries for their assistance: Drake Library, State University of New York at Brockport; New York Public Library, Library of Congress, Prendergast Library, Jamestown, N. Y.; and the State Education Department Library, Albany, N. Y. The following Canadian libraries were helpful, especially with British items: University of Guelph Library, Niagara Falls Public Library, and the Kitchener Public Library. Many libraries contributed to the success of this project by making books and journal articles available through Inter-Library Loan.

A number of individuals were also very helpful. They include Dr. Reinhold Aman, Editor of <u>Maledicta</u>; Dr. Grace Alvarez-Altman, Professor of Foreign Languages and Dr. George Cornell, Director of Libraries at State University of New York at Brockport; Richard Goff Smith, Reference Librarian at the University of Illinois, Urbana-Champaign; Alan Gailey, Acting Keeper, Ulster Folk and Transport Museum; Ralph Szymczak, Reference Librarian, Brandeis University; Valerie Fraser, <u>Christianity & Literature</u>;

Wilhelm (Bill) F. H. Nicolaisen, Department of English, State University of
New York at Binghamton; and Kelsie B. Harder, Department of English, State
University of New York at Potsdam.
      On my own campus, I am indebted to the Director of Libraries, John P.
Saulitis, for his strong encouragement and support, and also to the staff
of Reed Library.   Special thanks are due Margaret Pabst, in charge of
Inter-Library Loans, and her assistant, Janet Ferry, who were most patient
with my innumerable requests; Vincent Courtney who helped track down a
number of correct citations; and Gary Barber who answered a number of
reference questions and was most helpful with advice and encouragement.
Also, special thanks go to Dr. Edward N. Saveth, Distinguished Professor
Emeritus, who called my attention to several items dealing with historical
aspects of names.
      The staff of the Computer Center at Fredonia was most helpful in
preparing the data for classification and word processing.   I wish
particularly to thank Dr. Frederick D. Ullman, Director of the Center   and
Thomas H. Taylor, Academic Manager and those who helped in writing the
computer programs: Marcy L. Metivier, John F. McKenna, and Christine
Goggin.
      Finally, I would like to thank my wife, Irene Kentner Lawson, for
checking the entries in their final form.
      In any work like this, there are bound to be some errors.   I would
appreciate my attention being called to any of these. I hope that future
investigators will be assisted by this bibliography.

                                                    EDWIN D. LAWSON
State University of New York
   at Fredonia

SAMPLE BOOK ENTRY

```
1           2                    3        4                    5
[43.1.17]   Smith,  Elsdon  C.  (1969).  American  surnames.  Philadelphia:
Chilton, 370 p.
6        7
```

8
Gives introduction to surnames. Then, treatment of names developed as patronyms, from occupations, from nicknames (developed from description or action), and from sources. Listing of the 2000 most common surnames from records of the Social Security Administration. Approx 7500 names covered. 47 refs.
9

1. Item number
2. Author(s)
3. Year of publication
4. Title of book
5. Place of publication
6. Publisher
7. Number of pages (or specific pages referred to)
8. Annotation
9. Number of bibliographical references

SAMPLE JOURNAL ENTRY

```
1           2                 3        4
[34.1.5]    Seeman, Mary V.  (1983).  The  unconscious  meaning of  personal
names. Names, 31, 237-244.
4        5        6    7
```

8
Systematic discussion of the psychological purposes (conscious and unconscious) that names serve. Among these purposes are: commemorative (after a dead ancestor), connotative (where the name gives information about genealogy and social standing), induction (wished-for qualities), nicknames, and pseudonyms. Also discussed are name changes and rites of passage. Examples given of each type of name. 19 refs. French abstract.
```
                                                  9           10
```

1. Item number
2. Author(s)
3. Year of publication
4. Title of article
5. Name of journal
6. Volume number
7. Inclusive pagination
8. Annotation
9. Number of bibliographical references
10. Indication of foreign language abstract if present

1. NAMES, GENERAL WORKS

[1.1]   Adler, Max K. (1978). <u>Naming and addressing: A sociolinguistic study</u>. Hamburg: Helmut Buske Verlag, 281 p.
Discussion of the history of naming, magic and myth, taboos, lists of Czech names derived from nouns, forms of address. Scholarly presentation. Approx 360 refs.

[1.2] Cottle, Basil. (1983). <u>Names</u>. London: Thames & Hudson, 224 p.
A wide-ranging witty and entertaining coverage of many aspects of names. Three of the 10 chapters deal with words from names, first names, and surnames. 16 onomastic refs in these chapters.

[1.3] Dunkling, Leslie Alan. (1974; 1983; 1986). <u>The Guinness book of names</u>. Guinness Superlatives: Enfield, Middlesex, England, 1974, 256 p. (2nd ed., 1983; rev. and updated ed., 1986)
Wide coverage of many aspects of names and naming. Includes first name origins, fashions, nicknames, trade names. Many examples. Tables of popular names. Glossary of name terms. Index. 210 refs.

[1.4] Highet, Gilbert. (n. d.). <u>Lifetime labels</u>, Audio-Forum No. 23323. New York: Jeffrey Norton. (cassette recording)
Introduction to naming. Surnames are based upon 4 major sources: father (patronyms, ex., Johnson), occupation (Taylor), place (DuPont, "at the bridge"), and appearance (Grant, "grand"). First names often come from the Bible or the Calendar of Saints (John, Mary, Elizabeth, Charles).

[1.5] Hook, J. N. (1983). <u>The book of names</u>. New York: Franklin Watts, 288 p.
This general work, written with a light touch, has 15 chapters on first names and surnames. Among them are those that deal with: choosing the name for a child, fads and fancies, changing names, national origins of surnames, and unusual names. Approx 60 refs.

[1.6] Jacobs, Noah Jonathan. (1958). <u>Naming day in Eden</u>. New York: Macmillan, 159 p.
A light general introduction to onomastics. Begins with naming in the Garden of Eden and expands to different naming practices in other cultures and times.

[1.7] Lambert, Eloise & Pei, Mario. (1960). Our names: Where they came
from and what they mean. New York: Lathrop, Lee, & Shepard, 192 p.
A general book in a popular style. Covers first names, family names, thing
names (including animal names & trade names), and names that have become
words.

[1.8] McDavid, Raven I., Jr. (1967). Mencken's   onomastics.   Orbis
(Louvain), 16, 93-100.
Description and comment on the 10th chapter of the abridged version of
Mencken's (1963) The American language. This chapter deals with first
names and surnames as well as placenames and other proper names.

[1.9] Rudnyckyj, Jaroslav Bohdan. (1966). Typology of namelore.
Proceedings of the Eighth International Congress of Onomastic Sciences,
Amsterdam, pp. 433-441
Has some material on name change and also some on proverbs using names such
as "Like St. George who is always on horseback and never rides." 1 ref on
this material.

[1.10] Sherif, Muzafer & Cantril, Hadley. (1947). The psychology of
ego-involvements. New York: Wiley, 525 p.
Passages on p. 202 and pp. 352-356 have material on names. A description
of naming practices, acquisition, change, and change at marriage is drawn
from Holt [34.1.3]. Description of primitive cultures that have change of
name. Mention of close association of name and status which is a problem
in the Romeo and Juliet play. 3 refs to these pages.

[1.11] Scheetz, George H. (1981). An onomastic onomasticon. ANS Bulletin,
No. 65, 4-7.
Definitions of 52 terms used in onomastics such as anthroponym (a personal
name), aptronym (a name which is also an occupation (Hunt, Chase), eponym
(a person for whom something is named). 15 refs.

[1.12] Slovenko, Ralph. (1983). The destiny of a name. Psychiatry and
Law, 11, 227-270.
General article on naming practices. Extensive coverage of unusual names,
Dr. Coffin, a physician, Carl Bank, vice president of a bank; other
physicians: Belcher and Rumble in gastroenterology; Prettyman in plastic
surgery; and Strange in psychiatry; in law, judges named Wisdom and
Friendly; and in politics, men named Pepper and Pickle. 87 refs.

[1.13] Smith, Elsdon C. (1950). The story of our names. New York:
Harper, 296 p.
General introduction to first names, surnames, and nicknames. Other topics
include names in other countries, biblical names, and change of name.
Index. 61 refs.

[1.14] Smith, Elsdon C. (1966). The significance of name study.
Proceedings of the Eighth International Congress of Onomastic Sciences
Amsterdam, pp. 492-499.
Points out the contributions names have made to understanding culture,
history, religion, philology, social behavior, and business, 8 refs.

[1.15] Smith, Elsdon C. (1967). Treasury of name lore. New York: Harper
& Row, 246 p.
Covers about 175 categories of the social aspects of names and naming.
Sample topics include acronyms, acrostics, aliases, Armenian names,
metronymics, ruined names, and twins' names.

[1.16] Staff. (1962, December 29). U. N. names. New Yorker, 133-134.
A reporter's brief interview with delegates from Ceylon and the United Arab
Republic on their names.

[1.17] Stewart, George R. (1963). Names: In linguistics. Encyclopedia
Britannica, Vol. 16, pp. 62-63D.
Brief overview of personal names from cultural, historical point of view.
9 refs.

2. FORMS OF ADDRESS AND NAMES

[2.1] Brown, Roger. (1965). Social psychology. Chicago: Free Pr., 785 p.
Integrates the research (pp. 51-100) of Brown & Ford [2.2] on the forms of
address, John or Mr. Jones, in terms of the basic dimensions of
interpersonal relations. 43 refs.

[2.2] Brown, Roger & Ford, Marguerite. (1961). Address in American
English. Journal of Abnormal and Social Psychology, 62, 375-385.
Evaluation of patterns of address involving first name (John) vs. title
and last name (Mr. Smith), whether reciprocal or not. Research was based
on field work and the analysis of dramatic plays. Concludes that a person
uses the first name with an intimate of equal status or a subordinate;
title and last name are used with a superior or in an equal status
interaction with a stranger. 14 refs.

[2.3] Hook, Donald D. (1984). First names and titles as solidarity and
power semantics in English. International Review of Applied Linguistics in
Language Teaching, 22, 183-189.
Semantic solidarity refers to the reciprocal use of T (the familiar
pronoun) or V (the polite pronoun), the power semantic is the
non-reciprocal use of T or requirement of T. English cannot distinguish
solidarity and power by use of pronouns. Therefore, it uses first names
and titles as markers. The hierarchy from greater to lesser power is: (1)
title, (2) title + last name, (3) short title + last name, (4) last name
only, (5) first name only, and (6) names of endearment, diminutives.   10
refs.

[2.4] Kroger, Rolf O. (1982). Explorations in ethogeny with special
references to the forms of address. American Psychologist, 37, 810-820.
Gives the rationale for the study of forms of address (first name or title
+ last name) in social interaction as a non-laboratory and valuable way of
studying social behavior in a variety of contexts including
cross-culturally. 42 refs.

[2.5] Kroger, Rolf O., Cheng, Ken, & Leong, Ishbel. (1979). Are the rules of address universal? A test of Chinese usage. Journal of Cross-Cultural Psychology, 10, 395-414.
Testing a Chinese sample in Toronto provides confirmation of Brown's [2.1] concept of Invariant Forms of Address. 7 refs.

[2.6] Kroger, Rolf O., Wood, Linda A., & Beam, Thelma. (1984). Are the rules of address universal? II, Greek usage. Journal of Cross-Cultural Psychology, 15, 259-272.
Empirically tested with a Greek sample whether formal (e. g., sir) or informal terms (e. g., John) are used in a variety of family, work, and social situations. Confirms Brown's assertion [2.1] of the universality of patterns of address. 10 refs.

[2.7] Kroger, Rolf O., Wood, Linda A., & Kim, Uichol. (1984). Are the rules of address universal? III, Comparisons of Chinese, Greek, and Korean usage. Journal of Cross-Cultural Psychology, 15, 273-284. Similar to studies above of Kroger et al., results with Koreans in Korea and Canada showed no significant differences. In 3-way comparisons of Chinese, Greek, and Korean samples, the Chinese sample was more conservative. 12 refs.

[2.8] Kaufmann, Harry. (1973). Social psychology: The study of human interaction. New York: Holt, Rinehart & Winston, 557 p.
Discussion of forms of address and name, stereotyping of names (pp. 95-96; 352-353). Describes Kaufmann's shock at first hearing the excellent English of labor leader Cesar Chavez, having expected just the opposite. 1 ref.

[2.9] Slobin, Dan I., Miller, Stephen H., & Porter, Lyman W. (1968). Forms of address and social relations in a business organization. Journal of Personality and Social Psychology, 8, 289-293.
Research with employees of a large insurance company confirms the results of Brown and Ford [2.2] and goes on to conclude that forms of address and other forms of communication can give a picture of the general climate of an organization. 12 refs.

3. ALIAS NAMES

[3.1] Hartman, A. Arthur. (1951). Criminal aliases: A psychological study. Journal of Psychology, 32, 49-56.
Work with prisoners at Joliet, Illinois showed that 97% of the repeaters and 55% of the first offenders used an alias. The alias group had more personality difficulties. Discussion of use of an alias, change of name, or use of a pseudonym. 14 refs.

[3.2] Lazard, Didier. (1946). Two years under a false name (Jerome S. Bruner, Trans.). Journal of Abnormal and Social Psychology, 41, 161-168.
Story of a Jewish intellectual who changed his identity and lived underground in France during WWII.

4. ALPHABET POSITION AND NAMES

[4.1]   Autry, J. W., & Barker, D. G. (1970). Academic correlates of alphabetical order of surname. Journal of School Psychology, 8, 22-23.
Some observers have felt that individuals whose surnames begin with a letter early in the alphabet do better in academic work. To test this hypothesis, the Iowa Test of Educational Development was used with seniors in a high school in Texas. Of the 11 abilities measured (social science background, vocabulary, reading etc.), there were 22 correlations (11 for boys, 11 for girls). One correlation was significant at the .05 level (and this was in the direction opposite to the hypothesis), about what one would expect by chance. 5 refs.

[4.2] Dietrich, Richard V. & Reynolds, Larry T. (1973). The name is not the thing. Names, 21, 277-280.
While it has been asserted that there are more superior achievers among those whose surnames are in the first half of the alphabet, data from the Social Security Administration on frequencies of names compared with data from American Men of Science, Who's Who in America, and the National Union Catalog of Authors do not confirm this hypothesis. 10 refs.

[4.3] Felton, Gary S. (1975). Addendum to "The name is not the thing." Names, 23, 57-59.
Extended the work of Dietrich and Reynolds [4.3] to determine whether low achievers (academic dropouts) at Los Angeles City College had a pattern of surname initial letters which differed from that of the general population. Concluded that there is no relationship between surname first letter and low achievement. 8 refs.

[4.4]   Ring, Erp. (1981). Hat der Anfangsbuchstabe des Familiennamens wirklich etwas mit der Karriere zu tun? (Is there really a connection between the initial letter of a person's surname and his career?). Zeitshrift fuer Soziologie, 1980, 9, 285-289. (From Sociological Abstracts, 1981, 29, Abstract No. 81L5810; original article in German)
Concludes that people whose surnames begin with letters in the first third of the alphabet have a higher level of education. This is attributed to teachers paying more attention to people/names at the beginning of the alphabet.

[4.5]   Segal, Mady Wechsler. (1974). Alphabetical attraction: An unobtrusive measure of the effect of propinquity in a field setting. Journal of Personality and Social Psychology, 30, 654-657.
Trainees in the Maryland State Police Training Academy were assigned rooms and lockers by surname. Results indicate that this proximity had a greater effect on friendship choice than a wide variety of other characteristics. 12 refs.

[4.6] Williams, Stephen M. (1985). Alphabetical name-order and memory for sentences. Perceptual and Motor Skills, 60, 994.
This Northern Ireland study indicates that memory performance for simple items was better for those whose surnames were early in the alphabet. 1 ref.

5. BIBLICAL NAMES

Note: The Religion Index has hundreds of further items under a search for the word name in titles.

5.1. Old Testament

[5.1.1]   Abba, Raymond. (1962). Name. In George Arthur Buttrick (Ed.), Interpreter's dictionary of the Bible, Vol. 3, pp. 500-508. New York Abingdon Pr.
An overview of names in both the Old and New Testaments.   Included is coverage of the names of God, Jesus, and biblical figures. 12 refs.

[5.1.2] Archi, Alfonso. (1979). The epigraphic evidence from Ebla and the Old Testament. Biblica, 60, 556-566.
Cuneiform archives at Ebla (in what is now Syria) date back to the 3rd millenium BC. Discussion and comment on names ending in -il and -ya which are understood by some to refer to El or Yahweh, as well a other names. 75+ refs.

[5.1.3] Encyclopedia Judaica. (1972). 16 Vols. Jerusalem: Keter.
Has definitive entries for most Bible figures.

[5.1.4]   Goldman, Solomon. (1958). From slavery to freedom. New York: Abelard-Schuman, pp. 133-215.
Detailed, scholarly description and analysis of the various meanings and names of God associated with Moses. Hundreds of citations and refs.

[5.1.5] Griffiths, J. Gwyn. (1953). The Egyptian derivation of the name Moses. Journal of Near Eastern Studies, 12, 225-231.
Marshaling of linguistic evidence from a number of sources, Egyptian, Hebrew, Greek and others, leads to the conclusion that the name is of Egyptian origin. 80+ refs.

[5.1.6]   Key, Andrew F. (1964). The giving of proper names in the Old Testament. Journal of Biblical Literature, 83, 55-59.
Categorizes the patterns with 7 tables of about 100 names. 4 refs.

[5.1.7] Lachs, Samuel T. (1979). "Hadassah that is Esther." Journal for the Study of Judaism, 10, 219-220.
Hadassah is the Hebrew for myrtle. Suggests that in the revision of the original story, the myrtle which was associated with Aphrodite/Venus was introduced as the Hebrew name for Esther. 26 refs.

[5.1.8]   Millard, A. R. (1977). The Persian names in Esther and the reliability of the Hebrew text.   Journal of Biblical Literature, 96, 481-488.
After surveying the evidence presented by C. A. Moore, concludes that Hebrew scribes worked with care in transcribing foreign names into Old Testament Hebrew. It was Greek scholars who distorted the names. 35 refs.

[5.1.9] Murtonen, A. (1952). A philological and literary treatise on the Old Testament divine names, El, Eloah, Elohim, and Yahweh. Studia Orientalia, Societas Orientalis Fennica, Helsinki, 18, 105 p.
Exhaustive evaluation from sources where these names occurred in the

various languages of the Ancient Middle East (includes Ugaritic, Arabic, Hebrew, Old Aramaic, Akkadian, Amoritic, and others). Indexes of Bible references. 350+ refs.

[5.1.10] Patai, Raphael. (1959). Sex and family in the Bible and the Middle East. Garden City, NY: Doubleday, pp. 188-192, 268.
This brief section on naming comments on the origin of the names of about 35 Bible personalities such as Abner, Benjamin, and Gershom. Appropriate Bible citations are made. Concludes that in the majority of cases it was the mother who chose the child's name. 2 refs.

[5.1.11] Reik, Theodor. (1959). Mystery on the mountain. New York: Harper, 210 p.
A well-known psychoanalyst gives his evaluation of the various names of God in the Bible, with special reference to Moses in Chapter 29, The name ineffable, pp. 149-159. 18 refs on pp. 202-203.

[5.1.12] Stamm, Johann Jakob. (1972). Names: In the Bible. Encyclopedia Judaica, Vol. 12, pp. 803-806, 811-812. Jerusalem: Keter.
Brief systematic description of Hebrew names. 75+ examples. 7 refs.

[5.1.13] Taylor, John. (1963). Name: Personal names. In James Hastings (Ed.) Dictionary of the Bible, (rev. ed.), Frederick C. Grant & H. H. Rowley, (Eds.), pp. 643-644. New York: Scribner's.
Background material on naming in the Old Testament with reference to naming practices of modern Arabs.

[5.1.14] Zadok, Ran. (1981). Notes on the biblical and extra-biblical lexicon. Jewish Quarterly Review, 71, 101-117.
The increase of West Semitic names reported from recent research has led to the reinterpretation of some 45 non-Israelite names of nethinim (temple slaves) and slaves of Solomon. Another name, Cimber, is interpreted as possibly from Latin referring to a drunkard. Approx 57 refs.

5.2. New Testament: See also--5.1. Old Testament

[5.2.1] Arbeitman, Yoel. (1980). The suffix of Iscariot. Journal of Biblical Literature, 99, 122-124.
Critique and approving comment on Ehrman below. 10 refs.

[5.2.2] Ehrman, Albert. (1978). Judas Iscariot and Abba Saqqara. Journal of Biblical Literature, 97, 572-573.
Proposes that the name Iscariot means "red dyer." 9 refs.

[5.2.3] Fitzmyer, Joseph A. (1963). The name Simon. Harvard Theological Review, 56, 1-5.
Roth [5.2.5] contended that the name of the apostle Peter dominated over Simon because of the tendency of the then current Jewish practice to avoid the name Simon. Fitzmyer provides evidence that the name was greatly used. 12 refs.

[5.2.4] Fitzmyer, Joseph A. (1964). The name Simon--A further discussion. Harvard Theological Review, 57, 60-61.
A reply to Roth's reply [5.2.6] to Fitzmyer's reply above. 2 refs.

[5.2.5] Roth, Cecil. (1961). Simon-Peter. Harvard Theological Review 54, 91-97.
Presents the view that Simeon (Simon) had a nickname Kaipha (Aramaic for Rock). The name Simeon was not used at this time since it was borne by several patriotic leaders. Therefore, the name Kaipha (Peter) was left. 7 refs.

[5.2.6] Roth, Cecil. (1964). The name Simon--A further discussion. Harvard Theological Review, 57, 60.
Reply to Fitzmyer [5.2.3]. 2 refs.

6. BIBLIOGRAPHIES

[6.1] Allen, Irving Lewis. (1983). The language of ethnic conflict: Social organization and lexical culture. New York: Columbia University Pr., 162 p.
The extensive references (pp. 143-162) contain an excellent bibliography on epithet nicknames directed at ethnic groups. About 200 refs.

[6.2] Barnhart, Clarence L. (1967). Index. Names, 15, 245-340.
Index of articles, reviews, and notices which have appeared in the journal Names from 1953-1967 (Vols. 1-15).

[6.3] Dabbs, Jack A. (1953). Namelore in Latin America. Names, 1, 177-187.
Introduction. Helpful background information for the study of personal, family, and placenames in Latin America. 81 annotated bibliographic references.

[6.4] Dabbs, Jack A. (1954). Namelore in Latin America II. Names, 2, 234-248.
Continues previous annotated bibliographic material with about 200 entries, mostly in Spanish, and mostly placenames, but does include some work on personal names.

[6.5] Dabbs, Jack A. (1956). Namelore in Latin America III. Names, 4, 18-38.
Provides 465 annotated references, mostly Spanish, on aspects of personal, family, and place names in Latin America.

[6.6] Dabbs, Jack A. (1956). Name lore in Latin America 1954-1955. Names, 4, 168-176.
Continues annotated bibliographies with 52 sources on names, mostly in Spanish and mostly on surnames. Extensive listing of surnames covered.

[6.7] Harder, Kelsie B. (1982). Index. Names, 30, 235-329.
Index of articles, reviews, and notices which have appeared in the journal Names from 1968-1982 (Vols. 16-30).

[6.8]   Jensen, Gillian Fellows. (1980). On the study of Middle English by-names. Namn och Bygd, Tidskrift for nordisk ortnamnsforskning, 68, 102-115.
Critical evaluation of the work of a number of investigators including: Selten, Tengvik, and Jonsjo. 43 refs.

[6.9] Lawson, Edwin D. (1984;1986). Personal names: 100 years of social science contributions. Names, 32, 45-73; 34, 89-90.
A survey of over 260 contributions from the fields of anthropology, psychology, psychiatry, psychoanalysis, and sociology, as well as geography and history. Includes first names, alias names, hypocoristic (short names such as Bill), Jrs., nicknames, surnames, twin names, and unique names. Psychiatrists/psychoanalysts include Abraham, Freud, Kraepelin, and Reik; psychologists, Allport, Bruning, Busse, English, Garwood, Holt, and Zweigenhaft. 260+ refs.

[6.10]   MacDougall, Priscilla Ruth. (1981). Women's, men's, children's names: An outline and bibliography. Family Law Reporter, 7, 4013-4018.
A bibliography of name-change litigation from 1859-1981 at the state and federal levels. Includes 125 legal citations, about 25 selected readings, and about 50 informal and formal opinions of state attorneys general.

[6.11]   Markey, Thomas L., Kyes, R. L., & Roberge, Paul T. (1977). Germanic and its dialects: A grammar of Proto-Germanic, III, Bibliography and indices. Amsterdam: John Benjamins, 504 p.
A bibliography of over 8000 items, mostly non-English, with a number on personal names, some of which are in English.

[6.12]   Mieder, Wolfgang. (1976). International bibliography of explanatory essays on proverbs and proverbial expressions containing names. Names, 24, 253-304.
A collection of over 1500 citations from many sources relating to names in about 500 proverbial expressions such as "Abraham's bosom" and "robbing Peter to pay Paul."

[6.13] Sadowski, Cyril J. & Wheeler, Karen J. (1980). A bibliography on the psychology of names. JSAS Catalog of selected documents in psychology, 10(4), 86. (Ms. No. 2158).
Lists 84 theoretical, empirical, anecdotal, and popular reference items from psychology, sociology, and onomastics.

[6.14]   Singerman, Robert. (1977). Jewish and Hebrew onomastics: A bibliography. New York: Garland, 132 p.
Lists under appropriate topic or category 1195 reference sources. Also gives an index of Jewish surnames which appeared in Norbert Pearlroth's "Your Name" column in Jewish Post and Opinion, 1945-1976.   General subject and author index.

[6.15]   Smith, Elsdon C. (1953). Books in English on personal names. Names, 1, 197-202.
Review article commenting on over 50 books on names from William Camden's Remaines to Elizabeth G. Withycombe's Oxford English dictionary of christian names (see Smith [6.16], Nos. 437 and 565). 50+ refs.

[6.16] Smith, Elsdon C. (1965). Personal names: A bibliography, Detroit: Gale Research, 226 p. (Originally published in 1952 by the New York Public Library)
Over than 3400 references on names with complete citations plus a brief comment. Covers all areas of names and naming from animals to Bible to nicknames to psychology.

7.CHANGE OF NAME: See also--20. LAW AND LEGAL ASPECTS OF NAMES

[7.1] Alia, Valerie. (1985). Changing names: Clues in the search for a political onomastics. Onomastica Canadiana, 67(1), 25-34.
Gives examples of name-change among several groups (Inuit, Kurds, South Africans et al.) and with individuals such as Stokely Carmichael to indicate that name-change can be an act of political and social equality and is a component of social change. 17 refs.

[7.2] Ashley, Leonard R. N. (1971). Changing times and changing names: Reasons, regulations,and rights. Names, 19, 167-187.
Wide-ranging discussion of name-changing in many ethnic groups. Includes changes in England, France, Ireland, Germany, and the US. 38 refs.

[7.3] Ashley, Leonard R. N. (1975). Flicks, flacks, and flux: Tides of taste in the onomasticon of the moving picture industry. Names, 23, 221-280.
Comprehensive survey of name-change patterns of show business people from silent films to today. There are hundreds of examples and references to specific films.

[7.4] Broom, Leonard; Beem, Helen P., & Harris, Virginia. (1955). Characteristics of 1,107 petitioners for change of name. American Sociological Review, 30, 33-39.
A sample of 1107 petitions for change of name in Los Angeles was analyzed. There was a high percentage of Jewish name-changers. Among the non-Jewish petitioners, ethnic considerations appeared to play a minor role. Major considerations were familial or dissatisfaction with the name itself, either because it is difficult to pronounce or has humorous or obscene connotations. 10 refs.

[7.5] Champlin, Charles. (1985, April). A name by any other name would sell as sweet. Smithsonian, 16(1), p. 216.
Points out that years ago Hollywood stars such as John Wayne and Joan Crawford changed to those from their original names of Marion Morrison and Gretchen Le Sueur. Now, stars such as John Hodiak and Meryl Streep keep their names.

[7.6] Cohn, Werner. (1983). The name changers. Forum, 50, 65-72.
Discusses name-changing among Jews in the United States. Concludes that those who change theirs (to Anglo-Saxon ones) are more anxious about outward appearance; non-changers have more of a basic sense of identity. 5 refs.

[7.7] Davidson, Sara. (1974, June 2). Notes from the land of the Cobra. New York Times Magazine, pp. 36-38, 40-42, 44, 46.
Refers to change of name by Patty Hearst to Tania commemorating Tania, the German woman who had loved, and died for, Che Guevara.

[7.8] Drury, Darrel W. & McCarthy, John D. (1980).The social psychology of name change: Reflections on a serendipitous discovery. Social Psychology Quarterly, 43, 310-320.
One-third of the American students at the University of Copenhagen shortened their names. Willingness to do so showed positive attitude toward Denmark, satisfaction with stay, positive evaluation by Danes and change in self-esteem. 28 refs.

[7.9] Falk, Avner. (1975). Identity and name changes. Psychoanalytic Review, 62, 647-657.
Literature survey. Discussion of 2 Israeli case histories involving name-change and identity. Discussion of name-changing in Israel by emigrants from the Diaspora. Analysis of name and identity of Erik Homburger Erikson. 38 refs.

[7.10] Feldman, Carol G. (1976). Social and psychological dynamics of name-change among American males. Dissertation Abstracts, 36, 4753B. (University Microfilms No. 76-6567, 147 p.)
Pairs of brothers were analyzed where one had anglicized his surname and the other had not. Results indicated a significant relationship between economic conditions and name-changing. Other factors also evaluated.

[7.11] Freud, Anna. (1956). Special experiences of young children articulated in times of social disturbance. In Kenneth Soddy (Ed.), Proceedings of the International Seminar held by the World Federation for Mental Health, 1, 151-155.
Describes the case of a 3-yr-old Jewish girl who was underground in Holland during WWII. She was able to suppress her real name successfully for 3 years until the Liberation. Also, describes experiences of those (mostly Jews, presumably) who took French names to survive during the war and then had the problem of going back to their original identities. 1 ref. See also--Lazard [3.2].

[7.12] Goffman, Erving. (1963). Stigma: Notes on the management of spoiled identity. Englewood Cliffs, NJ: Prentice Hall, pp. 58-59, 64.
Contains a discussion of legal and illegal change of name; right to privacy regarding one's past and original name. 3 refs.

[7.13] Kang, Tai S. (1971). Name change and acculturation. Pacific Sociological Review, 14, 403-412. Chinese students at the University of Minnesota in 1967 who were name-changers showed better socialization, economic adjustment, and social control than non-changers. 6 refs. (article is not clear whether first names, surnames, or both were changed)

[7.14] Kang, Tai S. (1972). Name and group identification. Journal of Social Psychology, 86, 159-160.
Apparently the same study as above but without refs.

[7.15] Manfred, Frederick Feike. (1954). The evolution of a name. Names, 2, 106-108.
How one man was able to reconcile his original Frisian surname (Feikema) to an acceptable replacement.

[7.16] Maass, Ernest. (1958). Integration and name-changing among Jewish refugees from Central Europe in the United States. Names, 6, 129-171.
Comprehensive overview, background, classification, reasons for, and the various patterns of change of name done by the small percentage of those who did. About 75 refs.

[7.17] Mencken, Henry Louis. (1963). The American language (4th ed. & 2 supplements, abridged, with annotations and new material by Raven I. McDavid, Jr.). New York: Knopf, pp. 572-642.
The pages cited above cover most of Chapter 10, Proper Names in America. Mencken devotes systematic and thorough coverage of how ethnic groups such as German, Czechs, Norwegians, Jews, Armenians, Greeks, Blacks, and others changed both their first names and surnames in the process of becoming Americanized. Also included is a section on American Indians. 200+ onomastic references in these pages.

[7.18] Moger, Art. (1983). Hello! my real name is.... Secaucus, NJ: Citadel Pr., 159 p.
Has an introduction by comedian George Burns. A popular presentation on about 480 entertainers whose names were changed. Each entry has a photograph of the star with 3 choices as to the original name. There is a key. Included are Shirley Booth (Thelma Ford), Kathryn Grayson (Zelma Hedrick), and Boris Karloff (William Pratt). 2 refs.

[7.19] Rennick, Robert M. (1969). Hitlers and others who changed their names and a few who did not. Names, 17, 199-207.
There were a number of individuals in the United States with the surname Hitler or one similar. Many (most?) changed their name. Rennick was able to identify only one person who bore the name who was not Jewish and he was Adolf's nephew. 36 refs.

[7.20] Rennick, Robert M. (1970). The inadvertent changing of names by newcomers to America: A brief historical survey and popular presentation of cases. New York Folklore Quarterly, 26, 263-282.
Describes some of the circumstances of inadvertent name-changing by immigrants. Most name-changing by officials and immigrants themselves took place before the 1890s. Phonetic and shortening changes as well as other types of modification were made. Examples: Yankele > John Kelly, Balotnikov > Balot. Anecdotal stories and examples. 17 refs.

[7.21] Room, Adrian. (1981). Naming names: Stories of pseudonyms and name-changes with a Who's Who. Jefferson, NC: McFarland, 349 p.
Systematic coverage of name-change in 4 major sections: (1) name-change in general, (2) stories on name change of approx 700 individuals, (3) 40 lists of changed names along with the original names, e. g., Sarah Fulks to Jane Wyman, Ethan Allen to Fred Allen, and (4) Who's Who and Index with information on over 4000 names. Appendices include synonyms of Voltaire, Defoe, Lovers, Wrestlers, and Real Names that sound to some as if they might have been made up. 100+ refs.

[7.22] Smith, Elsdon C. (1969). Influences in change of name.   Onoma, 14, 158-164.
Gives 16 reasons for change of name such as: difficulties in spelling, prejudice, religious conversion, and demand of an employer.

[7.23] Smith, William Carlson. (1939). Americans in the making: The natural history of the assimilation of the immigrants.   New York: Appleton-Century, pp. 130-132.
Examples of change of name by immigrant Swedes, Lithuanians, Hungarians, Jews, and others. 22 refs.

[7.24] Staff. (1966, August 27). 's' Vonderful. New Republic, p. 7.
A New York City judge refused to allow a petitioner to add a 'von' to his name on the grounds that it was a title of nobility.

[7.25] Strauss, Anselm. (1959). Mirrors and masks: The search for identity. Glencoe: IL: Free Pr., pp. 15-18.
These pages have a few general comments on name-change and how status is acquired by name-change. 1 ref.

8. ETHNIC, NATIONAL, AND REGIONAL NAMES

8.1. Acadian

[8.1.1] Loustalot, Kenneth. (1972). Acadian names and nicknames. Attakapas Gazette, 7, 170-181.
Naming customs among the Acadians of Breaux Bridge and other Louisiana communities. Some first names listed are: Anatol, Honor, and L'Odias. Some of the 100 nicknames are: Zoonta, Pee Shoot, and Carencro. The 57 clan names include: Foston Monet, and Rouge. 4 refs.

8.2. African

[8.2.1] Adefenmi, Baba Oseijeman. (n. d.). African names from the ancient Yoruba kingdom of Nigeria. New York: The Yoruba Academy, 4 p.
Brief introduction. Listing of 36 male and 31 female names with phonetic pronunciation and English translation.

[8.2.2] Adzei, Kwaku. (1962). The meaning of names in Ghana. Negro Digest, 12(November), 95-97.
Brief description of naming customs; day names, proverbial names.

[8.2.3] Akinnaso, F. Niyi. (1980). The sociolinguistic basis of Yoruba personal names. Anthropological Linguistics, 22, 275-304.
Comprehensive introduction to the sociocultural and linguistic aspects of Yoruba. Many examples of different types of name; how each individual is named according to special circumstances. 26 refs.

[8.2.4] Akinnaso, F. Niyi. (1981). Names and naming principles in cross-cultural perspective. Names, 29, 37-63.
Comparisons of the naming systems of the Delaware Indians with the Yoruba. Concludes that personal names not only identify individuals but serve to

describe the individual named as well as the community and the past. Extended information on the Yoruba. 48 refs.

[8.2.5] Akinnaso, F. Niyi. (1981). On the syntax and semantics of nominal compounds in Yoruba names. Semiotic Scene, 7, 1-12.
Examination of "the syntactico-semantic structure and naming function of nominal compounds by analyzing a productive subset of Yoruba personal names." Several categories are described with examples such as Okeowo = oke + owo = "bag + money" and Akinade = akin + ade = "valor + crown." 14 refs.

[8.2.6] Akinnaso, F. Niyi. (1983). Yoruba traditional names and the transmission of cultural knowledge. Names, 31, 139-158.
Focuses on ritually motivated subtypes of Yoruba names, (1) Amunterunwa, where a child is born under unusual birth circumstances (Ojo, "child born with the cord around its neck"), (2), Abiku, given to a child believed to be a reincarnation of a parent (Kusaanu, "death was merciful") and (3) Eya, a child believed to be a reincarnated ancestor (Babatunde, "Father has returned"). Comment on the effect of Christianity and Islam on current naming practices. Many examples. 31 refs.

[8.2.7] Beattie, J. H. M. (1957). Nyoro personal names. Uganda Journal, 21, 99-106.
Naming customs among the Nyoro, a Bantu-speaking people of W Uganda. Many of the first names deal with themes of death (Alifaijo, "he will die tomorrow"), sorrow (Kanwijamu: "he comes in it"), poverty (Tibaiseka, "they do not laugh at it), and neighborly spite (Ndyanabo, "I laugh at them." 2 refs.

[8.2.8] Beidelman, Thomas O. (1971). Kaguru descent groups (East-Central Tanzania). Anthropos, 66, 373-396.
Research on the Kaguru. Discussion of clans and listings of associated names with meanings. 19 refs; 36 footnotes, some with additional refs; map.

[8.2.9] Beidelman, Thomas O. (1974). Kaguru names and naming. Journal of Anthropological Research, 30, 281-293.
Description of naming customs of the Kaguru of Eastern Tanzania. Children are not named until the 4th day. Boys receive a new name at initiation circumcision rites. Women receive teknonyms at motherhood. Funeral names are also assigned. Some Kaguru also adopt foreign names such as Musa (Moses), or Helen. 17 refs.

[8.2.10] Carter, George F. (1974). Nigerian onomastics. In Fred Tarpley (Ed.), They had to call it something (pp. 13-24), Publication 3, South Central Names Institute. Commerce, TX: Names Institute Pr.
Description of Ibibio male and female names in these categories: (1) day or season of birth, (2) notable event commemorated, (3) praise to God, (4) expression of social relations, (5) birth order, and (6) titles. 11 refs.

[8.2.11] Chuks-orji, Oganna. (1972). African names. Edited and with a commentary by Keith E. Baird. Chicago: Johnson, 89 p.
Alphabetical listing by sex of first names. Name entries include pronunciation, meaning, language, and country of origin. Commentary and discussion. 11 refs.

[8.2.12]   Daeleman, Jan. (1977). Proper names used with 'twins' and
children succeeding them in Sub-Saharan languages. Onoma, 21, 189-195.
Reports a number of observations in 45 Bantu languages and 9 non-Bantu with
regard to twins. Some groups use a stereotype personal name such as in
Ntandu, a Koongo dialect, where all first-born twins are called Nsiimba
("wild-cat") and the last-born, Nzuzi ("serval"). In some groups, later
siblings have special names commemorating the twins. 8 refs.

[8.2.13] DeCamp, David. (1967). African day names in Jamaica. Language,
43, 130-147.
Day names indicating sex and day of the week of birth came from Africa to
Jamaica in the 17th and 18th centuries. These 14 names survive as
disparaging common nouns giving support to the subordination of semantic
features to syntactic ones. Map. 17 refs.

[8.2.14] Dillard, Joey Lee. (1971). The West African day-names in Nova
Scotia. Names, 19, 257-261.
Discussion of the evidence for the traces and survival of West African day
names in Nova Scotia. 15 refs.

[8.2.15] Ekpo, Monday U. (1978). Structure in Ibibio names. Names, 26,
271-284.
Description of the naming customs of the Ibibio who live in SE Nigeria.
Children are named after kinsmen, non-kinsmen and 18 categories of events
(ex., pleasant, harmonious, twins). Many examples plus a table of 50 names
with meaning and appropriate sex identification.

[8.2.16] Ekundayo, S. A. (1977). Restrictions on personal name sentences
in the Yoruba noun phrase. Anthropological Linguistics, 19, 55-77.
Explanation of the grammatical aspects of the Yoruba (Nigeria) personal
naming system. The most important principle of Yoruba name construction is
"the condition of the home determines a child's name." Rules and
restrictions discussed. 11 refs.

[8.2.17] Hertzog, John D. (1971). Fertility and cultural values: Kikuyu
naming customs and the preference for 4 or more children. Rural Africana,
14, 89-96.
Explains the Kikuyu interest in having 4 or more children as a result of
the naming tradition in which the 4 grandparents are memorialized before a
child could be named after a favorite brother or sister. Similar practices
in other tribes. 16 refs.

[8.2.18] Iwundu, Mataebere. (1973). Igbo anthroponyms: Linguistic evidence
for reviewing Ibo culture. Names, 21, 46-49.
Igbo is the language of the Ibo, an ethnic group in Nigeria. Explanation
of how Igbo names express ideas, ex., Eberechukwu ("mercy of God"),
Objijiaku ("the home has wealth"), and Ndukaaku ("life surpasses riches").

[8.2.19] Jahoda, Gustav. (1954). A note on Ashanti names and their
relationships to personality. British Journal of Psychology, 45, 192-195.
The Ashanti, a tribe in Nigeria, give their children names based upon the
day of the week the child was born. Many people believe that the specific
day born determines a person's character. To test this notion, male
delinquents were compared with normals. Results confirm that those days
associated with Wednesday's child, "bad," did have more delinquents than
Monday's child, "cool," "day of peace." 5 refs.

[8.2.20] Johnson, Samuel. (1960). The history of the Yorubas (O. Johnson, Ed.). (first published, 1921) Lagos, Nigeria: C. M. S. Bookshops, pp, 78-89.
Description of the naming customs among the Yoruba. Children can have as many as 3 types of name: (1) the Amutorunwa, the name the child is born with (Oke, "curly-headed"), (2) the Abiso, christening name (Ogundalenu, "our home has been devastated by war"), and (3) the Oriki, attributive name (Ajamu, "one who seizes after a fight). 100 examples. Comment on naming practices.

[8.2.21] Kilson, Marion. (1968/1969). The Ga naming rite. Anthropos, 63-64, 904-920.
Reports on a people in Ghana. The child receives its name at a ceremony on the 8th day. The name is determined by sex and birth order among the mother's children. 22 refs.

[8.2.22] Kirk-Greene, Anthony H. M. (1964). A preliminary inquiry into Hausa onomatology. Zaria, Nigeria: Institute of Administration, 56 p.
Systematic description, pp. 1-11, of the naming practices of Muslims and Christians of the Hausa people of Northern Nigeria. Included are given names, father's name, occupational names, father's title, nicknames, and day names. Examples. 5 refs. on p. 55.

[8.2.23] Koopman, Adrian. (1979). The linguistic difference between names and nouns in Zulu. African Studies, 38, 67-80.
Zulu is a Bantu language which has 5 types of name: a personal traditional Zulu, a European, a nickname, a clan-name, and a clan praise-name. Analysis of 465 male and 312 female names in terms of structure. 13 refs.

[8.2.24] Madubuike, Ihechukwi. (1976). A handbook of African names Washington, DC: Three Continents Pr., 1976, 233 p.
Introduction. Discussion of the influence of Christianity. Description of the use of first names, middle names, nicknames, and surnames. Listing and description of names by 21 tribes and regions such as Igbo, Yoruba, Ivory Coast, Rwanda, and Zaire. Pronunciation guide. 6 refs.

[8.2.25] Mafukidze, Takawira. (1970, July). The origin and significance of African personal names. Black World, pp. 5-6.
Introduction to African naming. Some information on day names and surnames as well as ceremonies of name bestowal.

[8.2.26] Marshall, Lorna. (1957). The kin terminology system of the !Kung bushmen. Africa, 27, 1-25.
Description of the very complex naming system of this society in SW Africa. Among the customs: no surnames, sex-linking of names, parent and child cannot have the same name, children are always named for relatives, fathers have the right to name all children. 3 refs.

[8.2.27] Marshall, Lorna. (1966). The !Kung Bushmen of the Kalahari desert. In James L. Gibbs, Jr. (Ed.), Peoples of Africa. New York: Holt, Rinehart & Winston, pp. 243-378.
Describes naming customs of this tribe in SW Africa. First sons and 1st daughters are named after paternal grandparents. Other children for maternal grandparents, parental siblings, and other relatives. 43 refs.

[8.2.28]   Middleton,   John.   (1961). The   social   significance of Lugbara
personal names. Uganda Journal, 25, 34-42.
The Lugbara are a Sudanic-speaking people of the West Nile district.
Personal names are given by the mother. There are special names for twins.
Names fall into 4 categories: moral attributes of parents, those associated
with death, non-moral attributes of parents, and attributes of the child.
850 names listed. 1 ref.

[8.2.29]   Migeod, F. W. H.   (1917). Personal names among some West African
tribes. Journal of the African Society, 17, 38-45.
Some general statements about the naming processes for the tribes speaking
the Twi, Ga, Mende, Hausa, and other languages. 1 ref.

[8.2.30] Mohome, Paulus M. (1972). Naming in Sesotho: Its cultural and
linguistic basis. Names, 20, 171-185.
Description of naming customs in Sesotho, a Bantu language of southern
Africa, spoken by members of the Basotho tribe who live in Losotho. Many
examples of names with translations. 10 refs.

[8.2.31]   Ndoma,   Ungina. (1977). Kongo personal names: A sketch. Names,
25, 88-98.
Review of the personal naming system used by the Bakongo who speak Kikongo,
a Bantu class language. Effect of the government's 1972 decision not to
allow use of foreign first names. Influence of Portuguese on Kongo names.
7 refs.

[8.2.32] Nsimbi, N. B. (1950, Baganda traditional personal names. Uganda
Journal. 14, 204-214.
Brief description of the major classes of naming such as proverbial,
nicknames, title, automatic, and locative names. 1 ref.

[8.2.33] Oduyoye, Modupe. (1972). Yoruba names: Their structure and their
meanings. Ibadan, Nigeria: Daystar Pr., 108 p.
Focuses on the structure of Yoruba names. Not a dictionary as such.
However, the reader can determine meanings of many names with the aid of
this book. Includes a number of footnotes and references.

[8.2.34]   Ojoade,   J. Olowo. (1980). African proverbial names: 101 Ilaje
examples. Names, 28, 195-214.
The Ilaje are a sub-section of the Yoruba. Among the 12 types of name are
proverbial names such as Tamuno, a shortened form of Tamunonengiyeofori
("there is nothing greater than God"). Usually, only the first half or the
2nd half of the name is employed. 30 refs.

[8.2.35] Omari, C. L. (1970). Personal names in socio-cultural context.
Kiswahili, 40, 65-71.
Describes naming practices in Tanzania. Some names describe social or
political events, others recall ancestors or prominent people or show
religious conversion; effect of foreign names. Listing of some traditional
names.

[8.2.36] Osuntaki, Chief. (1970). The book of African names. Washington,
DC: Drum and Spear Pr., n. p.
Naming ceremonies and legends. Lists of names with meanings from West,
Central, East, and South Africa.

[8.2.37] Quartey-Papafio, A. B. (1914). The use of names among the Gas or Accra people of the Gold Coast. Journal of the African Society, 13, 167-183.
Description of the naming system among a tribe in what is now part of Ghana. Includes tribe names, day names, fetish names, nicknames, and Kra (soul) names. Some examples. 2 refs.

[8.2.38] Ryan, Pauline M. (1981). An introduction to Hausa personal nomenclature. Names, 29, 139-164.
Description of the naming system of the Hausa, both Muslim and non-Muslim, who live in Northern Nigeria. Each child is given a secret name and a public name. For Muslims, the public name is taken from the Koran. Children are also given nicknames. Among the classes of nickname are phrase names (Karba Gari, "receive the town"), and slave names (Allah Magani "God the remedy for all things"). Other types of names included sunan kakani, names given by grandparents, suna wasa, play names, kirari, praise names, and Christian names. 9 refs.

[8.2.39] Sanyika, Beckthemba. (1975). Know and claim your African name. Dayton, OH: Rucker Pr., 40 p.
Personal names in Swahili, Yoruba, Arabic, and other African languages. Entries show name, pronunciation, meaning, language, and country. Approx 540 male, 315 female names. Additional names from Ethiopia and East Africa.

[8.2.40] Sholola, Bandele. (1971). Some African names for your baby. African Progress, 12(June), 36-37.
Discussion of African naming customs. Listing of over 60 names with meaning and country of origin. West, Central, East, and South Africa represented.

[8.2.41] Sholola, Bandele. (1971). More African names: The Yoruba way African Progress, 12(Sept-Oct), 28-29.
Popular description of the naming ritual of the Yoruba; 24 names listed with meaning of each.

[8.2.42] Tonkin, Elizabeth. (1980). Jealousy names, civilized names: Anthroponymy of the Jlao Kru of Liberia. Man (N. S.), 15, 653-664.
Description of the naming system of the Kru community of Jlao (Eng. Sasstown). One type of name is the jealousy name (ex., Kpawin, "carrier of sound" meaning someone who gives false reports). The jealousy name has sardonic rhetorical questioning. The system also has horn names (secret names with a tune for signal in battle), praise names, nicknames, and "civilized" names. 28 refs.

[8.2.43] Uchendu, Victor. (1965). The Igbo of Southeast Nigeria. New York: Holt Rinehart & Winston, 111 p.
A child is given many names, by birth marks, by diviner's opinion, by the market day of birth, and others. 1 ref.

[8.2.44] Zawawi, Sharifa. (1971). Kiswahili kwa Kitendo: An introductory course. New York: Harper & Row, 290 p.
Swahili is spoken in the East African countries of Tanzania and Kenya and the Congo province of Katanga. Basic name patterns are described. Listing of some names on pp. 3-5.

8.3. <u>American Indian</u>: See also--8.12. <u>Canadian</u>

[8.3.1]   Bodine, John J. (1968). Taos names: A clue to linguistic
acculturation. <u>Anthropological Linguistics</u>, <u>10</u>, 23-27.
Research with 1357 Indians of the Taos (New Mexico) Pueblo, indicates a
generational shift from Spanish first name dominance to English. 1 ref.

[8.3.2] Bright, William. (1958). Karok names. <u>Names</u>, <u>6</u>, 172-177.
The Karok live along the Klamath River in California. Analysis of 19 male
and 6 female names shows 4 patterns: (1) doer names ("bad talker"), (2)
physical characteristics ("tall, young man"), (3) location ("he of the
creek edge"), and (4) miscellaneous. 3 refs on names.

[8.3.3] Bright, William. (1967). Karok makkay < Scottish McKay. <u>Names</u>,
<u>15</u>, 79-80.
Explains that the Karok Indian word makayva.s ("cloth") really comes from
the name of a man highly regarded by them who was named McKay. 4 refs.

[8.3.4] Casagrande, Joseph B. (1955). Comanche linguistic acculturation
III. <u>International Journal of American Linguistics</u>, <u>21</u>, 8-25.
Pp. 12-20 contains a systematic presentation on personal names. Using 1940
census rolls, the pattern of 2394 Comanche names was traced from the older
to the younger generations showing the shift to white styles for first
names and patronyms. 4 refs in this section.

[8.3.5] Cooke, Charles A. (1952). Iroquois personal names: Their
classification. <u>Proceedings of the American Philosophical Society</u>, <u>96</u>(4),
427- 438.
The Iroquois consisted of 8 nations: Mohawk, Oneida, Onandaga, Cayuga,
Seneca, Huron-Wyandot, Tuscarora, and Cherokee. The classification covers
6200 names (in English, some also in Iroquois) with frequencies for men and
women. Among the categories are: occupational, plant, animal, heavens,
religious, and abstract.

[8.3.6] Dabbs, Jack A. (1985). Spanish treatment of names of the Apache
Indians. <u>XV, Internationaler Kongress fuer Namenforschung</u>, 1984, Leipzig,
<u>5</u>, 32-41.
Going back to the 17th century, explores the various possibilities of how
Spanish names were acquired by the Apaches. Possibilities include:
bestowal by missionaries, translation by interpreters, and assignment by
the military. Listing of 250+ Indian names. 13 refs.

[8.3.7] de Laguna, Frederica. (1954). Tlingit ideas about the individual.
<u>Southwestern Journal of Anthropology</u>, <u>10</u>, 172-191.
Naming customs of this Alaskan tribe. Each person may have 4 names: a
birth name, a pet name, a nickname, a big or potlatch name. Teknonymy is
practiced. 8 refs.

[8.3.8] Dubois, Betty Lou. (1976). Mescalero Apache personal names in the
early period of United States domination (1846-1880). <u>Names</u>, <u>24</u>, 327-328.
Five types of Spanish names were used by Mescalero males: (1) Christian
names (Mateo, Francisco), (2) surnames (Gomez, Barela), (3) double names
(Simon Manuel, Simon Parade), (4) Nicknames (Negrito), and names of objects
(Cigarito, "little cigar"), "private-names" were also maintained. 3 refs.

[8.3.9] Jones, William, (1939). Ethnography of the Fox Indians, Margaret Welpley Fisher (Ed.). Smithsonian Institution, Bureau of American Ethnology, Bulletin 125. Washington, DC: United States Government Printing Office, pp. 117-143.
Appendix A gives an extensive listing of Indian names based on the tribal roll of 1906. Appendices C and D along with other information furnish some translations of gens names such as Kiskinenuswa ("half buffalo"), Mamawa ("woodpecker"), and Nasapipyata ("the one who went in the water"). 4 refs.

[8.3.10] Kenny, Hammill. (1956). Names, 4, 54-58.
Point by point criticism of Taube's thesis (Names, 1955, 3, 65-81) that the Algonquian placenames of the Atlantic coastal area are corrupted tribal names. 7 refs.

[8.3.11] Kroeber, Alfred Louis. (1953). Handbook of the Indians of California. Berkeley: CA, 995 p. (originally published as Bulletin 78, Bureau of American Ethnology of the Smithsonian Institution, 1925)
Describes the naming customs of the following tribes on the pages shown: Yurok, p. 38, 47-49; Karok, 107-108; Yuki, 180-181; Huchnom, 210-211; Maidu, 403; Yokut, 499; Juaneno, 646; Mohave, 741-744, 749. This book is considered by many a classic in the field. 415 refs.

[8.3.12] Markey, Thomas L. (1983). Totemic typology. Quaderni di semantica, 4, 367-394.
Description of naming customs among the Fox Indians of Iowa. Names are variations on the clan totemic name; thus for the Thunder clan, Sharp Thunder, Splitting Thunder, and Rolling Thunder. Names are assigned by women. Fox family names as such do not exist but names such as Brown or Buffalo are taken to satisfy the authorities. 57 refs.

[8.3.13] Mithun, Marianne. (1984). Principles of naming in Mohawk. In Elisabeth Tooker (Ed.), Harold C. Conklin (Symposium Organizer), 1980 Proceedings of the American Ethnological Society (pp. 40-54). Washington, DC: American Ethnological Society,
Description of the naming system (placenames as well as personal names) of the Mohawk, a division of the Iroquois. Personal names, as with other Iroquoian tribes, were assigned by a clan name-keeper. As the Mohawk were converted to Catholicism by French missionaries, names such as Catherine were modified into Mohawk as Kateri; Pierre became Tie:r. Several examples. 7 refs.

[8.3.14] Pearce, T. M. (1963). Naming customs among Southwestern Indians. New Mexico Folklore Record, 11, 33-37.
Naming customs among the Navaho, Pueblo, and Mohave. Some mention of Spanish baptismal names and how bestowed and recent trend of anglicizing Spanish names. 7 refs.

[8.3.15] Shaul, David L. (1972). The meaning of the name Sacajawea. Annals of Wyoming, 44, 237-240.
Sacajewea was the Indian woman guide of the Lewis & Clark expedition. The "South Dakota" theory of her name gives it the Hidatsa meaning of "bird woman." The "Wyoming" theory is that it means "boat launcher" in Shoshone. Suggests that the Shoshones approximated the original Hidatsa name and gave it a meaning. 14 refs.

[8.3.16] Skinner, Alanson. (1925, Oct. 3). Observations on the ethnology of the Sauk Indians. Bulletin of the Public Museum of the City of Milwaukee, 5(1), pp. 119-180.
Listing on pp. 151-152 of some 17 names indicating that the proper names are derived from the clan, as White-Tail < deer clan.

[8.3.17] Spier, Leslie & Sapir, Edward. (1930). Wishram ethnography. Publications in Anthropology, 3, 153-299.
Pp. 258-260 decribes the naming ceremony of the Wishram of Washington State.   Names did not have meaning and were different for each sex. Wishram were reticent about names. No 2 people bore the same name. A name was always that of a dead older relative. Short listing of names. 2 refs.

[8.3.18] Sturtevant, William C. (1960). In J. B. Casagrande (Ed.), In the company of man (pp. 506-532). New York: Harper.
Example of the Seminole custom of forming adult names by employing several series of elements without regard to meaning, a moral series, a morphological, and a zoological leading to a name such as "crazy-spherical-puma" (pp. 507-508).

[8.3.19] Underhill, Lonnie E. (1968). Indian name translation. American Speech, 43, 114-126.
Traces the problems faced by Indian agents in the period 1870-1900 in assigning Indians surnames that were considered appropriate. One of the more successful efforts was that of Dr. Eastman, a Sioux himself, who renamed the entire tribe. 20 refs.

[8.3.20] Vickers, Ovid. (1983). Mississippi Choctaw names and naming: A diachronic view. Names, 31, 117-122.
The Choctaws, a branch of the Muscogee, now live in E Central Mississippi and number about 4100.   Describes the pattern of transition from pre-1830 animal/incident naming pattern without surnames to the current pattern of names such as Gregory Tubby. 9 refs.

[8.3.21] Weeks, Thelma E. (1971). Child-naming customs among the Yakima Indians. Names, 19, 252-256.
Description of naming customs among the Yakima who live in central Washington state. Those who live on the reservation have a ceremony (personal or Indian) where the child is named after a deceased relative. 3 refs.

[8.3.22] Weslager, C. A. (1959). European personal names given to the Eastern Indians. Names, 7, 54-56.
Indians in Maryland began replacing their Algonkian first names with English ones in 1704. Those in New York began to replace their Algonkian names with Dutch names in 1678. 8 refs.

[8.3.23] Weslager, C. A. (1971). Name-giving among the Delaware Indians. Names, 19, 268-283.
The naming traditions of those now living in Oklahoma maintain some traces of early Delaware Indian culture. Appendix listing some names. 21 refs.

8.4. Amish

[8.4.1] Enninger, Werner. (1985). Amish by-names. Names, 33, 243-25
Uses research on Amish names to develop the position that legal names
(first names and surnames) are markers of social identity and that by-names
are makers for personal identity. Concludes that by-names are a special
class of personal names characterized by: (1) a specific act of nomination,
(2) linguistic status, and (3) specific role. 34 refs.

[8.4.2] Mook, Maurice A. (1967). Nicknames among the Amish. Names, 15,
111-118.
Since the Amish have a limited number of surnames, nicknames help
differentiate individuals. There are 8 types of nickname including: (1)
name shortening, as Samuel to Sam, (2) physical trait, "Big Ben," (3)
behavior, "Grumpy Aaron," (4) relating to an incident, usually humorous,
and (5) using a middle initial with first name, "Iksie" (Isaac Z.).

[8.4.3] Smith, Elmer Lewis. (1968). Amish names. Names, 16, 105-110
The Amish, because of the rule of marrying within the group, have as few as
14 surnames which account for 90% of the names used. For first names, 20
biblical names account for 80% of the men; another 20 names account for 88%
of the women. To cope with identification problems, middle names,
nicknames, and other techniques are used. 8 refs.

[8.4.4] Troyer, Lester O. (1968). Amish nicknames from Holmes County,
Ohio. Pennsylvania Folklife, 17, 24.
In the Amish community nicknames are important because of the frequency of
identical names.   Ten colorful nicknames are listed with descriptions of
their bearer such as Duwak Ksicht (Tobacco Face, "he chewed tobacco and was
an accurate spitter").

8.5. Ancient Middle Eastern

[8.5.1] Albright, William F. (1954). Northwest Semitic names in a list of
Egyptian slaves from the 18th century BC. Journal of the American Oriental
Society, 74, 222-233.
A recently-discovered Egyptian 13th Dynasty papyrus (circa 1740 BC) shows
95 slave names, 37 of which were originally labeled Semitic. Analysis of
these names throws light on several biblical names including Jacob and Job.
78 refs.

[8.5.2] Bennett, John. (1965). Meaning of the royal nomen and praenomen.
Journal of Egyptian Archeology, 51, 206-207.
Hypothesizes that when the name of a god is included along with a royal
name, it is meant to compare the king with a god. 3 refs.

[8.5.3] Bennett, John. (1965). Notes on the 'aten.' Journal of Egyptian
Archeology, 51, 207-209.
Believes that aten should be translated as "the sun-god" and is not a name
but a common noun. 9 refs.

[8.5.4] Benz, Frank L. (1972). Personal names in the Phoenician and Punic
inscriptions. Rome: Biblical Institute Press, 511 p.
A collection of personal names in 2 ancient Semitic languages, Phoenician
from the Eastern Mediterranean, and Punic, a dialect of Phoenician from the

Western Mediterranean. Information is arranged by location of inscription and by name. Form and grammar of names are also considered.   Apparently, hundreds of names are covered. Approx 400 refs.

[8.5.5] Coogan, Michael David. (1976). West Semitic personal names in the Murasu documents. Missoula, MT: Scholars Pr., University of Montana, 142 p.
Based upon over 700 tablets from the 5th century BC found in a room at Nippur, the onomasticon is considered unparalleled as a source of West Semitic, especially of Biblical personal names of post-exilic period. Extensive documentation. 200+ refs.

[8.5.6] Gelb, Ignace J. (1956). The names of ex-voto objects in Ancient Mesopotamia. Names, 4, 65-69.
Inscriptions found on statues, bowls, weapons, and the like bore names of the divinities and the offerers such as "Entemena is the beloved of Enlil," the name of a statue dedicated by Entemena to Enlil. 18 refs.

[8.5.7] Gelb, Ignace J. (1962). Ethnic reconstruction and onomastic evidence. Names, 10, 45-52.
Discusses the difficulties of trying to reconstruct the ethnic traditions of the Middle East on the basis of personal names and toponyms. Contrasts the problem with trying to understand the city of Chicago on the basis of names in the telephone directory and local toponyms. 4 refs.

[8.5.8] Gelb, Ignace J. (1968). An old Babylonian list of Amorites. Journal of the American Oriental Society, 88, 39-46.
Deciphering and translation of a tablet at Tell Asmar from the Ur III period has produced 31 personal names, 29 Amorite, 2 Akkadian. Concludes that the tablet is the missing link between the Ur III and Old Babylonian periods and that Ur III and Old Babylonian West Semitic belonged to the same Amorite group. 29 refs.

[8.5.9] Harris, Rivka. (1972). Notes on the nomenclature of Old Babylonian Sippar. Journal of Cuneiform Studies, 24, 102-104.
Analysis of personal names from ancient Sippar, a community of several thousand, indicates that no 2 men had the same name and patronomy in the same generation. Questions whether there was a central office for name registration. 3 refs.

[8.5.10] Harris, Rivka. (1977). Notes on the slave names of Old Babylonian Sippar. Journal of Cuneiform Studies, 29, 46-51.
Analysis of female and male slave names indicates that some names are more characteristic of slaves, others of free men. Suggests that some persons born free were sold into slavery or sold themselves to pay debts. Many slave names are theophoric. 6 refs.

[8.5.11] Huffmon, Herbert Bardwell. (1965). Amorite personal names in the Mari texts: A structural and lexical study. Baltimore: Johns Hopkins University Pr., 304 p.
Analysis of personal names from ancient documents. Lists of names. Glossary. Thoroughly documented with hundreds of citations and references.

[8.5.12] Lipinski, Edward. (1975). Studies in Aramaic inscriptions and onomastics, Orientalia Lovaniensia Analecta, Leuven, Belgium: Leuven University Pr., 240 p.

Evaluates personal names appearing in Aramaic texts dating back to the first millenium BCE. Among the sources of the approximately 800 personal and divine names are the inscriptions from Bar-Hadad, Zakire, Assur, Tell Halef, and Lachish. Hundreds of refs. (For a summary see--Lipinski (1974), Studies in Aramaic inscriptions and onomastics, Onoma, 18, 421-425)

[8.5.13] Quaegebeur, Jan. (1974). Studies in Aramaic inscriptions and onomastics. Onoma, 18, 403-420.
Description of the Greek presence in Egypt going back as far as 663 BC; relevance of Egyptian names in Greek translation. One aspect of relevance is for research on population mobility and localization of persons and documents. Systematic reference to sources. 100+ refs, mostly non-English.

[8.5.14] Shevoroskin, V. (1978). Studies in Hittite-Luwian names. Names, 26, 231-257.
The onomastics of the Hittite-Luwian languages (spoken in Anatolia and other regions from BC 2000-AD 100) show a system close to other Indo-European languages. Many notes. Many examples. 17 refs.

[8.5.15] Silverman, Michael Henry. (1969). Onomastic notes to "Aramaica Dubiosa." Journal of Near Eastern Studies, 28, 192-196.
Evaluates onomastic evidence of some Egyptian-Aramaic documents that are possibly forged. Concludes that onomastic evidence alone is not sufficient to make a judgment. 17 refs.

[8.5.16] Stark, Jurgen Kurt. (1971). Personal names in Palmyrene inscriptions. London: Oxford University Pr., 152 p.
The research was based on ancient inscriptions in NW Semitic found in Palmyra, now Syria. Part I catalogs the occurrence of the names. Part II is a lexicon which gives the meaning of approx 1600 names, ex., MRWN ("Lord"), B ("Father"). Most of the names are Semitic but also there are some Greek, Latin, and Persian names included. Careful attention to the work of other scholars. 280+ refs + source materials.

[8.5.17] Ward, William A. (1976). Some personal names of the Hyksos. Ugarit-Forschungen, 8, 353-369.
Sophisticated analysis and speculation on the origin of names found on ancient scarabs. 50+ refs. Figures show 67 scarabs.

8.6. Arabic

[8.6.1] Al-Ja'fari, Fatima Susan. (1977). Muslim names. Indianapolis, IN 46231: American Trust Publications, 10900 W. Washington St., 45 p.
Listing in English alphabetical order of about 320 men's and 230 women's names with meaning and Arabic spelling for each entry.

[8.6.2] Allen, Harold B. (1956). Nicknaming in Egyptian Arabic. Names, 4, 75-82.
Most Egyptian nicknames have a direct relationship with the first name (Hamada for Hamdi or Mohammed), others have no direct relationship to the name itself but to the person's physical appearance, being called Filfil ("black pepper"). Girls' nicknames also included, about 100 in all.

[8.6.3] Antoun, Richard T. (1968). On the significance of names in an Arab village. Ethnology, 7, 158-170.
The study was conducted in the Arab Muslim village of Kufr al Ma which is located in the eastern foothills of the Jordan Valley. There is a complete and systematic coverage of naming patterns in the community covering such topics as nicknames which express character, physical and personal traits, occupations, hostility, and places of origin. Some coverage also of title and teknonyms. 6 refs.

[8.6.4] Campbell, C. G. (1953). Girl's names of possible Arabic origin. Names, 1, 48-49.
Suggests that Norah, Leila, Lulu, and Adela are of Arabic origin.

[8.6.5] Geertz, Clifford. (1975). On the nature of anthropological understanding, American Scientist, 63, 47-53.
Description of the nisba, a type of personal name used in the Middle East in which the individual can be identified by region, tribe, or occupation. The nisba indicates how the society categorizes its members. 3 refs.

[8.6.6] Hakim, Dawud. (1970). Arabic names and other African names with their meanings. Philadelphia: Hakim's Publications, 214 S. 60th St., 19139, 28 p.
Lists approx 200 Arabic names for boys and girls with meaning and Arabic written form. Some names have pronunciation indicated. Also included are about 100 names from West Africa and some from the Congo and East Africa.

[8.6.7] Harding, G. Lankester. (1971). An index and concordance of Pre-Islamic names and inscriptions, Near and Middle East Series, Vol. 8. Toronto: University of Toronto Pr., 943 p.
This is a reworking and expansion of Prof. Gonzague Ryckmans' Les names propres sud-semitiques. The index of 9,000-10,000 names involves 7 dialects: Lihyanite, Safaitic, Thamudic, Hadrami, Minaean, Qatabanian, and Sabaean, indicating in which dialect each name is found. A solid background in Arabic is probably necessary to appreciate this contribution. 800+ refs.

[8.6.8] Oman, Giovanni. (1980). Personal names in the Southern Region (Zufar) of the Sultanate of Oman. Oriente Moderno, 60, 181-195.
Lists of names from the telephone directory in alphabetical order by Arabic roots and by frequency. Mostly male names. Over 27 refs.

[8.6.9] Oman, Giovanni. (1982). Personal names in the capital area of the Sultanate of Oman. In Jacqueline Sublet (Responsable), Cahiers d'onomastique Arab 1981 (pp. 95-113). Paris: Centre National de la Recherche Scientifique. (This article is in English)
Analysis of the Arabic personal names from the telephone directory. Listing includes English spelling, phonetic spelling, Arabic spelling, and the frequency of the names. Only a few female names. 5 refs.

[8.6.10] Yassin, M. Aziz F. (1978). Personal names of address in Kuwaiti Arabic. Anthropological Linguistics, 20, 53-63.
Systematic description of types of naming practice in Kuwait, a Persian Gulf Arab state. Categories include: personal names, teknonyms, patronyms, and brachynyms (which include nicknames and diminutives). Among the many examples of various types of nickname are: bu beela ("a man with a drum") and bu tamba ("the fat one," lit., "father of the stomach"). 4 refs.

8.7. Armenian

[8.7.1] Atikian, Martha B., & Atikian, Hagop. (1973). Armenians' names. No city listed: published by author, 71 p.
Contains entries with meaning for about 360 male and 260 female Armenian names with culture/language group of origin (most are Armenian). Included are Ardamis (Diana), Maro (Mary), Levon (Leon), and Mooshegh (Moses).

[8.7.2] Avakian, Anne M. (1982). Armenian name changes. ANS Bulletin, No. 67, 32-38.
After describing some aspects of Armenian name change, lists about 140 Armenian surnames in original and adapted forms, such as Casabian to Cass. Some name changes such as Ekzoozian to Orphan represent translations. Some mention of reverse name change, as Taylor to Terzian. 3 refs.

[8.7.3] Hewsen, Robert H. (1963). Armenian names in America. American Speech, 38, 214-219.
While there have been some changes of Armenian surnames in the United States and children of Armenian parents tend to have Anglo-Saxon first names, Armenian surnames appear to have had less change than might have been expected. 3 refs.

[8.7.4] Jeryan, Puzant. (1981). Those unwieldy surnames. Ararat, 22(4), 41.
Armenians from Turkey bear names derived from Turkish expressions. These names are difficult to pronounce for non-Turkish speaking people. Sugggests changing to shorter names with traditional Armenian identification.

8.8. Australian

[8.8.1] Clyne, Michael. (1972). German surname changes in Victoria, Australia, 1937-39: A study in integration. Linguistics: An International Review, No. 87, 37-46.
Systematic study of 129 surname changes. Systematic categorization in terms of spelling, expression, and content. 7 refs.

[8.8.2] Greenway, John. (1959). Australian nicknames. American Speech, 34, 224-226.
Listing with some background of the nicknames of 17 Sydney dockworkers. Included are: The London Fog (a lazy worker, "he never lifts") and Blue-Tongued Lizard ("he nervously licked his lips"). 1 ref.

[8.8.3] Hart, C. W. W. (1930). Personal names among the Tiwi. Oceania, 1, 280-290.
Describes the complex naming system of the Tiwi of the Melville and Bathurst islands. An individual may have a number of unique names. There are some types of taboo names. Individuals have several names associated with initiation grades and age grades. 1 ref.

[8.8.4] Hernandez, Theodore. (1941). Social organization of the Drysdale River tribes, North-West Australia. Oceania, 11, 211-232.
Personal names are derived from the totem of a moiety (pp. 218-219). Tribesmen have other names as well.
[8.8.5] Kelly, C. Tennant. (1935). Tribes on Cherburg Settlement,

Queensland. Oceania, 5, 461–473.
Each person has 3 names: a Yamba name which indicates the spirit home, the
Kujal name which is held in common with brothers and sisters, and the Kyi
name which is a personal and secret name (p. 468). 1 ref.

[8.8.6] Pink, Olive M. (1933–1934). Spirit ancestors in a Northern Aranda
horde country. Oceania, 4, 176–186.
Brief mention (p. 176) that if one knew the Aranda language, one could
determine the totem of an individual by deduction from the name.

[8.8.7] Radin, Paul. (1957).   Primitive religion: Its nature and origin.
New York: Dover, pp. 85–95. (Reprint of Viking, 1937)
Description of an initiation ceremenony among the Arunta, a tribe of
central Australia, in which the boy goes through a laborious initiation
ceremony in which he gets different names at different phases. 13 refs.

[8.8.8] Thomson, Donald E. (1946). Names and naming in the Wik Monkan
tribe.   Journal of the Anthropological Institute of Great Britain and
Ireland, 76, 157–167.
Description of the naming customs of an aboriginal tribe of Cape York,
Queensland, Australia. The complex system of naming includes kinship terms
(names which express relationship), transition names, nicknames, and
personal names. Taboo names. 7 ref notes.

[8.8.9] Warner, William Lloyd. (1958). A black civilization (rev. ed.).
New York: Harper Torchbook.
Brief reference (p. 380) to the Murngin of Arnhem Land, Northern Australia
whose names are all taken from the totem complex.

8.9. Black

[8.9.1] Bennett, Lerone, Jr. (1969). What's in a name? Negro vs.
Afro-American vs. Black. ETC: A Review of General Semantics, 26, 399–412.
Examination of various positions on the use of these terms. 2 refs.

[8.9.2] Brown, Barbara W., & Rose, James M. (1980).   Black roots in
southeastern Connecticut, 1650–1900. Detroit: Gale Research, 722 p.
This is the result of an immense project in which hundreds of court and
other records were searched for references to blacks. It appears that
approx 8500 persons are listed, some without any surname.   Approx 1500
surnames are included. This is a reference for those interested in slave
names and genealogy. 300+ refs. Several indexes.

[8.9.3] Byrd, James W. (1978). Dracula! What kind of name is that for a
niggah? In Fred Tarpley (Ed.), Ethnic names (pp. 19–25), Publication 6,
South Central Names Institute. Commerce, TX: Names Institute Pr.
Considers that stereotype first names of blacks such as Sam, Rastus, Liza,
and Mandy are the work of both black and white writers. In actual practice,
blacks and whites draw on the same pool of first names. 3 refs.

[8.9.4] Closson, David L. (1977). Onomastics of the rabble. Maledicta, 1,
215–233.
The term rabble refers to the campus oral tradition regarding nicknames at
Lincoln University during 1961–1965. There were over 450 of these names

which fell into the physical or personality trait category. About 300 of these names with an explanation are listed including: Duke ("his last name was Wellington"), Foothill ("he had big feet"), Gator ("from the swamps of Florida"), and Stumpy ("like a tree trunk"). 5 refs.

[8.9.5] Cody, Cheryll Ann. (1982). Naming, kinship, and estate dispersal: Notes on slave family life on a South Carolina plantation, 1786-1833. William and Mary Quarterly, 39, 192-211.
Reports that the slaves of Peter Gaillard frequently named their children for: (1) both paternal and maternal kin, (2) siblings, (3) to symbolically mend broken family times. 5 tables. 14 refs.

[8.9.6] Cohen, Hennig. (1952). Slave names in colonial South Carolina. American Speech, 27, 102-107.
Overview of slave names indicating there was a dual system of naming: (1) "proper" names (those given by the owner) and (2) "country names" (those of African origin). Many examples of different names given including: Cuffee, Calabar, Ketch, Embro, York, and Ponpon. 14 refs.

[8.9.7] Dillard, Joey Lee. (1972). Black English, New York: Random House, pp. 123-135.
These pages describe West African naming practices outside Gullah territory. Focuses on day names. Attention to names such as Cuffee, Phoebe, and Sambo. 33 refs.

[8.9.8] Dillard, Joey Lee. (1976). Black names. The Hague: Mouton. 114 p.
Shows the survival of African patterns in the naming of black Americans. Covers music, folklore, nicknames, and vehicle names. Many page notes. Over 140 refs.

[8.9.9] Eby, Cecil D., Jr. (1961). Classical names among Southern Negro slaves. American Speech, 36, 140-141.
Suggests that the practice of naming black slaves after figures of Roman history such as Caesar and Cato goes back to the 18th century British practice of naming animals for classical figures. 5 refs.

[8.9.10] Ellison, Ralph (Waldo). (1964). Shadow and act. New York: Random House, pp. 144-166.
Describes the reactions of a black boy growing up in Oklahoma with a European surname and with first and middle names of a famous writer. Description of how these names influenced him.

[8.9.11] Gutman, Herbert G. (1976). The Black family in slavery and freedom, 1750-1925. New York: Pantheon, pp. 185-256.
Extensive discussion with documentation of naming practices for first names and surnames. Stronger role of father for first names is shown. Choice of surnames in many cases was actually different than the common perception. 100+ refs.

[8.9.12] Moore, Richard B. (1960). The term "Negro" its origin and evil use. New York: Afroamerican Publishers, 82 p.
After relating the history of the term Negro, concludes that Afroamerican is the most acceptable descriptor.

[8.9.13] Paustian, P. Robert. (1978). The evolution of personal naming practices among American blacks. Names, 26, 177-191.

Brief history of black naming in the United States. Contrasts with naming practices in Africa. Many examples. 43 refs.

[8.9.14] Puckett, Newbell Niles. (Murray Heller, Ed.). (1975). **Black names in America: Origins and usage**. Boston: G K Hall, 561 p.
A presentation of specialized lists of names based upon a collection of 340,000 black and 160,000 white names from 1619 to the mid-1940s. There are 22 categories of source lists. Each of these categories has 2-6 sub-categories. Among the categories are: black (slave, free), white, first name, surname, common, unusual, and college student. Includes a dictionary of black and white names of African origin and the language source(s). Index. 75 refs plus a list of a number of college student and city directories.

[8.9.15] Williams, George Walton. (1958). Slave names in Ante-Bellum South Carolina. American Speech, 33, 294-295.
Responding to the work of Cohen [8.9.6], notes that records of 600 slaves from a black church in Charleston did not indicate a dual system of naming; some slaves did have a surname; and some had double names. 2 refs.

8.10. Bulgarian

[8.10.1] Danchev, Andrei. (1985). For a complex approach to the standardization of proper names. XV, Internationaler Kongress fuer Namenforschung, 1984, Leipzig, 8, 19-23.
Linguistic, sociolinguistic, and psycholinguistic factors in problems of interlingual transcription. Bulgarian orientation. 8 refs.

[8.10.2] Nicoloff, Assen. (1983). Bulgarian folklore. Cleveland, OH: Assen Nicoloff, 1990 Ford Dr., Apt. 1115, Cleveland, OH, 44106, pp. 280-309.
Covers first names and surnames. Historical background. Listings of male and female names, most with derivation and meaning. Listings of names typical of districts.

8.11. Burmese

[8.11.1] Khaing, Mi Hi. (1958, February). Burmese names. Atlantic Monthly, p. 108.
Brief description of Burmese names with a few examples.

8.12. Canadian

[8.12.1] Chaput, Donald. (1966). From Indian to French: A female name curiosity: Algonquian. Names, 14, 143-149.
Indian women, especially Algonquian, who married Frenchmen in the 17th century assumed new first names and surnames. Common surnames were Panis ("Slave") and Sauvegesse ("Savage"). List of 30 representative Indian-to-French female names. 18 refs.

[8.12.2] Columbo, John Robert. (1978). Columbo's names and nicknames, Toronto: NC Pr., 212 p.
Over 4000 entries including 2000 Canadians. Section 1 shows names to

nicknames; Section 2, nicknames to names. Thus, Graham Kerr = The Galloping Gourmet, George Imlach = Punch, Bobby Orr = Number 4.

[8.12.3] Creighton, Helen. (1962). Cape Breton nicknames and tales. In Horace P. Beck (Ed.), Folklore in action: Essays for discussion in honor of MacEdward Leach (pp. 71-76). Philadelphia: American Folklore Society.
Nicknames are extensively used in Cape Breton, Nova Scotia by Scots-descended people since there is a limited number of surnames such as, MacDonald, MacIsaac, and MacMillan. About 50 nicknames are listed including: Big John, Jack the Butcher, Maggie the Lighthouse, and Jim the Wig.

[8.12.4] Goldenweiser, Alexander A. (1914). On Iroquois work: Summary report of the Geological Survey of Canada, Department of Mines 1913, Sessional Paper No. 26, pp. 365-372, Ottawa: King's Printer.
Naming examples and uses of names of tribes including the Senecas, Onondagas, Tuscaroras, Cayugas, Oneidas, and Mohawks. Only a few examples and these are in English. Examples are: He-raises-the-Sky, She-works-in-the House. Some names are newly-created such as She-is-in-Want who was born to a poor mother.

[8.12.5] Klymasz, Robert B. (1963). The Canadianization of Slavic surnames: Part I, A study in language contact. Names, 11, 81-105; Part II, 182-195; Part III, 229-253.
Part I outlines the background of Canadianization of Slavic surnames. Part II is a systematic exposition of the phonological changes with many examples, as Sutoff to Sutton, Jentke to Jenkins, Przednovak to Novak. Part III is a classification with comment of morphological changes, as Dobruskin to Ruskin, Ozarow to Arrow, Worobec to Worobey. 50+ refs.

[8.12.6] Lehiste, Ilse. (1975). Attitudes of bilinguals toward their personal names. American Speech, 50, 30-35.
Deals with the difficulties of Canadian Estonian-English bilinguals in dealing with how the public pronounces their Estonian first names.

[8.12.7] Mingall, Constance. (1977). Changing your name in Canada: How to do it legally. North Vancouver, BC: International Self-Counsel Pr., 132 p.
Description of the procedures, province by province, for change of name. Apparently directed mainly at married women. Samples of legal applications for change of name.

[8.12.8] Pike, Robert E. (1956). Further mutations on French-Canadian proper names. American Speech, 31, 153.
Mention of some changes of French-Canadian names such as Grandmaison to House, Buisson to Bushey, and Lenoir to Black.

[8.12.9] Rudnyckyi, Jaroslav Bohdan. (1976). Anthroponyms in contact: Canadian pattern. Berichte des XII. Internationaler Kongresses fuer Namenforschung, 1975, Bern, 3, 261-264.
Patterns of assimilation of Slavic European first names with Canadian English. Examples include: Nadia to Hope, Stanislaw to Stanley, and Jaroslav to Jerry. 8 refs.

[8.12.10] Seary, E. R., & Lynch, Sheila M. P. (1977). Family names of the island of Newfoundland. St. John's, Newfoundland: Memorial University, 544 p.

The surnames were drawn from a 1955 list of electors (voters). The introduction gives background information on surnames. The main part of the work consists of a comprehensive dictionary of over 3700 surnames with important information on meaning, prominent holders of the name, location, along with appropriate citations. The appendix includes 816 surnames with 50 entries or more. Exhaustive list of references.

[8.12.11]   Thomas, Gerald. (1982, Dec.) Some Acadian names in Western Newfoundland. Onomastica Canadiana, No. 62, pp. 23-34.
Information and comments on Acadian French surnames in Western Newfoundland. 18 refs. Appendix of other French or Acadian names. Map.

[8.12.12]   Thomas, Gerald. (1986). French family names on the Port-au-Port Peninsula, Newfoundland. Onomastica Canadiana, No. 68(1), pp. 21-31.
Using oral data from French-speaking Newfoundlanders, surveyed metropolitan French surnames in areas of current French settlement. Over 50 surnames (with variations) are individually discussed with current listings of holders of that surname in telephone directories. Names included are: Dubois, Felix, and Perrier. 8 refs. Map.

[8.12.13]   Voorhis, Paul. (1985). The Kickapoo diminutive, with notes on the formation of personal names. Algonquian and Iroquoian Linguistics, 10(2), 11-15.
Explains with examples some of the ways personal names are formed from diminutives. 6 refs.

[8.12.14]   Wallis, Wilson D. (1947). The Canadian Dakota. Anthropological Papers of the American Museum of Natural History, 41, Part 1, 38-40.
The ordinal position of birth is used a basis for naming children of both sexes. Other names are also used. Children are not named after a living person. The area of the Canadian Dakota is Manitoba. 2 refs.

[8.12.15]   Wells, Evelyn. (1980). Baby names from A to Z. Toronto: Coles, 326 p.
A popular dictionary especially for those wishing to choose a name for a child.

8.13. Caribbean

[8.13.1]   Crowley, Daniel J. (1957) Plural and differential accommodation in Trinidad. American Anthropologist, 59, 817-824.
Pp. 820-821 briefly describe the varied ethnic mix of Trinidad, Creole, Spanish, Hindu, Muslim, and others and their naming customs.

8.14. Celtic

[8.14.1]   Evans, David Ellis. (1967). Gaulish personal names: A study of some Continental Celtic formations. Oxford: Clarendon Pr., 492 p.
Lists Celtic personal names found in Celtic inscriptions of Ancient Gaul, Caesar's Commentaries on the Gallic War, and in the graffiti of La Graufesenque (site of a factory which made vases). Entries are presented in alphabetical order giving details of where information was recorded, meanings and interpretations. Thorough documentation. Hundreds of references and citations.

8.15. Chicano

[8.15.1]   Coltharp, Lurline. (1981). Dual influences on Chicano naming
practices. Names, 29, 297-312.
Comparisons were made of first name preferences by American, Chicano, and
Mexican students at the University of El Paso. Concludes that both
American and Mexican cultures have influence on Chicano naming practices.
1 ref.

8.16. Chinese

[8.16.1] Berlitz, Charles F. (1972). Hwang it all which Wong are you.
Horizon, 14(Summer), p. 236.
Explains that in Chinese a name can be pronounced in one way yet spelled
differently (and with different meanings). Several examples of how
American names such as Nixon, Reagan, and Kennedy can be translated into
Chinese.

[8.16.2] Chao, Yuen Ren. (1956). Chinese terms of address. Language, 32,
217-241.
Includes explanations of affectionate names, surnames, school names,
"courtesy" names, and title names. 8 refs.

[8.16.3] Chen, Charles K. H. (Compiler). (1972). A standard romanized
dictionary of Chinese and Japanese popular surnames. Hanover, NH: Oriental
Society, 681 p.
Contains 3 main sections. Part 1 is a listing of romanized Chinese surnames
in 700 patterns. Part 2 lists about 11,000 Chinese surnames in oriental
stroke order. Part 3 lists about 10,000 Japanese names in oriental stroke
order. Meanings of the names are not included.

[8.16.4] Kehl, Frank. (1971). Chinese nicknaming behavior: A
sociolinguistic pilot study. Journal of Oriental Studies, 9, 149-172.
Systematic presentation of the dimensions of Chinese nicknaming. These
include phonological processes, semantic materials, sociological functions,
nickname use in reference and address, and others. Many examples. 5 refs.

[8.16.5] Lo, T. Y. (1925). Correlation of name and fame. Chinese Journal
of Psychology, 3(4), 1-10. (From Psychological Abstracts, 1927, 1,
Abstract No. 1386; original article is in Chinese)
Four factors of a name were found related to fame: number of strokes
(negative correlation), meaning, a single name (vs. a first name with a
middle name), and a name derived from a noun or adjective.

[8.16.6] Smith, F. Porter. (Compiler). (1870). A vocabulary of proper
names in Chinese and English. Shanghai: Presbyterian Mission Pr., 81 p.
Although primarily a placename dictionary, personal names in Chinese
characters are included. Examples are An-Tan (Marcus Aurelius Antoninus),
A-tan (the Muslim name for Adam), Ching-kih-sz'han (Genghis Khan).

[8.16.7] Yutang, Lin. (1962). The pleasures of a nonconformist. New York:
World, pp, 225-227.
This chapter contains comments in a light vein on Chinese name styles.

8.17. Christian, Early

[8.17.1]   Kajanto, Iiro. (1963). Onomastic studies in early Christian
inscriptions of Rome and Carthage, Acta Instituti Romani Finlandiae, Vol.
2(1)), 141 p.
Detailed description of the complicated Latin naming system as shown in
Christian catacomb inscriptions from the 3rd to the 5th century.   The data
from Carthage are somewhat later. Approx 1200 names discussed. 130+ refs.

8.18. Classical (includes Ancient Greek and Roman)

[8.18.1]   Ashley, Leonard R. N., & Hanifin, Michael J. F. (1978).
Onomasticon of Roman anthroponyms: Explication and application (Part I).
Names, 26, 297-401.
Comprehensive treatment of many aspects of Roman names. Main sections are:
Nomina, Praenomina, and Cognomina. Many examples. Many footnotes.   50+
refs.

[8.18.2]   Ashley, Leonard R. N., & Hanifin, Michael J. F. (1979).
Onomasticon of Roman anthroponyms: Explication and application (Part II).
Names, 27, 1-45.
Continues from Part I above.   Describes words in English that come from
Roman names, ex., vulcanize, Junoesque, and bacchanal; names and titles in
Roman history; how Shakespeare and Ben Jonson used Roman names; and
classical pseudonyms at the time of the Reformation. Wide-ranging. Many
footnotes. 77 refs plus many from literature.

[8.18.3] Astour, Michael C. (1964). Greek names in the Semitic world and
Semitic names in the Greek world. Journal of Near Eastern Studies, 23,
193-201.
Research analysis applying the method of vestiges (where the myth is
evaluated in terms of names in parallel languages, in this case Greek vs.
West Semitic) to the myth of Cadmon and the Cadmids provides evidence that
Semitic myths were important prototypes of many Greek myths.

[8.18.4]   Bailey, David Roy Shackleton. (1976). Two studies in Roman
nomenclature, American Classical Studies No. 3, American Philological
Association (no city listed), 135 p.
The first study "Onomasticon Pseudotullianum" cites and gives comments on
about 200 errors involving names in the works of Cicero. The 2nd essay
"Adoptive Nomenclature in the Late Roman Republic" deals with system of
naming used in adoptions. There is also a register of adoptions that gives
background information on names during the period 130-43 BC. 24 refs.

[8.18.5] Jones, Arnold Hugh, Martingale, J. R., & Morris, J. (1971). The
prosopography of the Later Roman Empire, Vol. 1, A. D. 260-315. Cambridge,
England: University Pr., 1152 p.
Listing of names of senators, equestrians, and officials of the Empire
(NCOs and privates not included) from remaining records along with
available information on each person. Section on family trees. Estimated
5000 individuals listed. Hundreds of refs and citations.

[8.18.6]   Kajanto, Iiro. (1965). The Latin cognomina. Commentationes
Humanorum Litterarum, Vol. 36(2). Helsinki: Societas Scientarum Fennica,
418 p.

The cognomen is the last element in Latin nomenclature and refers to the individual's surname. This research reports on a study of 133,000 Latin cognomina mostly from the 5th century BC to 600 AD largely collected from inscriptions categorized into 15 major groups, ex. Theophoric, Iuppiter; Body/Mind, Velox ("Fast"). There are 5783 different names with citations and frequencies. Index. 140 refs.

[8.18.7] Kajanto, Iiro. (1967). Supernomina: A study in Latin epigraphy. Commentationes Humanorum Litterarum. Helsinki: Societas Fennica, 40(1), 1-114.
A supernomen is a personal name apart from other names an individual has. There are 2 types: an agnomen, given at birth or later in life, and a signum, which appears to be an appellation indicating various types of identification such as a club. The 502 agnomina and 417 signa are taken from Roman inscriptions. An example of an agnomen is Flavinus Flavii Clovii f. Salditanus ("Flavinus, son of Flavius Clovius from Saldea"); of a signum, Cn. Lurius Abascantius--venator Taelegeniorum, where the Taelegeniorum refers to his membership in a hunters' club. 6 types of index. 110+ refs and sources.

[8.18.8] Kajanto, Iiro. (1968). On the origin of the Latin cognomen Piso. Names, 16, 43-50.
Examines conflicting views as to whether the name Piso is of Etruscan, Greek, or Latin origin. Concludes that it is of Latin origin. 14 refs.

[8.18.9] Swanson, Donald C. (1967). The names in Roman verse. Madison: University of Wisconsin Pr., 425 p.
Has about 24,000 names from the works of Roman poets such as Cicero, Horace, and Plautus. Examples include Fabius, Laurens, and Marcellus. Each entry lists the author who cited the name with available information. 40+ refs.

[8.18.10] Weaver, P. R. C. (1964). The status nomenclature of the Imperial slaves. Classical Quarterly, 58 Old Series, 14 New Series, 134-139.
Research on status nomenclature of the slaves of Ancient Rome is important because it helps date slave sepulchral inscriptions and also shows the status of Imperial slaves. Approx 13 refs.

8.19. Cypriot

[8.19.1] Michaelidou-Nicolaou, Ino. (1976). Prosopography of Ptolemaic Cyprus, Studies in Mediterranean Archeology, Vol. 44. Goteborg, Sweden: Astroms, 172 p.
Gives available information from inscriptions (steles, epitaphs, dedications etc.) on approx 1200 individuals during Ptolemaic times. Ability to read Greek script for names is necessary. 88 refs.

8.20. Czech

[8.20.1] Salzmann, Zdenek. (1981). Nicknaming in Bigar: A contribution to the anthroponymy of a Czech-speaking village in the Southern Romanian Banat. Names, 29, 121-137.
Patterns of nicknaming in a small Czech-speaking isolated mountain community of 340 people. Nicknames are used when at least 2 individuals

have the same given and family names. A person may have more than 2 nicknames, as Lupu ("wolf"), Burtanos ("big-bellied"), 7 refs.

8.21. Danish

[8.21.1] Kisbye, Torben. (1979). Osgod/Osgot on early Anglo-Danish coins. Claus Faerch, Torben Thrane & Graham D. Caie (Eds.), Essays presented to Knud Schibsbye, Publications of the Department of English, University of Copenhagen, vol. 8, pp. 12-26.
After review of a great deal of data on Danish coins concludes that the t-d interchange can be extended to other names such as Algod/Algotn; and Durgod/Dorgut(r)/Durgot. The Anglo-Saxon form in -d predominated in the early period of Danish history. 50+ refs.

[8.21.2] Kisbye, Torben. (1979). A thousand years of English influence on Danish masculine nomenclature. Nomina, 3, 61-77.
Traces English influences on Danish naming. Included are early moneyers' names, church influences (clerics and saints), Celtic names, names of authors, and other prominent persons. 45 refs.

[8.21.3] Kisbye, Torben. (1981). Name-borrowing mechanisms: The impact of English masculine personal names on a major Danish town community 1800-1950. Proceedings of the 13th Congress of Onomastic Sciences, 1978, Cracow, 1, pp. 599-607.
Using data from Aarhus, describes trends in naming due to foreign influence and socioeconomic status. Among these influences are: (1) imitation of upper-class patterns, (2) English literature, and (3) the entertainment industry.

[8.21.4] Kisbye, Torben. (1985). The Ossianic names: A contribution to the history of Celtic names in Scandinavia. Nomina, 9, 93-102.
The heroes and heroines of Scotsman James Macpherson's romantic sagas The poems of Ossian (allegedly translated from Gaelic) had an impact on naming practices in Europe. The incidence of the Ossianic names Oscar, Orla, Ossian, Fingal, Selma, Malvina, and Minona was traced in Denmark, from 1790 to the present, with some reference to modern Swedish frequencies. 14 refs.

[8.21.5] Sondergaard, George. (1979). General outline of a computational investigation of Danish naming practice. Onoma, 23, 1-32.
Examination of a Danish sample of 10,000 first names for naming motives with special attention to the problems of work with computers. 7 refs + several diagrams & tables.

8.22. Dutch

[8.22.1] Van Langendonck, Willy. (1982). Socio-onomastic properties of by-names. Onoma, 26, 55-62.
Using the Flemish dialect of Dutch, systematically discusses and evaluates binary combinations of first names, by-names, and collective (family) names. Concludes that the name-giving system shows a shift from male dominance to equalization between the sexes. Attention also focused on social aspects of naming. 5 refs.

[8.22.2] Zabriskie, George Olin. (1962). Genealogist gives help on early Dutch American names. The Genealogical Helper, 16, 251.
Some of the problems of tracing early Dutch names involving patronyms and surnames from places.

8.23. English

8.23.1. English, General

[8.23.1.1] Barley, Nigel. (1974). Perspectives on Anglo-Saxon names. Semiotica, 11, 1-31.
Analysis, discussion, and comment on Anglo-Saxon names and naming. Place and function of nicknames. Extensive references to other scholars. 100+ refs.

[8.23.1.2] Beeaff, Dianne Ebertt. (1978). Aelfraed and Haranfot: Anglo-Saxon personal names. History Today, 28, 688-690.
Background material on name-bestowal and meaning in England to the 13th century. 1 ref.

[8.23.1.3] Bennett, Michael. (1979). Spiritual kinship and the baptismal name in traditional European society. In Leighton O. Frappell (Ed.), Principalities, powers, and estates, Studies in medieval and early government and society (pp. 1-13). Adelaide, Australia: University of Adelaide Pr.
Evaluation of the documentation of spiritual kinship in western Europe between the 5th and the 18th centuries, locates late medieval English evidence "linking spiritual kinship with patterns of personal nomenclature..." Evidence suggests that as many as 90% of the nobility and gentry shared the same first name as that of their godparents (14th century). 33 refs.

[8.23.1.4] Clark, Cecily. (1978). Thoughts on the French connections of Middle-English nicknames. Nomina, 2, 38-44.
Discussion and comment on why there appears to be such a strong French influence on ME nicknames. 60+ refs.

[8.23.1.5] Clark, Cecily. (1978). Women's names in post-Conquest England: Observations and speculations. Speculum: A Journal of Medieval Studies, 53, 223-251.
Extended discussion and comment with documentation on the various influences on women's names in post-Conquest England. Concludes that Norman women played little part in the post-Conquest settlement of England. 120+ refs.

[8.23.1.6] Clark, Cecily. (1981). Nickname-creation: Some sources of evidence, 'naive' memoirs especially. Nomina, 5, 83-94.
Draws on sources from as far back as the 12th century to provide examples of nicknames and explanations on how the names were bestowed. The 100+ names include: Paul Bootlace, Slap-arse Wharton, and Searchlight Charlie. 25 refs.

[8.23.1.7] Clark, Cecily. (1982). The early personal names of King's Lynn: An essay in socio-cultural history. Nomina, 6, 51-71.
King's Lynn, in Norfolk County, was at one time an important port with a

number of foreign contacts. Using a number of sources, baptismal names were analyzed in terms of: (1) Pre-Conquest elements (Old English and Scandinavian), (2) Continental influences (French, Flemish, and German), and (3) women's names. Approx 140 refs.

[8.23.1.8] Clark, Cecily. (1985). The Liber Vitae of Thorney Abbey and its "catchment area." Nomina, 9, 53-72.
Analysis of the confraternity lists of this document of 40,000 names from the 11th and 12th centuries indicates the localities from which people came by their by-names. 100+ English by-names are evaluated. 20 refs.

[8.23.1.9] Colman, Fran. (1981). The name element Aethel- and related problems. Notes and Queries, 28, 295-301.
(The th in Aethel is more accurately represented by the OE letter thorn) Systematic evaluation of the various forms of Aethel from pre-Conquest times including those found on coins. Attention also to French, German, Danish, and various English influences. 40 refs.

[8.23.1.10] Cunnington, C. Willett. (1959). Fashions in Christian names. In J. Hadfield (Ed.), The Saturday book, Vol. 18, pp. 285-291. London: Macmillan.
Comment on fashions in English names associated with royalty, saints, Protestantism, Puritanism, and literature.

[8.23.1.11] Dodgson, John McNeal. (1985). Some Domesday person-names, mainly Post-Conquest. Nomina, 9, 41-52.
Discussion of the types of error that appear to have arisen in the compilation of the Domesday book such as those of scribes in copying and transcribing. Many examples. 38 refs.

[8.23.1.12] Insley, John. (1979). Regional variation in Scandinavian personal nomenclature in England. Nomina, 3, 52-60.
Elaboration on the complexities of tracing Scandinavian names from the 9th-13th centuries in the Danelaw (the area of England at one time under Danish rule). Many examples. 34 refs.

[8.23.1.13] Insley, John. (1982). Some Scandinavian personal names from South-West England. Namn och Boyd, 70, 78-93.
Uses late OE vernacular records, moneyers' names on coins, and other records to evaluate Scandinavian personal nomenclature in Devon and Cornwall, areas outside of the Danelaw. Comment and discussion of about 30 names such as Old Norse Atli which is derived from the Gothic Attila. 30+ refs.

[8.23.1.14] Jackson, Kenneth. (1979). Queen Boudicca? Britannia, 10, 255.
The name Boadicea, Boudicea or other spellings, is now written as Boudicca. It should be pronounced as Bowdeekah (bow as to tie a bow). 1 ref.

[8.23.1.15] Jensen, Gillian Fellows. (1968). Scandinavian personal names in Lincolnshire and Yorkshire. Copenhagen: Akademisk forlag, 374 p.
Historical background of Danish and Norwegian settlements in Lincolnshire and Yorkshire followed by a dictionary of approx 1360 major name headings derived from old sources, ex., Drengr ("warrior"). Listings of 1st and 2nd elements in personal names. 100+ refs + source documents.

[8.23.1.16] Jensen, Gillian Fellows. (1976). Some problems of a maverick anthroponymist. In Herbert Voitl (Ed.), The Study of the personal names of the British Isles (pp. 43-62). Erlangen, Germany: Institute fuer Anglistik und Amerikanistik, Universitaet Erlangen--Nurnberg.
Relates some of the difficult problems in identifying the personal name origins of English placenames especially those of Scandinavian origin. Also, the problem of defining forename, surname, by-name, and occupational name. 7 refs.

[8.23.1.17] Jensen, Gillian Fellows. (1985). On the identification of Domesday tenants in Lincolnshire. Nomina, 9, 31-40.
Uses several names such as Adestan, Edric, and Vlgrim to demonstrate possible etymology and changes. 28 refs.

[8.23.1.18] Jonsjo, Jan. (1979). Studies on Middle English nicknames: I. Compounds (Lund Studies in English No. 55). Lund: CWK Gleerup, 227 p.
After an introduction to ME (AD 1100-1400) nicknames, gives background, meaning, and citations for approximately 1200 "nicknames" from 6 northern counties and Lincolnshire. Examples are: Barlicorn ("one who sells corn"), Barfoot ("one who walks barefoot") and Wytekake ("one who sells white bread"). It appears that many of these nicknames are now surnames. Hundreds of citations for names. 100+ refs. List of OE and Middle English name elements.

[8.23.1.19] Kristensson, Gillis. (1976). Computer processing of Middle English personal-name materials. In Herbert Voitl (Ed.), The study of the personal names of the British Isles (pp. 62-74) Erlangen, Germany: Institute fuer Anglistik und Amerikanistik, Universitaet Erlangen--Nurnberg.
Description of computer project involving ME names at the University of Lund.

[8.23.1.20] McClure, Peter. (1981). Nicknames and petnames: Linguistic forms and social contexts. Nomina, 5, 63-76.
Discussion of sociolinguistic aspects of naming and sets up a classification. There are 2 major sub-types of nicknames: secondary forms of official names and primary nicknames (4 categories). Against this system the work of the Opies [26.1.18] and Morgan et al. [26.1.16] is evaluated. 21 refs.

[8.23.1.21] Nightingale, J. Leslie. (1959). Puritans at the font. History Today, 9, 195-197.
General comments on naming practices of the periods before, during, and after the Commonwealth.

[8.23.1.22] Pine, Leslie Gilbert. (1984). A dictionary of nicknames. London: Routledge & Kegan Paul, 207 p.
Contains approx 2800 (mostly British) nickname entries. Many are now considered as surnames, such as Grice (gray-haired). Another example is Soapy Sam (Samuel Wilberforce, 1805-1873; Bishop of Oxford), so named because of his way of speaking. 6 refs.

[8.23.1.23] Selten, Bo. (1965). Some notes on Middle English by-names independent use. English Studies, 46, 165-181.
Systematic coverage mainly from East Anglia of ME by-names. Examples are for nicknames: Brunerobin; for local by-names, Claverying; for genealogical

by-names, Howissune (son   of High); and for   occupational by-names,
Wytbredman. Approx 120 names covered. 56 refs.

[8.23.1.24]   Selten,   Bo. (1968-1969).   Early   East-Anglian nicknames:
'Shakespeare names.' Scripta Minora (Lund), 3, 1-27.
Shakespeare-type names are compound names consisting of a formless verb and
its direct object, ex., Spillewit (scatterbrain). Approx 100 names are
discussed for possible meaning with citations. Nicknames are in 3
categories: nicknames proper (ex., Dolitel "idler,") occupational (ex.,
Planterose, "gardener"), and local nicknames (ex., Passelwe, "ferryman").
57 refs.

[8.23.1.25] Selten, Bo. (1972). The Anglo-Saxon heritage in Middle
English personal names: East Anglia 1100-1399. Lund, Sweden: Berlingska
Boktrycheriet, 187 p.
Careful analysis of how personal names of Anglo-Saxon origin survived in
the Middle English period in East Anglia. 150+ refs.

[8.23.1.26] Selten, Bo. (1975). Early East-Anglian nicknames: Bahuvrihi
names. Lund, Sweden: CWK Gleerup, 1975, 69 p.
A bahuvrihi is a name compounded of 2 nouns or adjectives, as Prudfot "one
who had proud feet," i. e., a proud gait. Approximately 250 names are
evaluated and explained with citations. The time period covered is from
1100-1400. 80+ refs.

[8.23.1.27] Sheppard, David. (1964). Fashions in Christian names. Durham
Research Review (England), 4, 140-144.
Presents tables of most   common first names from birth and death
announcements in 2 British newspapers, The Times and The Guardian and also
from electors lists. Discussion of fashions in names. 5 refs.

[8.23.1.28] Smart, Veronica. (1979). Moneyers' names on the Anglo-Saxon
coinage. Nomina, 3, 20-28. Extensive data on coins of the Anglo-Saxon,
Norman, and early Plantagenet periods. 36 refs.

[8.23.1.29] Thomson, R. L. (1985). Manx surnames. Nomina, 9, 89-92.
Description of the transformation of Gaelic surnames from the 15th century.
Prefixes such as Mac or O' have been subjected to lenition with examples
such as Quiggin, (Viking), Crebbin (Robbin), and Quine (Matthew). Other
surnames are drawn from occupations (Taggart, "priest"). Concludes that
there has been "a creeping anglicization and europeanization in first
names." 2 refs.

[8.23.1.30] Van Els, T. J. M. (1972). The Kassel manuscript of Bede's
'Historia Ecclesiastica Gentis Anglorum' and its Old English material.
Assen, Netherlands: Gorcum, 277 p.
Van Els has examined the OE material of the 8th century Kassel ms. In
addition to extensive background material, there is a listing of about 500
personal names, placenames, and prominent people with meaning, etymology,
and other information. Examples include; Balthild ("bold in combat"), a
one-time Anglo-Saxon slave who married Clovis; and Coelred ("red ship"),
son of King Aedilred of Mercia, reigned from 709 to 716. 350+ refs.

[8.23.1.31] Voitl, Herbert. (Ed.). (1976). The study of the personal
names of the British Isles. Erlangen, Germany: Institute fuer Anglistik und
Amerikanistik, Universitaet Erlangen--Nurnberg, 135 p.

Report of a conference to coordinate and exchange information on British name research. For contributions by von Feilitzen, Fellows Jensen, Redmonds, and Voitl see individual entries in this section and 8.23.2. 85 refs.

[8.23.1.32]   von Feilitzen, Olof. (1968). Some Old English uncompounded personal names and bynames. Studia Neophilologica, 40, 5-16.
Elaborates on 25 personal names not previously described such as Aedding which is an -ing derivative of Aedda and Edor from hedge and prince; 16 by-names such as braders from OE brad ears, ("broad arse") and clenehand from claene hand ("clean hand"). 75 refs.

[8.23.1.33]   von Feilitzen, Olof. (1976). The personal names and bynames of the Winton Domesday. In Martin Biddle (Ed.), Winchester in the Early Middle Ages (pp. 143-229).
Scholarly presentation based upon the 1066, 1110, and 1148 surveys of Winchester. Has approximately 600 personal names with derivations, also tables of local by-names, occupational by-names, and nicknames. Many refs and citations.

[8.23.1.34]   von Feilitzen, Olof. (1976). Planning a new Old English Onomasticon. In Herbert Voitl (Ed.), The Study of the personal names of the British Isles (pp. 16-42). Erlangen, Germany: Institute fuer Anglistik und Amerikanistik, Universitaet Erlangen--Nurnberg.
Criticizes Searle's Onomasticon Anglo-Saxicum (see Smith--[6.16], No. 1657) for: (1) normalizing names, (2) omissions, (3) failure to identify people, and (4) use of irrelevant material. Calls for a new Onomasticon to rectify errors. 39 refs. 5 appendixes.

[8.23.1.35]   von Feilitzen, Olof & Blunt, Christopher. (1971). Personal names on the coinage of Edgar. In Peter Clemoes & Kathleen Hughes, England before the Conquest (pp. 183-214). Cambridge, Eng: University Pr.
Systematic evaluation of approx 250 personal names found on coins of the late 10th century. 150+ refs.

[8.23.1.36] Withycombe, Elizabeth Gidley. (1977). The Oxford dictionary of English Christian names, (3rd ed.). Oxford: Clarendon Pr., 310 p.
Scholarly description and derivation of names. Listing of rolls with the name. Also a section on common words derived from Christian names. 60+ refs.

[8.23.1.37]   White, G. Pawley. (1972). A handbook of Cornish names. Camborne, England: G. Pawley White, 70 p.
Cornwall is on the SW coast of England. Following an introduction to Cornish names, there is a listing of about 800 items. Among the names included are Moyle ("bald"), Rouse ("heath"), and Tremayne ("homestead of stones"). Items show origin, meaning, and where found. 16 refs.

8.23.2. English: Surnames

[8.23.2.1] Addison, Sir William. (1978). Understanding English surnames. London: Batsford, 176 p.
Discussion of surnames in England within 8 major regions such as Wessex, the West Midlands, and Lancashire and Yorkshire. Many stories especially about more unusual names such as Catchpole and Cokinbred. Index has about 1100 surnames. 47 refs.

[8.23.2.2] Ashley, Leonard R. N. (1963). French surnames and the English.
Names, 11, 177-181.
Comment on the number of English names such as Algernon, Balliol, Haig, and
St. Clair that are of French origin.

[8.23.2.3] Barber, Henry. (1968). British family names: Their origin and
meaning with lists of Scandinavian, Frisian, Anglo-Saxon, and Norman names,
2nd ed. Baltimore: Genealogical Publ., 286 p. (Originally published in
London, 1903)
Gives Domesday names, Old Norse, and personal names. Major part of the
book is an alphabetic list of British surnames and meanings with attention
to Scandinavian and Frisian names.

[8.23.2.4] Clark. Cecily. (1976). Some early Canterbury surnames. English
Studies, 57, 294-309.
Gives background on about 75 surnames. Some are occupational such as
Feiner (hay-dealer) and Wolmongere (wool-merchant); others are patronymic
such as Munin from Simon, Colle from Nicolas. 85+ refs.

[8.23.2.5] Clark, Cecily. (1980). An anthroponymist looks at   an
Anglo-Norman new town.   Proceedings of   the Battle Conference on
Anglo-Norman Studies, 2, 21-41; 168-172.
Discussion of the principles and methodology of name study in 12th century
England. This is followed by a listing from a British Museum manuscript of
115 householders at Battle. Each entry contains available information,
ex., No. 21, Wilelmi Pinel. The Wilelmi is from Continental German; the
Pinel is a nickname or toponym from the Old French pinel (small pine-tree).
Approx 80 refs.

[8.23.2.6] Cottle, Basil. (1967). The Penguin dictionary of surnames.
Hammondsworth, Middlesex, England: Penguin, 234 p.
Surnames of the British Isles and those of British stock in the US.
Surnames derived from first names, location, occupation and other sources.
Includes over 8000 surnames. 30 refs.

[8.23.2.7] Dolan, J. R. (1972). English ancestral names: The evolution of
the name from medieval occupations. New York: Clarkson N. Potter, 381 p.
Gives historical background of 5000 names developed from occupations.
Organized into 189 groups. Comprehensive, scholarly. Index. 58 refs.

[8.23.2.8] Dolley, Michael. (1983). Toponomic surnames and the pattern of
pre-1830 English immigration into the Isle of Man, Peter McClure (Ed.).
Nomina, 7, 47-64.
Draws from the work of John Joseph Kneen's The personal names of the Isle
of Man (see Smith--[6.16], No. 1893) to evaluate about 400 surnames
according to area of England and time period. 2 appendices. 12 refs.

[8.23.2.9] Ekwall, Eilert. (1957). Some cases of initial variation in
medieval London surnames. Moderna Sprak, 51, 21-27.
Explanation of how names with an initial H such as Horsham were modified in
spoken English. Thus, Horsham--of Horsham--Forsham. Other names were
similarly changed as Heston to Feston. Loss of initial N was observed in
some names as, Neceton to Eketon. Initial T has also been lost as
Trippelawe to Riplawe. 6 refs.

[8.23.2.10] Ekwall, Eilert. (1965). Some early London bynames and
surnames. English Studies, 46, 113-118.
Gives derivations of 20 names such as Singemasse ("singer of masses"),
Musege ("mouse-eyed person"), and Wombestrong ("one with a strong worm," i.
e. a good appetite). 13 refs.

[8.23.2.11] Forster, Klaus. (1977). English family names from places in
England. Nomina, 1, 23-26.
A thesis abstract based on 1200 surnames and associated placenames focusing
on how the differences arose, i. e., surname Chillinton vs. placename
Chillington.

[8.23.2.12] Hassall, W. O. (1967). History through surnames. Oxford:
Pergamon, 224 p.
Draws from Ekwall's Oxford dictionary of place-names, Withycombe's Oxford
dictionary of English Christian names (see Smith [6.16], No. 565 and
[8.23.1.36]), and Reaney's Dictionary of British surnames [8.23.2.31].
Directed primarily at "younger readers." Describes the development of
mostly British surnames through historical periods. Gives information and
meaning on approximately 16,000 names and variations. Index. 4 refs.

[8.23.2.13] Holt, J. C. (1982). What's in a name? Family nomenclature and
the Norman Conquest. Reading, England: University of Reading, 23 p.
Through a critical discussion of a number of families such as Arundel,
Beaumont, Montgomery, and Mowbray, demonstrates the linkage of toponyms
with hereditary names. Approx 66 refs.

[8.23.2.14] Hoskins, W. G. (1972). The homes of family names. History
Today, 22, 189-194.
General description of some of the methodology of doing research on
surnames with comments on names research in Leicestershire,
Gloucestershire, Norfolk, and other areas. 2 refs.

[8.23.2.15] Hughes, James Pennethorne. (1961). How you got your name: The
origin and meaning of surnames, (rev. ed.). London: Phoenix, 169 p.
Concise treatment of the origin of surnames from patronyms, locations,
occupations, and nicknames. Mostly English. Index. 17 item biblio.

[8.23.2.16] Lenfest, Donald E. (1980). Lenfestey-Lenveiset: A case of
mistaken identity. Names, 28, 32-42.
Reacting to the listing by Reaney in his Dictionary of British surnames
[8.23.2.31] that Lenfestey is associated with Lenveiset, Lenfest provides
substantial evidence that the names have different origins. 12 refs.

[8.23.2.17] Matthews, Constance M. (1966). English surnames. London:
Weidenfeld & Nicolson, 359 p.; New York: Scribner's, 1967.
Covers topics of family relationships, local names, Pre-Conquest names,
surnames from women's first names. Tables from London telephone directory.
Approx 2250 items in index. 100+ refs.

[8.23.2.18] Matthews, Constance M. (1967, Winter). History in the
telephone book. Horizon, 9, 105-111.
Background material on surnames, especially common ones. Included are
Lewis (Welsh from Llewellyn), Rosenbaum (rose tree), and Webster (weaver).

[8.23.2.19] Matthews, Constance M. (1967). How surnames began.   London: Butterworth, 148 p.
General introduction to surnames. A simplified version of the author's English surnames [8.23.2.17] above. British emphasis.

[8.23.2.20] McClure, Peter. (1978). Surnames from English placenames as evidence for mobility in the Middle Ages. Local Historian, 13, 80-86.
Discussion of some of the difficulties and their resolution of using surnames as evidence of mobility. 18 refs.

[8.23.2.21] McClure, Peter. (1982). Onomastic notes: The origin of the surname Waterer. Nomina, 6, 92.
Concludes that the origin of the name is topographical ("at the water") rather than occupational ("one whose occupation is to water"). 4 refs.

[8.23.2.22] McClure, Peter. (1983). The ME. occupational term Ringere Nomina, 7, 102.
Suggests that the surname could also refer to a person who makes rings and that the final -er is explained as misinterpretation of a copyist's final flourish. 4 refs.

[8.23.2.23] McKinley, Richard Alexander. (1969). Norfolk surnames in the sixteenth century.   Department of English Local History, Leicester University, Occasional Papers, Second Series, No. 2, 60 p.
Norfolk is a county a little NE of London. Analyses of subsidy rolls, military surveys, and other records yielded a list of 18,500 surnames. These may be classified as: (1) locative, 17%; (2) topographical, 11%; (3) patronymic or metronymic, 26%; (4) other relationships, 0.5%; (5) occupational, 19%; (6) based on physical characteristics, 3%; and (7) others, 23.5%. Approx 300 specific names are mentioned. 100+ refs.

[8.23.2.24] McKinley, Richard Alexander. (1975).   Norfolk and Suffolk surnames in the Middle Ages.   Vol. 2, English Surnames Series. London: Phillimore, 175 p.
Comprehensive description and analysis of surnames in East Anglia. Topics include surnames derived from occupation, location, personal names, and the influence of social class on surnames. Examples. Tables. 200+ refs.

[8.23.2.25] McKinley, Richard Alexander. (1977). Surnames of Oxfordshire, Vol. 3, English Surnames Series. London: Leopard's Head Pr., 311 p.
Oxfordshire is a region NW of London. Comprehensive description and analysis of surnames of that region derived from location, occupation, first names, and nicknames. There are also chapters on names of married women and of bondsmen. Index of names. Hundreds of references.

[8.23.2.26] McKinley, Richard Alexander. (1980). Social class and the origin of surnames. Genealogists' Magazine, 20(2), 52-56.
Lists from the 12th and 13th century from East Anglia, Suffolk, and Norfolk show that there was a high percentage of surnames derived from placenames among the land-owning classes. Similar findings are shown in data from Oxfordshire and Lancashire somewhat later. Among bondsmen, surnames derived from topological features (Field, Brooks etc.) and from Christian names were more common. 10 refs.

[8.23.2.27] McKinley, Richard Alexander. (1981).   The surnames of Lancashire, Vol. 4, English Surnames Series. London: Leopard's Head Press,

501 p.
Lancashire is on the W coast of England and includes the cities of
Manchester and Liverpool. There is extensive coverage of surnames in the
region. Major sections include: development of hereditary names, surnames
derived from location (Ashton, Furness), topography (someone who lived near
a feature of the land, ex., Cross, Crabtree), occupation, relationship
(Cousins, Brothers), personal names, and nicknames (Stringfellow
"strong-fellow," Whitehead). Also included are sections on the Salford
Hundred and Rochdale parish. Hundreds of citations and refs.

[8.23.2.28] Parish, William Douglas. (1967). A dictionary of the Sussex
dialect and collection of provincialisms in use in the county of
Sussex, (new ed., Helena Hall, Ed.). Boxhill, England: Gardners, 185 p.
(Originally published by Farncombe at Lewes, 1875)
Pp. 157-160 give a listing of surnames derived from Anglo-Saxon words.

[8.23.2.29] Padel, O. J. (1985). Cornish names in 1327. Nomina, 9, 81-87.
An analysis of surnames of the 1327 Lay Subsidy Roll concludes that an
"overwhelming majority of people with place-name surnames bore names which
were those of farms in the parishes where they were living." 10 refs.

[8.23.2.30] Pine, Leslie Gilbert. (1965). The story of surnames. London:
Country Life, 152 p. (Also published by Tuttle: Rutland, VT in 1966)
General introduction to British surnames. In addition to patronymic,
location, occupation, and nickname types of surnames includes chapters on
Norman, Welsh, Scottish, and Irish surnames. Index. 35 refs.

[8.23.2.31] Reaney, Perry Hide. (1961). A dictionary of British surnames.
London: Routledge & Kegan Paul, 1961, 366 p. (with corrections).
(Originally published in 1958)
Scholarly introduction. Names are given in alphabetical order with
citations of first historical usage. Probably over 11,000 entries. 250+
ref/biblio items.

[8.23.2.32] Reaney, Perry Hide. (1967). The origin of English surnames.
London: Routledge & Kegan Paul, 415 p.
An interpretation and extension of the author's A dictionary of British
surnames above. Covers local surnames; those of office, occupation, and
relationship, and those derived from physical and social characteristics.
Index. 68 item biblio.

[8.23.2.33] Redmonds, George. (1973). Yorkshire West Riding, Vol. 1,
English Surnames Series. Chichester, England: Phillimore, 314 p.
A study of 4 categories of surname developed from nicknames, relationship,
occupation and office, and geographical from the areas of Bradford, Leeds,
York, and Sheffield. Materials from 1300 to 1969 are used to classify and
identify patterns of English surnames. Approx 3400 surnames in index.
Maps. 150+ refs + parish registers.

[8.23.2.34] Redmonds, George. (1976). English surnames research. In
Herbert Voitl (Ed.), The Study of the personal names of the British Isles
(pp. 75-86). Erlangen, Germany: Institute fuer Anglistik und
Amerikanistik, Universitaet Erlangen--Nurnberg.
Criticizes Reaney's Dictionary of British surnames [8.23.2.31]. Recommends
tracing of modern surnames by genealogical methods. 4 refs.

[8.23.2.35] Redmonds, George. (1981). Migration and the linguistic development of surnames. Family History, 11, Nos. 77-78, New Series, 53-54, 173-180.
Develops the position that as bearers of a surname migrate, there are variations in the name. Traces the Lightowler family in Rochdale parish from 1246 to Yorkshire, Bradford and the Colne Valley as Lightoller and Lightholder. Hinchcliffe and other names are also discussed. 4 specific refs.

[8.23.2.36] Redmonds, George. (1985). Personal names and surnames in some West Yorkshire 'Royds.' Nomina, 9, 73-80.
Discussion and comment on the suffix -royd which arose in the 13th century (a royd refers to land that was cleared from the forest). However, the name element declined after 1350 when land-clearing also declined. 19 refs.

[8.23.2.37] Ruckdeschel, Gisela. (1980). Secondary motivation in English family names. Nomina, 4, 64-66.
Abstract of a doctoral dissertation at the Universitaet Erlangen--Nurnberg. Focuses on 887 English surnames, mostly ME, with aspects of secondary motivation (introduction of "unknown, unfamiliar, and isolated words into the vocabulary of a language with known and familiar words, although no etymological relation exists among the words").

[8.23.2.38] Scheetz, George H. (1981). Wrights wrought: The history of a word. In Lawrence E. Seits (Ed.), The dangerous, secret name of God Fartley's compressed gas company: the barf'n'choke; and other matters. onomastic, Papers of the North Central Names Institute, 2, 52-70.
History of the surname Wright in various forms such as Boltwright, Housewright, and Cartwright. 26 refs.

[8.23.2.39] Verstappen, Peter. (1980). The book of names: Origins and oddities of popular names. London: Pelham, 256 p.
Gives background information on 76 of the most common English surnames and their variations. These names account for 50% of the population. Thus, for the name Moore ("dark-complected"), there are 16 variations including Morecraft, Morley, Moorcock, and Mocking.

[8.23.2.40] Voitl, Herbert. (1976). A computer archive of present-day British and Early Modern English family names. In Herbert Voitl (Ed.), The Study of the personal names of the British Isles (pp. 87-110). Erlangen, Germany: Institute fuer Anglistik und Amerikanistik, Universitaet Erlangen--Nurnberg.
Describes a computer archive with 2 main parts: modern British family names from a number of sources (last 100 years) and selective listings of names from the early modern period beginning with 1598. 33 refs + sources.

Eskimo: See--8.35. Inuit
8.24. Estonian

[8.24.1] Must, Hildegard. (1962). The names of the Apostles as Estonian Christian names. Names, 10, 260-264.
Listing of names of the Apostles, Andreas (Andrew), Bartholomaeus (Bartholomew) et al., as used in various foreign forms and in Estonian forms. 6 refs.

[8.24.2]   Must, Hildegard. (1964). Trends in Estonian name-giving from
1900-1945. Names, 12, 42-51.
In reaction to the monotonous pattern of traditional saints' names, new
patterns of name-giving arose in Estonia at the beginning of the 20th
Century. By 1945, there was a new stock of names which included: revived
short forms of saints' names, recently adopted Finnish names,
newly-invented Estonian names, and revived pre-Christian native names. 9
refs.

[8.24.3]   Must, Hildegard. (1965). English Christian names in Estonian
anthroponymy. In Victor Koresaar and Alexis Rannit (Eds.), Estonian poetry
and language: Studies in honor of Ants Oras (pp. 125-135). City not
listed: Estonian Learned Society in America.
Comment and discussion of English names that became popular in Estonia
after the beginning of the 20th century. Examples include English names of
Germanic origin such as, Edgar, Edward, Alfred, Edith, Daisy, and Maud; and
English names of non-Germanic origin such as John, Tom, Allan, Betty,
Jenny, and Nancy. 11 refs.

[8.24.4] Must, Hildegard. (1970). Scandinavian Kalf and Estonian Kalev.
Names, 18, 1-8.
Examination of the evidence that there once was an historical Viking name
Kalev but the true story is forgotten and blurred by mythical features. 38
refs.

8.25. Finnish

[8.25.1] Larmouth, Donald W. (1967). Finnish surname change in Minnesota.
American Speech, 42, 31-37.
First, gives the general rationale of Finnish names. Examples being:
Seppala (smithy), Saarinen (island), and Makinen (hill). Then, gives a
description of patterns of phonological and morphological surname change in
Northern Minnesota. 50+ examples.

[8.25.2]   Narhi, Eeva Maria. (1984). Changes in surnames in bilingual
Finland during the twentieth century: The year 1906. XV, Internationaler
Kongress fuer Namenforschung, 1984, Leipzig, 5, 133-140.
In 1906, approx 100,000 non-Finnish surnames were finnicized (Swedish had
been the official language). Analysis of the shift patterns indicates; (1)
no preference for a name at the beginning of the alphabet, (2) a preference
for shorter names. Specific patterns also analyzed. 2 refs.

8.26. French

[8.26.1] du Gard, Rene Coulet. (1979, Dec.). French eponyms. Onomastica,
No. 56, 13-24.
Lists and defines about 80 eponyms of French origin in 6 categories:
literary, inventor, mythological, historical, religious, and dynastic.
Some eponyms are human such as a Catalina ("troublemaker") and a Benjamin
(referring to the youngest son in a family or group). 1 ref.

[8.26.2] Dupaquier, Jacques. (1981). Naming-practices, godparenthood, and
kinship in the Vexin, 1540-1900. Journal of Family History, 6, 135-155.
The research is based upon data from the Vexin (a region NW of Paris)

between 1600 and 1872. The results indicate that the number of first names became restricted from 1600 to the end of that century. Then, the number of names increased with the introduction of double and triple names. The romantic period saw a large increase in names. Some comparisons are made with French Canada 1621-1699. Naming fashions were spread from the upper to the lower classes and from urban to rural areas. Discussions, examples, and tables. 11 refs, all in French.

[8.26.3] Johnson, E. D. (1956). First names in French Louisiana. Names, 4, 49-53.
Describes shift away from traditional French first names to common English ones. Discussion of current pronunciation of French names. 1 ref.

[8.26.4] Ketcham, Rodney K. (1967). Investigation of surnames as a cultural hobby. French Review, 40, 368-376.
Explanation of 50+ surname root names, each with a number of variations. For example, Champ (field), Alcam, Cam, Camps, DeCamp, Descamps, and others. 7 refs.

[8.26.5] Leon, Monique. (1976). Of names and first names in a small French rural community: Linguistic and sociological approaches. Semiotica, 1976, 17, 211-231.
Systematic introduction and analysis of the naming practices in a small French Catholic community near Tours; forms of address. 23 refs.

[8.26.6] Morgan, M. R. (1979). The meaning of Old French Polain, Latin Pullanus. Medium Aevum, 48, 40-54.
Polain is the term that was used to describe a 12th century Latin Christian crusader who was a permanent inhabitant of the Latin kingdom of Jerusalem. By the 13th century, however, the term had acquired a negative meaning related to the military failure against the Muslims. 36 refs.

[8.26.7] Speer, David G. (1957). Given names in Strasbourg. Names, 5, 71-79.
Gives tables of the 100 most common male and female names in that city on information from birth notices.

[8.26.8] Van Eerde, John. (1959). Names in Provence. CLA Journal, 3, 119-122.
Provence is a district of SE France. Reports on the etymology of some of the epithet names used by people of towns and villages. People in Pernes have been called Li Luneu (the Lunatics); in St. Dedier, lis Arrougant (the Swaggerers), and Mormoiron, li Dent-Rousso (The Red Tooths). 1 ref.

[8.26.9] Wakefield, Walter L. (1979). Pseudonyms and nicknames in Inquisitorial documents of the Middle Ages in Southern France. Names, 27, 188-197.
Draws on 12th and 13th century material from 5 sources to show the use of pseudonyms and nicknames in 150 entries, ex., "Arnaldus de Sus qui vocabatur" (Arnaldus de Sus who by his proper name is Pepi). 15 refs.

8.27. Frisian

[8.27.1] Droege, Geart B. (1955). Frisian family and place names. Names, 3, 89-97.

Frisian family names are mostly derived from patronymics and end in a_. Examples are Tolsma, Alena, Dijkstra, and Boonstra. 12 refs on surnames.

[8.27.2] Droege, Geart B. (1978). Frisian family names: Borne by Jews only. Names, 26, 27-39.
Historical notes on Jews with characteristic a_ endings to their surnames. Names include Leefsma, Drilsma, and van Biema. Map. Table. Many notes. 50 refs.

8.28. German/Germanic/Gothic

[8.28.1] Droege, Geart B. (1966). *Fris-/*Fre2s- in two-stemmed West Germanic given names. Names, 14, 169-174.
Traces various forms of the root as the first part of dithematic names back to the year 840. Evaluates different positions on the root's origin. 30 refs, mostly non-English.

[8.28.2] Graham, Robert Somerville. (1955). The anglicization of German family names in western Canada. American Speech, 30, 260-264.
Relates how a number of German surnames in W central Saskatchewan kept their spelling but changed their pronunciation. Thus, Hauk became Hook; Heidt, Hyde; and Wierhacke, Wierhockey. Analysis of the patterns of vowel, consonant, spirant, and other changes.

[8.28.3] Hartmann, Torsten. (1985). Ratings on German personal names and E, P, and A. Psychological Reports, 56, 859-862.
Use of the semantic differential with German first names provides confirmation for the E (Evaluation), P (Potency), and A (Activity) factors of Osgood. Specific names used are not listed. 14 refs.

[8.28.4] Johnson, Arta F. (1981). A guide to the spelling and pronunciation of German names. Columbus, OH: The Copy Shop, 52 p.
Describes patterns of how German names came to be respelled in the US, ex., Ku"hle to Keeley, Eberle to Everly, Dresch to Tresh, Hund to Hunt. Many examples. Index. 6 refs.

[8.28.5] Marchand, James W. (1959). Names of Germanic origin in Latin and Romance sources in the study of Germanic philology. Names, 7, 167-181.
Concludes that data from inscriptions and early writings provide valuable evidence of great value for the history of Germanic names and name-giving. 35 refs, mostly German.

[8.28.6] Nicolaisen, Wilhelm F. H. (1985). Recent German publications in onomastics. Names, 33, 158-168.
Reports some major ideas of 9 recent books. Among them (titles translated) are: Rainer Wimmer's Proper names in German, Reinhard Krien's Name physiognomy, and Reiner Frank's On the question of a stratum specific personal name nomenclature. 13 refs.

[8.28.7] Penzl, Herbert. (1966). Early Germanic names and vowel shifts. Names, 14, 65-68.
The diachronic study of spelling of name forms provides phonemic data. Discussion of shift from long e_ to long a_. 7 refs, mostly non-English.

[8.28.8] Penzl, Herbert. (1977). Names and historical Germanic philology:
The bilingual sixth century Ravenna deeds. Names, 25, 8-14.
Evaluation of 11 names which appeared on a land contract in both Gothic and
Latin. Gives evidence for double names (Danihel and Igila) and some for
morpheme replacement (Mirica: Mirila). 16 refs.

[8.28.9] Penzl, Herbert. (1982). Personal names and Germanic noun
inflection. Names, 30, 69-75.
Discussion of the inflection patterns used with names in Old High German,
Middle High German, Early New High German, and New High German. 20 refs.

[8.28.10] Schwartz, Stephen P. (1968). The use of onomastics in
linguistics: The first steps. Names, 16, 119-126.
Discussion of how knowledge of an ancient language such as West Germanic,
East Germanic, or North Germanic can be obtained from the ways that then
contemporary writers, such as Tacitus, described aspects of those cultures,
especially names. 10 refs, mostly non-English.

[8.28.11] Sotiroff, George. (1968). Onomastic and lexical curiosities in
early Gothic.   Etudes slaves et est-europeenes: Slavic and East European
Studies, Revue Universitaire, 13, 53-62.
Develops the position that Gothic up to the 13th century in the treatment
of names shows some Hunnic or Slavonic features, but few Germanic ones.
Research was based upon examination of Chanson de la Croisade Albigeoise,
the Ravenna ms. and other sources. 14 refs.

[8.28.12] von Feilitzen, Olof. (1963). Some Continental Germanic personal
names in England. In Arthur Brown & Peter Foote (Eds.), Early English and
Norse studies (pp.46-61). London: Methuen.
Listing with sources of over 80 names not listed in the work of Thorvald
Forssner (1916). 47 refs.

8.29. Greek

[8.29.1] Alatis, James E. (1955). The Americanization of Greek names.
Names, 3, 137-156.
Comprehensive presentation on the patterns of Greek surname changing. Data
were obtained in Columbus, Ohio. Some names were translated as Chrysoules
(from Chryso "gold") to Golding. Other names have been modified in various
ways as Balasopoulos to Wallace. 8 refs.

[8.29.2] Astour, Michael C. (1967). Hellenosemitica: An ethnic and
cultural study in West Semitic impact on Mycenaean Greece. London: Brill,
424 p.
Extensive analysis of a number of Greek myths and legends such as
Bellerophon, Cadmos, and Asclepios reveals their Semitic roots. 558 refs.

[8.29.3] Bernard, Russell H. (1968). Paratsoukli: Institutionalized
nicknaming in rural Greece. Ethnologia Europaea, 2, 65-74.
Kalymnos is a small island 90 miles N of Rhodes among the Dodecanese. Its
pattern of nicknaming is assumed to be similar to that of other Greek rural
communities.   Nicknames are: (1) personal identifiers, and (2) always
descriptive of outstanding physical characteristics, peculiar behavior
characteristics, or of unusual events in the person's life.   Several
examples. 9 refs.

[8.29.4] Bialor, Perry A. (1967). What's in a name? Aspects of the social organization of a Greek farming community related to naming customs. Kroeber Anthropological Papers, Special Publication No.1, 95-108.
Results confirm that the tradition of naming the first-born of each sex after the paternal grandparents is followed. Discussion of names from saints, role of godparents, nicknames. 8 refs.

[8.29.5] Ilievski, Petar. (1981). Mycenean-Greek personal names as a lexical stock. Proceedings of the 13th Congress of Onomastic Sciences, 1978, Cracow, 1, pp. 529-534.
Description of the translation of Mycenean Greek Linear B script inscriptions involving personal names with special reference to the intensive prefixes eri- and ari-. 6 refs.

[8.29.6] Kulukundis, Elias. (1967). The feasts of memory: A journey to a Greek island: New York: Holt, Rinehart & Winston, pp. 55-77.
A Greek-American tries to find the roots of his surname.

[8.29.7] Lindgren, Margareta. (1973). The people of Pylos: Prosopographical and methodological studies in the Pylos archives. Boreas: Uppsala Studies in Ancient Mediterranean and Near Eastern Civilization, Acta Universitatis Upsaliensis, 3, Part I, 191 p., Part II, 228 p.
Pylos, a town on the W coast of Messinia, Greece has a number of tablets from Mycenean times. From these, information has been developed on approximately 1900 names which have been transliterated into English. 400+ refs.

[8.29.8] Tavuchis, Nicholas. (1971). Naming patterns and kinship among Greeks. Ethnos, 30, 152-162.
Second generation Greek Americans tend to show a shift in the naming pattern from paternal kin to paternal and maternal kin similar to other American groups. 6 refs.

8.30. Huguenot

[8.30.1] Mayrant, Drayton. (1958). French Huguenot names and their mispronunciation. Names in South Carolina, 7(Winter), 51.
Explains how about 14 French Huguenot surnames have had their pronunciation modified as the bearers lived first in England and then in South Carolina, ex., DuPre is now DuPree; Gourdin, Gud-dine.

8.31. Hungarian

[8.31.1] Kalman, Bela. (1978). The world of names: A study in Hungarian onomatology (Zsolt Viragos & Michael Laming, Trans.). Budapest: Akademiai Kiado, 199 p.
Besides placenames, there is extensive coverage of first names, hypocoristic names, surnames, and change of name. Systematic scholarly background on Hebrew, Greek, Latin, Germanic, Slavic, Turkic, and other languages in relation to names. Tables of fashions in Hungarian first names from the 16th century. Map. Index. 100+ refs, almost all in Hungarian.

[8.31.2] Nogrady, Michael. (1979, June). Ancient Sumerian names in modern Hungary. Onomastica, No. 55, 5-13.
Discussion of evidence and conclusion that some modern Hungarian surnames such as Guti and Ugi go back 5000 years to ancient Sumerian. Both languages originate from an older common language. 7 refs.

8.32. Icelandic

[8.32.1]   Bessason, Haraldur.   (1967). A few specimens of North American-Icelandic. Scandinavian Studies, 39, 115-146.
Pp. 132-144 describe Icelandic surnames. Most immigrants kept their Icelandic names (ex., Sveinn Grimsson) within the Icelandic community but used a name such as John Anderson in the general community. Listing of surnames derived from Icelandic names such as Hofteig from Hofteigur and Benson from Benediktsson. 50+ surnames mentioned. 6 refs in this section.

[8.32.2] Hale, Christopher S. (1981). Modern Icelandic personal bynames. Scandinavian Studies, 53, 397-404.
Classification and description of 8 categories of by-names (some authors would call these nicknames) from NW Iceland. Many of the names are derogatory, ex., Gopgi, goes (goose), Kitti, krungar (hump). 3 refs.

[8.32.3] Tomasson, Richard F. (1975). The continuity of Icelandic names and naming patterns. Names, 23, 281-289.
Comparisons of the most frequent 25 or so male and female first names from Saga times (870 AD to 1030 AD) to 1970 at 6 intervals show striking continuity Other naming trends discussed include alliteration, variation, and commemoration. 23 refs.

[8.32.4] Wolf-Rattkay, W. H. (1971). Some onomastic and toponomic aspects of Icelandic traditionalism. Names, 19, 229-239.
Information on current Icelandic naming practices and how foreign names are treated in Icelandic. Indicates that traditional patronymic naming practices are maintained. 15 refs.

Indian, American: See--8.03. American Indian
8.33. Indo-Pakistani Sub-Continent
(includes India, Pakistan, and Bangladesh)

[8.33.1]   Emeneau, Murray Benson. (1974). Ritual structure and language structure of the Todas. Transactions of the American Philosophical Society, New Series, 64(Part6), 1-103.
The Todas are a small pastoral tribe (about 800) in S India who are oriented around buffalo herds and dairies. A systematic description of naming patterns is followed by 819 men's and 275 women's names with information on origin and meaning. 33 refs.

[8.33.2]   Gonda, Jan. (1970). Notes on names and the name of God in Ancient India, Verhandlingen der Koninklijke Nederlandse Akademie van Wetenschappen, AFD. Letterkunde Nieuwe Reeks, Deel 75, No. 4). Amsterdam: North Holland.
Extensive scholarly treatment of naming and the name of God in Ancient Indian religious writings. Hundreds of specific refs.

[8.33.3] Huq, A. M. Abdul. (1970). A study of Bengali personal names to ascertain the feasibility of application of a mechanistic rule for their   arrangement, Dissertation   Series.   Pittsburgh: University of Pittsburgh, Graduate School of Library and Information Sciences, 87 p.
The data used in the investigation are from East Pakistan, now Bangladesh. The problem was to set up some sort of computer system to handle the various types of names found in Bengali. Many of the names are from non-Bengali sources, Arabic, Persian, Urdu and Turkish. Individuals may use several names and titles as well. A few names occur over a million times in the population and the order of names is not consistent as in Western countries. For these and other reasons, Huq concludes that strict automation is not possible at this time. However, he does propose 10 rules for setting up alphabetical files. 94 refs.

[8.33.4] Junghare, Indira Y. (1975). Socio-psychological aspects and linguistic analysis of Marathi names. Names, 23, 31-43.
Marathi is an Indo-Aryan language spoken by people in the state of Maharashtra (roughly W central India) of which Bombay is the capital. Factors involved in naming children include: religion, grandparents, protection from death, twins, movies, literature, nature, and personal qualities. Two sets of phonological rules are followed, one from Marathi, one from Sanskrit. 17 refs.

[8.33.5] Khurshid, Anis. (1964, August). Cataloging of Pakistani names. Occasional Papers. Karachi, Pakistan: University of Karachi Library Science Department, 60 p.
Pakistan has special problems in cataloging since it has a number of languages and cultural groups. The structure of a person's name varies considerably. A name can appear as Mir Alam, Mir Taqi; Mir; S. M. Mir, or Syed Muhammad Mir Soz. In addition, libraries in different parts of the world use 6 ways of grouping Muslim names. Recommendations are made for guiding principles in cataloging Muslim names. 24 refs.

[8.33.6] Masani, Rustom Pestonje. (1966). Folk culture reflected in names. Bombay, India: Popular Prakashan, 120 p.
Description of Hindu naming customs set in a context of those of the West. Chapters of special interest include those on opprobrious (epithet) names, change and exchange of names, and tabooed names (deities, priest-kings, and the deceased). About 50 refs.

[8.33.7] Mehrota, R. R. (1982). Impact of religion on Hindi personal names. Names, 30, 43-47.
Description of the naming system for children. Five categories of names are explained each with several examples:(1) deities, (2) saints and philosophers, (3) sacred towns, (4) zodiac, and (5) modern secular. 3 refs.

[8.33.8] Pilai, Dorai Rangaswamy & Pilai, M. Appaswamy. (1968). The surnames of the Cankam age. Madras: University of Madras, 205 p.
Analysis and comment on the names of the hundreds of poets who wrote the early Tamil poems. Tribal surnames are also covered. 80+ refs.

[8.33.9] Radcliffe-Brown, A. R. (1922). Andaman Islanders. Cambridge, England: University Pr., pp. 89-95, 117-121, 294-297.
Naming customs in these islands belonging to India located in the Indian Ocean between Burma and Sumatra. Children bear names before they are born.

A girl will take a flower name at puberty. When she has a child she reverts to her prepuberty name. Boys also acquire a new name around puberty but this name does not appear to be permanent. Nicknames are also used.

[8.33.10] Shanta, M. A. (1969). Handbook of Hindu names. Calcutta, India: Arnica, 201 p.
Introduction to Hindu names followed by a listing of about 5500 Hindu names. Each entry contains the name in English followed by the Hindi equivalent, gender, and meaning. The source of non-Hindi names is given, i. e., English, Persian, French, etc. Popular names such as Moti ("a pearl") for a male or Indira ("the goddess Lakshami") are marked with an asterisk.

[8.33.11] Sharma, Mohan Lal. (1968). Meaning and origin of "Menon." Names, 16, 183.
Describes the origin of the title Menon. One source attributes it to a contraction of Menavan (a superior person). Another explanation is that it refers to a village accountant. 1 ref.

[8.33.12] Sharma, Mohan Lal. (1969). Origin and meaning of some Indian names. Names, 17, 199-207.
Introduction to Indian names. Explanation of the meaning of names of some prominent people as Jawahar ("jewel" in Urdu), Lal ("precious stone" in Arabic; "a little child" in Sanskrit), and Nehru ("one who lives near a canal"). Treatment of Hindu, Sikh, Muslim, funny, and feminine names. Many examples. 1 ref.

[8.33.13] Thundy, Zacharias P. (1981). The new Malayalee personal names. Proceedings of the 13th Congress of Onomastic Sciences, 1978, Cracow, 2, 539-548.
Malayalee is the language of Kerala, a state in SW India. This is a report on a survey of naming patterns among Christians, Muslims, and Hindus. Results indicate a generational shift from ethnophilia to anglophilia to indophilia in name choices.

8.34. Indonesian

[8.34.1] Brewer, Jeffrey D. (1981). Bimanese personal names: meaning and use. Ethnology, 20, 203-215.
Description and analysis of the system of naming among the Bimanese, a people living in the eastern half of Sumbawa, an island in Indonesia E of Java. Each person has a nym or given name plus other nyms, a patronym from one's father, a teknonym from one's child, and a paidonym from one's grandchild. Nyms have 3 forms, a proper form, a common form, and a respect form. Many examples are given along with other name usages. 11 refs.

[8.34.2] Uhlenbeck, E. M. (1969). Systematic features of Javanese personal names. Word, 25, 321-335.
Systematic description of the process of naming and the 6 types of name in Java. Males have 2 names, the 1st is replaced by a 2nd usually at marriage. Females have only 1 name. Both male and female have a status level. Thus, there are 2 types of female name and 4 types of male. Other aspects of names also described. Many examples. 19 refs.

8.35. Inuit (Eskimo)

[8.35.1] Guemple, D. L. (1965). Saunik: Name sharing as a factor governing Eskimo kinship terms. Ethnology, 4, 323-335.
Description of naming practices among the Qiqiktamiuk, a group of about 200 who inhabit the Belcher Islands in Hudson Bay W of Quebec. Each person has 2 names: a Christian first name usually of biblical origin, and an Inuit one. The Qiqiktamiut child does not acquire the name from parents or from someone even closely related. The name-giver must be willing and from then on has a close relationship with the namesake. Other naming customs are also described. 36 refs.

8.36. Iranian

[8.36.1] Aiken, Lewis R., Jr. & Zweigenhaft, Richard L. (1978). Signature size, sex, and status in Iran. Journal of Social Psychology, 106, 273-274. Results with faculty members, graduate students, undergraduates, and servants in Teheran indicates signature patterns similar to the US in that men and higher status persons used more space for signature. 5 refs.

8.37. Irish

[8.37.1] Adams, G. B. (1979). Prolegomena to the study of names in Ireland. Nomina, 3, 81-94.
A systematic presentation on Irish names. Topics include: the peoples of Ireland (Old Irish, Anglo-Normans, English, Scots, Huguenots, Palatines, Jews, and others), the languages of origin of surnames, typology of surnames, anglicization of Irish names, gaelicization of imported names, and an annotated listing of references. 27 refs.

[8.37.2] Adams, G. B. (1980). Surname landscapes in Fermanagh. Bulletin of the Ulster Place-Name Society, Second Series, 3, 56-68.
Extensive listing of surnames in 3 sections of this county and also the town of Enniskillen. Tables show name frequencies and distribution.

[8.37.3] Black, J. Anderson. (1974). Your Irish ancestors. New York: Paddington Pr., 253 p.
Has about 100 entries of well-known and most common Irish surnames (O'Brady, O'Flynn et al.). Maps show location where family is found. Photographs, pictures of Ireland. 50 refs.

[8.37.4] Burke, John E. (1978). The historical significance of early Irish immigrant names. In Fred Tarpley (Ed.), Ethnic names (pp. 49-68), Publication 6, South Central Names Institute. Commerce, TX: Names Institute Pr.
Surname evaluation for 19 wealthy Irish-American families including Nicholas Brady, John Buckley, John F. FitzGerald, and Thomas Fortune Ryan. 5 refs.

[8.37.5] Coghlan, Ronan. (1979). Irish Christian names. London: Johnston & Bacon, 140 p.
Lists approx 800 male and female first names with derivation, pronunciation, and meaning. In some cases the entry also includes location of the name in Ireland and prominent bearers. 28 refs.

[8.37.6] Fox, J. R. (1963). Structure of personal names on Tory Island.
Man, 63, 153-155.
Confirms writer Synge's 1898-1902 observations of the naming practices on
the Arran Islands with Tory Island, Donegal in [8.37.20]. Each person has
3 sets of names, a Gaelic ceremonial, an English practical, and a
Gaelic-English personal. Several examples. 2 refs.

[8.37.7] Grehan, Ida. (1973). Irish family names: Highlights of 50 family
histories. London: Johnston & Bacon, 160 p.
Background on some Irish names. 25 refs.

[8.37.8] Aer Lingus. (1977). Irish ancestral map.
Map of Ireland. Shows over 1000 Irish surnames with county of origin.

[8.37.9] Kelly, Patrick. (1976). Irish family names. Detroit: Gale, 136
p. (Originally published by O'Connor & Kelley, Chicago, 1939)
Gives origin of mottos, anglicized forms, and script of about 500 surnames.
Extensive list of associated names. Index. About 50 biblio items.

[8.37.10] MacLysacht, Edward (1957). Irish families: Their names, arms,
and origins. Dublin: Hodges Figgis, 366 p.
Background material on Irish names. Systematic coverage of over 200
prominent family names, etymology, prominent family members, crests etc.
such as O'Rourke and O'Kelleher. Several tables showing county of location
of the names as well as English imports. Maps. 900+ refs.

[8.37.11] MacLysacht, Edward. (1964). Supplement to Irish families
Baltimore: Genealogical Pr., 163 p.
Gives the derivation and meaning of over 500 surnames plus some notes on
previous volumes by the same author, see--[8.37.10], [8.37.13].

[8.37.12] MacLysacht, Edward. (1965). A guide to Irish surnames, (2nd
ed.). Dublin: Helicon, 256 p. (1st ed. 1964; also published as The surnames
of Ireland by Cahill in Dublin)
Introduction and listing of approximately 3500 surnames also giving the
location.

[8.37.13] MacLysacht, Edward. (1982). More Irish families (rev. ed.
Dublin: Irish Academic Pr., 254 p.
According to the editor, this volume incorporates the author's More Irish
families (1960; Galway: O'Gorman) and Supplement to Irish families
([8.37.11]; Dublin: Helicon) and is a companion book to Irish families
[8.37.10]. Background information, derivation, and meaning of 900-1000
Irish surnames. 55+ refs.

[8.37.14] O'Brien, Michael A. (1973). Old Irish personal names, Rhys
Memorial Lecture, Rolf Baumgarten (Ed.), Celtica, 10, 211-236.
Posthumous publication of the work of an outstanding scholar. Presents
classified lists of 1200 names under headings of Introduction, Typology
Morphology, Common Elements, Female Names, Borrowed Names. 14 refs.

[8.37.15] O'Brien, Michael A. (1976). Corpus genealogiarum Hiberniae,
Vol. 1. Dublin: Dublin Institute for Advanced Studies, 764 p.
Editing the 12th century Rawlinson ms. and some 15th century mss. has
provided an extensive listing of genealogical material including at least
12,500 personal names plus names of tribes and families. 8 refs.

[8.37.16] O Corrain, Donnchadh. (1979). Onomata. Eriu, 30, 167-180.
Scholarly tracing of 10 old Irish names including Dar Oma, Tairdelback, O
Luith, and Ui Chobtaigh. Much material on each. 58 refs.

[8.37.17] O Corrain, Donnchadh & Maguire, Fidelma. (1981). Gaelic
personal names. Dublin: Academy Pr., 188 p.
Contains about 1100 (mainly Gaelic) entries plus an index of variant forms.
Each entry contains main forms, pronunciation, origin of name and/or
prominent bearers and anglicized forms. Thus Conall (kun-al, "strong as a
wolf") is an old Celtic name borne by several kings and other prominent men
who are listed. It can be anglicized as Conall or Connell. 29 refs.

[8.37.18] O Cuiv, Brian. (1979). Borrowed elements in the corpus of Irish
personal names from medieval times. Nomina, 3, 40-51.
Foreign influences on Irish names from the time of Christianization through
Scandinavian, pre-Norman, and post-invasion periods. 17 refs.

[8.37.19] O Cuiv, Brian. (1980). Topographical elements in Irish personal
names. Bulletin of the Ulster Place-Name Society, Second Series, 3, 8-12.
Lists 150 non-Indogermanic personal names with some information about
topographical elements. These names were used up to about 1100 AD.   5
refs.

[8.37.20] Synge, John M. (1911). The Aran Islands. Boston: Luce, pp.
156-158.
Relates the naming practices on this island off the W coast of Ireland.
Epithet names such as Seaghan Ruadh ("Red John") are used. His children
are Mourteen Seaghan Ruadh etc.   In school children go by 2 names, the
official one in English and the other one in Gaelic, as Patrick O'Flaharty
and Patch Seaghan Dearg.

8.38. Italian

[8.38.1] Caldiero, Allisandru. (1983). Nciurii: Sicilian nicknames.
Maledicta, 7, 217-218.
Listing of 13 colorful Sicilian nicknames with explanations, ex., Vincenzo
Aricchiazza: Era ladiu cu l'aricchi 'ranni (Vinny Bigears, "He was ugly and
had big ears"). 1 ref.

[8.38.2] Ciardi, John. (1964, Sept. 26). Of onomastics, foibles, and
mercy. Saturday Review, 47, p. 24.
For those who are not familiar with Italian, this contribution gives
understanding to the work of Fucilla below on names of foundlings. Ciardi
explains the meaning of names such as della Chiesa (of the Church), della
Croce (of the cross) and di Dio (gift of God) along with other names such
as Cicoria (chicory) and Giudette Oloferni (Judith Holofernes). 1 ref.

[8.38.3] Fucilla, Joseph G. (1963). New names in the making in Italy.
Orbis (Louvain), 12, 456-462.
Description of some of the types of surname used to identify infants who
were left at a foundling home in Todi from 1805-1959. These names were all
assigned by the director and included fruit names (Persichetti), bird names
(Falconi), calendar names (Settembri), and many other types. These names
were all assigned by the director. See also Ciardi above.

[8.38.4] Gerardi, Robert J., & De Frank, Russell. (1982). Italian nicknames as surnames. ANS Bulletin, No. 70, 27-31.
Classification of surnames derived from nicknames. Examples include: for compound names, Giangrosso ("fat John"); from insects, Puccio ("bug"); from a domestic quadruped, Agnello ("lamb").

8.39. Japanese

[8.39.1] Gillis, Irvin V., & Pai, Ping-ch'i. (Compilers). (1939). Japanese surnames. Peking, China: Hwaihsing Pr., 381 p.
Part 1 lists 9173 Japanese surnames arranged by number of strokes in Japanese script. The number of strokes varies from 1-27. Part 2 lists the names by English transliteration. The names are also coded with 4-digit numbers so that telegrams can be sent. 2 refs.

[8.39.2] Gillis, Irvin V., & Pai, Ping-ch'i. (Compilers). (1940). Japanese personal names. Peking: no publisher listed, 142 p. (OCLC listings show this also being published by Edwards Brothers in 1939, 1940, and 1944)
This seems to be a companion volume to Gillis and Pai above. Part I has 3511 names which are grouped in order of number of strokes in Japanese script which range from 1-33. Part 2 has the names transliterated into English alphabet order.

[8.39.3] Kiley, Cornelius J. (1969). A note on the surnames of immigrant officials in Nara Japan. Harvard Journal of Asiatic Studies, 29, 177-189.
The officials referred to were officials of non-Japanese origin of this important center in 8th century Japan. Prestige of a name was indicated by the final element of a name called a kabane. Some officials changed their names to get the kabane and the prestige. Approx 40 refs.

[8.39.4] O'Neill, P. G. (1972). Japanese names. New York: John Weatherhill, 359 p.
Refers to over 36,000 names including 11,000 personal names, 13,500 surnames, and 6800 literary, historical, and artistic names. Names are indexed by number of strokes in Japanese and by romanization. 20 refs.

[8.39.5] Sibata, Takesi. (1975). Lexical system of personal names in an idiolect. Berichte des XII. Internationaler Kongresses fuer Namenforschung, Bern, 3, 333-339.
How names are bestowed in Okinawa. Types of name include childhood name, kinship term, registered name, house-name, occupational name, and surname.

[8.39.6] Tanaka, Yasuhito. (1985). On the frequency of the same family and personal names. XV, Internationaler Kongress fuer Namenforschung, 1984, Leipzig, 3, 269-280.
Empirical results in Japan with large samples indicates there are a number of individuals who have identical first names and surnames. This is a potential source for confusion. Suggests adding 1 or 2 digits for additional information.

8.40. Jewish (includes Hebrew, Israeli, and Yiddish)
See also--7. CHANGE OF NAME

[8.40.1] Adler, Cyrus. (1954). Name changes in Israel. Names, 2, 38-39.
Brief description of the pattern of Jews immigrating to Israel shedding
their Diaspora names and choosing new ones with a Hebrew root as Golden to
Sahavy (from the Hebrew for "golden").

[8.40.2] Brookes, Reuben S., & Brookes, Blanche. (1967). A guide to
Jewish names. Birmingham, Eng.: privately printed, 44 p.
Listing of Hebrew names and meaning with Western name equivalents and
meanings for both sexes. Thus, Leslie = meadows as does the Hebrew, Karmel;
Malcolm = dove as does the Hebrew, Jonah.

[8.40.3] Chazan, Robert. (1972). Names: Medieval period and establishment
of surnames. Encyclopedia Judaica, Vol. 12, pp. 809-813. Jerusalem: Keter.
Description of cultural, historical, and religious pressures that have led
to modern Jewish names. 13 refs.

[8.40.4] Chelminsky-Lajmer, Enrique. (1975). London, Berlin, and other
surnames. Names, 23, 59-60.
Explanation of how Jewish names such as London, Berlin, Gordon, Atlas,
Gross, and Pfeffer have meanings other than what is immediately apparent,
ex., Atlas is an acronym derived from the Hebrew of the first words of
Psalm 73:1 "Surely (God) is good to Israel, forever." 1 ref.

[8.40.5] Cohn, Werner. (1984). What's in a name: A comment on Himmelfarb,
Loar, and Mott. Public Opinion Quarterly, 48, 660-665.
Disagrees with the methodology used by Himmelfarb et al. [8.40.14] who
concluded that Jews with distinctive Jewish names do not differ
significantly in their Jewish identification from other Jews. 2 refs.

[8.40.6] Dalven, Rachel. (1977-1978). The names of the Jannina Jews. The
Sephardic Scholar: Journal of the American Society of Sephardic
Studies, 3, 9-23.
Jan(n)ina is a town and region NW of Athens. This is a description of the
naming customs of the Jews of that area. Among other customs, offspring
are/were named after living relatives. The influences of Greek, Turkish,
Spanish, and Hebrew languages are discussed. 4 refs.

[8.40.7] Eliassaf, Nissim. (1981). Names survey in the Population
Administration: State of Israel (Edwin D. Lawson & Batsheva Taube, Trans.).
Names, 29, 273-284.
Analysis of the name records of over 4 million individuals in Israel.
Statistical tables show distributions of first names and surnames by number
of letters and frequency. Also includes the 100 most frequent names in
various categories. Arab names are also included. 1 ref.

[8.40.8] Gaster, Theodor H. (1980). The holy and the profane. New York:
William Morrow, pp. 33-38.
This chapter has a description of Jewish naming customs from biblical days
to the present. These customs are related to those of other cultures.
Also contains a statement (p. 120) that the Jewish custom of smashing a
glass at a wedding goes back to magic customs of the ancient Middle East,
that Egyptians used to write the names of their enemies on clay pots and
then break the pots into pieces. 30 refs. Most appear on pp. 230-231.

[8.40.9] Glanz, Rudolf. (1961). German-Jewish names in America. Jewish Social Studies, 23, 143-169.
Historical survey and commentary. Among the major topics are: (1) distinctive German-Jewish names, (2), names of German-Jewish pioneers, (3), German-Jewish names in the German-American milieu, and (4) changes in the stock of names and name changes. 57 refs.

[8.40.10] Goitein, S. D. (1970). Nicknames as family names. Journal of the American Oriental Society, 90, 517-524.
Demonstrates that nicknames as family names go back to the Bible and that Rabbi Hanina (3rd century) and the Koran have injunctions against bad nicknames. Then shows that the Cairo Geniza (collection of Jewish documents from the 10th-13th centuries) contains cases where a nicknames has become a surname. Examples include: ibn Awkal ("dwarf"), ibn Misk ("dark-complexioned"), and Ben al-Khasisa ("son of the miserly, mean woman"). 25 refs.

[8.40.11] Goldberg, Harvey E. (1972). The social context of North African Jewish patronyms. In Issachar Ben-Ami (Ed.), Folklore Research Center Studies-Jerusalem, Vol. 3, pp. 245-257.
Explains that there are alternative ways that Jews in North Africa might have Berber names without having been directly descended from Berbers. 35 refs.

[8.40.12] Gottlieb, Nathan. (1960). A Jewish child is born: Laws and rites of circumcision, naming boys and girls. New York: Bloch, 160 p.
Circumcision rites. Also includes a short dictionary of Hebrew and Yiddish names with Hebrew and English spelling; Western names also included in a separate listing.

[8.40.13] Hazleton, Lesley. (1977). Israeli women: The reality behind the myth. New York: Simon and Schuster, pp. 95-96.
The Hebrew language has a sex-typing of nouns and verbs. This is reflected in the role expectations of first names. Men have names such as Dov (bear) and Aryieh (lion); women, Ayala (deer) of Shoshana (rose).

[8.40.14] Himmelfarb, Harold S., Loar, R. Michael, & Mott, Susan H. (1983). Sampling by ethnic surnames: The case of American Jews. Public Opinion Quarterly, 47, 247-260.
On the basis of a nationwide sample, concludes (with some reservations) that the use of distinctive Jewish surnames is a good way of selecting a Jewish sample. 18 refs.

[8.40.15] Kaganoff, Benzion C. (1977). A dictionary of Jewish names and their history. New York: Schocken, 250 p.
Part I, about half the book, gives history and background material on Jewish names, first names and surnames. Part II is a dictionary of approx 10,000 surnames, ex., Abrabanel is a diminutive derived from a patronymic for Abraham used by Spanish Jews; Katz is an acronym for Kohen Tzedek, "priest of righteousness." 28 refs.

[8.40.16] Klarberg, Manfred. (1981). Sound patterns and Hebrew names. Jewish Language Review, No.1, 97-107.
Discussion of the stress patterns in modern Hebrew, especially on names from other languages including Yiddish. Although the formal rules call for ultimate (last syllable) stress, most people pronounce such a name as

bri-TAN-ya (Britain) rather than bri-tan-YA. Several pages of comments by others. 17 refs.

[8.40.17] Kolatch, Alfred J. (1967). The name dictionary. Middle Village, NY: Jonathan David, 418 p.
Discussion of Jewish naming practices. Alphabetical listing by sex of Hebrew and Western names with appropriate English equivalents and vice versa. Hebrew name index.

[8.40.18] Kolatch, Alfred J. (1984). Complete dictionary of English and Hebrew first names. Middle Village, NY: Jonathan David, 488 p. (rev. ed. of: The names dictionary above)
A revision and expansion of the author's 1967 work. The total number of entries is about 11,000. The Hebrew spellings are now included along with the appropriate entries.

[8.40.19] Markrich, Max. (1958). A note on Jewish nicknames. Jewish Social Studies, 20, 232-233.
Olaf Gerhard Tychen (1734-1816) was a Christian orientalist who wrote Ockel-names (nicknames) of the Jews of Mecklenburg of 1769. Seventeen examples from this work are listed such as Mosche Lalle ("stammerer") and Moses Hackbart ("the invading Russians nailed his beard to a table and cut it off"). 2 refs.

[8.40.20] Massoutie, George. (1936, March). Jewish names. Central-Blatt and Social Justice (St. Louis), pp. 384-386. (Reprinted in ANS Bulletin, No. 50, 1977, pp. 14-16)
Systematic description of a number of Jewish first names and surnames. 6 refs.

[8.40.21] Memmi, Albert. (1966). The liberation of the Jew (Judy Hyun, Trans.). New York: Orion, pp. 31-42.
Analysis of the Jew in France who changes his name to conceal his Jewishness; the immigrant to Israel who gives up his Diaspora name.

[8.40.22] Rabinowitz, Louis I. (1972). Names: In the Talmud. Encyclopedia Judaica, Vol. 12, pp. 807-809, 812. Jerusalem: Keter.
Brief discussion of issues involving naming during the period 200 BCE-500 CE including pressures to use non-Jewish names. Notes that some names such as Moses and Joseph were conspicuously absent during this period. 2 refs.

[8.40.23] Rennick, Robert M. (1970). The Nazi name decrees of the nineteen thirties. (1970). Names, 18, 65-85.
Background and history of the Nazi name decrees which affected not only Jews but also non-Jews. Includes lists of the 185 male and 91 female names approved for Jews by Hans Globke of the Nazi Interior Ministry. 45 refs.

[8.40.24] Rennick, Robert M. (1984). What's in a "Jewish" name: Don't jump to conclusions. Bulletin of the Illinois Name Society, 2(4), 13-19.
There are a number of names which are often assumed to be Jewish but which, in fact, are not. Examples of individuals bearing these names are Felix Adler, Mr. Jerusalem, Ellen Hebrew, Thomas Jew, Norman Jewison, and a number of Chinese with the surname Jew. 19 refs.

[8.40.25] Rode, Zvonko R. (1976). The origin of Jewish names. Names, 24, 165-179.

Systematic presentation of Jewish surnames. Includes introduction and 15 major groups of surnames such as: names from the Bible in various forms (Abraham, Abram), translations of biblical names (Baruch "blessed" to Benedict), equivalents of Hebrew names (Abraham to Appel) and others. Many examples. 4 refs.

[8.40.26] Rottenberg, Dan. (1977). Finding our fathers: A guidebook to Jewish genealogy. New York: Random House, 401 p.
Following 8 chapters of background information, there are entries for about 8000 Jewish surnames. Entries show related names and some information on holders of the name. Many items list a reference source such as the Encyclopedia Judaica where further information may be obtained. Approx 500 refs.

[8.40.27] Sabar, Yona. (1974). First names, nicknames and family names among the Jews of Kurdistan. Jewish Quarterly Review, 65, 43-51.
Discussion and comment on Jewish naming patterns in Kurdistan. Lists of 37 common male and 17 common female names in everyday use plus short forms of the name. 17 refs.

[8.40.28] Sheby, David. (1979). In search of a Sephardic tradition: A family named Sheby. Toledot: The Journal of Jewish Genealogy. 2(3), 15-18.
An American Jew traces his ancestry back to Turkey. 4 refs.

[8.40.29] Silverman, Michael Henry. (1967). Jewish personal names in the Elephantine documents. Dissertation Abstracts International, 28A, 2233A-2234B. (University Microfilms No. 67-16,577)
Jewish names in this Jewish colony in Egypt were studied over 6 generations. The most important part of the research deals with theophorous names.

[8.40.30] Weil, Shalva. (1977). Names and identity among the Bene Israel. Ethnic Groups, 1, 201-219
The term Bene Israel refers to Indian Jews who settled originally on the Konkan coast and more recently were concentrated in the Bombay area. Now, the majority live in Israel. Indian Jews have first (personal) names, second names (patronyms or andronyms (husband's patronym), and -kar (village surnames). Although there has been much name-changing in Israel, Bene Israel maintain their village surnames in religious rituals as, for example, Michael ben Josef Thralkar. 20 refs.

[8.40.31] Wexler, Paul. (1979). Jewish onomastics: Achievements and challenges: Reflections on B. C. Kaganoff, A dictionary of Jewish names and their history, New York, 1977. Onoma, 23, 96-113.
Careful evaluation and comments on the book. 56 refs.

8.41. Korean

[8.41.1] Shin, Eui-Hang & Yu, Eui-Young. (1984). Use of surnames in ethnic research: The case of Kims in the Korean-American population. Demography, 21, 347-360.
Develops a method of estimating the size of the Korean-American population by extrapolation from the percentage of Kims (about 22%) in several samples from Chicago, New York, and other places. 39 refs.

8.42. Lebanese

[8.42.1] Halaby, Raouf J. (1983). Religion, politics, and linguistics: A study of Lebanese personal names. ANS Bulletin, No. 71, 39–46.
Describes some of the basic naming practices of Christians and Muslims in Lebanon. Short listing of Christian, Muslim and neutral names. 6 items.

8.43. Lithuanian

[8.43.1] Klimas, Antanas. (1981). Nicknames and family names: A case study of a Lithuanian village. Proceedings of the 13th Congress of Onomastic Sciences, 1978, Cracow, 1, 615–619.
Report on a Lithuanian village where 23 out of 41 of the farmers' families had nicknames. Examples include Spunta ("the man's wife was very fat and was compared to the stopper of a beer barrel") and Stepe ("the whole family was given this name from a bossy wife named Stefanija"). 5 refs.

[8.43.2] Senn, Alfred. (1969). An inventory of Lithuanian names. Names, 17, 127–137.
Though most of the information is on placenames, there is some information on Lithuanian personal naming practices. Many examples. 32 refs, mostly non-English.

8.44. Malaysian

[8.44.1] Benjamin, Geoffrey. (1968). Temiar personal names. Bijdragen tot de Taal-, Land- en Volkerkunde, 124, 99–134.
The Temiar, a preliterate society in Malaysia, have 6 classes of name: autonoyms, birth-order names, teknonyms, necronyms, burial names, and designations. The autonym is unique and is rarely revealed to others. 28 refs.

[8.44.2] Maxwell, Allen R. (1984). Kadayan personal names and naming. In Elisabeth Tooker (Ed.), Harold C. Conklin (Symposium Organizer), 1980 Proceedings of the American Ethnological Society (pp. 25–39). Washington, DC: American Ethnological Society.
The Kadayan are a Malay-speaking Muslim people who live in NW Borneo. The naming system has a first name (given at birth), a patronym which is a filial relator (son of, or daughter of), honorifics (Yang Mulia, "The Respected"), and a courtesy title (Haji, "Pilgrim"). Nicknames and epithet names are also used. 13 refs.

[8.44.3] Needham, Rodney. (1964). Temer names. Journal of the Malayan Branch, Royal Asiatic Society, 37, 121–125.
Some Temer names are the same as Malay ones. Discussion of death names and possible similarity to the Penan customs. 8 refs.

8.45. Maltese

[8.45.1] Aquilina, J. (1964). A comparative study in lexical material relating to nicknames and surnames. Journal of Maltese Studies, 2, 147–176.
Scholarly presentation of the evolution of Maltese surnames from Semitic

roots (Hebrew and Arabic) and later from Romance roots. Nicknames are included. Listings of names in several categories. 6 refs.

[8.45.2] Cassar-Pullicino, Joseph. (1976). Social aspects of Maltese nicknames. Studies in Maltese Folklore (Malta), 109-133.
Systematic classification and discussion of Maltese nicknames of individuals such as, Il-Ginger ("red-haired"), Tal-Prim ("well-built"), and Ix-Xellugi ("leftist"). Other nicknames such as for animals, fish, towns, and social groups are also included. 12 refs.

[8.45.3] Wettinger, Godfrey. (1978). Non Arabo-Berber influences on Malta's medieval nomenclature. Actes du deuxieme Congres International International d'etude des cultures de la Mediterraneane Occidentale (International Congress of Studies on Cultures of the Western Mediterranean, Second), 2, 199-213.
Discussion and comments on first names, nicknames, and surnames of Christian or other European origin in Malta. Hundreds of citations and references.

[8.45.4] Wettinger, Godfrey. (1980). The place-names and the personal nomenclature of Gozo, 1372-1600. In R. Y. Ebied & M. J. L. Young Oriental studies presented to Benedikt S. J. Isserlin. Leiden, Netherlands: Brill, pp. 173-198.
Gozo is an island just N of Malta proper. Church records and other documents contrast the pre-names (first names) and surnames with those of Malta. Some attention to Semitic and European names. 24 refs on personal names.

8.46. Mexican

[8.46.1] Collier, George A., & Bricker, Victoria R. (1970). Nicknames and social structure in Zinacantan. American Anthropologist, 72, 289-302.
Research in Zinacantan, a Mayan community in Chiapas, Mexico, suggests that nicknames whose initial use is informal are gradually being incorporated into the system of formal names replacing Indian names. 2 appendices of nicknames. 18 refs.

[8.46.2] Dabbs, Jack A. (1956). Family names in the Augustinian order. Names, 4, 138-145.
Evaluation of a register of the Augustinian order from Mexico City containing 843 names from 1536-1650 shows that most friars (56%) kept their family name, 14% took holy names, 14% took their mother's name. 4 refs.

8.47. Mongolian

[8.47.1] Krueger, John R. (1962). Mongolian personal names. Names, 10, 81-86.
Naming of children. Linguistic background of Mongolian names including Tibetan, Turkic, Chinese, Russian, and Sanskrit roots. 5 refs.

8.48. Muslim

[8.48.1] Ebied, R. Y., & Young, M. J. L. (1976). A list of appellations of
the Prophet Mohammed. Muslim World, 66, 259-262.
Leeds University ms. 12 from 1851 has a list of 201 names of the Prophet.
Among these are: Ajir ("hired"), Jabbar ("might"), and Muslih ("reformer").
4 refs.

[8.48.2] Ebied, R. Y., & Young, M. J. L. (1978). A note on Muslim
namegiving according to day of the week. Arabica, 24, 326-328.
The Leeds document of Safi'i jurisprudence by al-Nawawi gives directions
for naming children according to the day of the week on which they were
born. Thus, Sunday-born children were to have Old Testament names, Monday
children, names of Mohammed, etc. 5 refs.

[8.48.3] Qazi, M. A. (1974). What's in a Muslim name. Chicago: Kazi
Publications, 44 p.
Gives an introduction to Muslim names; 99 names of Allah; 56 names of
Mohammed; caliphs; and imans. The main entries are 396 common male and 220
common female names. There are also 33 biblical names (Arabic equivalents
of names such as Job, Moses, and Mary) and names of the wives and daughters
of Mohammed. The entries are listed according to the Arabic alphabet and
give the name transliterated into English along with the English meaning.

[8.48.4] Rudvin, Arne. (1978). A supplementary note to "A list of the
appellations of the Prophet Mohammed." Muslim World, 68, 57-60.
Asserts that the ms. referred to by Ebied & Young [8.48.1] was copied from
an earlier ms. by al-Jazuli Dala'il al-Khayrat. 14 refs.

8.49. Norse

[8.49.1] Janzen, Assar. (1954). The provenance of Proto-Norse personal
names I. Names, 2, 81-100.
Systematic analysis of personal names found on over 100 runic inscriptions
from 200-700 AD in Denmark and Sweden. Placename and various ethnic
influences are discussed. 11 refs.

[8.49.2] Janzen, Assar. (1954). The provenance of Proto-Norse personal
names II. Names, 2, 169-174.
Concludes previous article. Maintains that the naming structure of
Primitive Scandinavian partly reflects an old common-Germanic naming system
and partly a gradual development toward a specific Scandinavian type. 7
refs.

8.50. Oceania

[8.50.1] Bateson, Gregory. (1958). Naven (2nd ed.). Stanford, CA:
Stanford University Pr.
Brief mention (p. 127) of the Iatmul society in New Guinea where there is a
totemic system of naming of totemic ancestors--spirits, birds, stars,
animals, etc. An individual may have 30 or more such names.

[8.50.2] Bikajle, Tion & deYoung, John E. (1960). Marshallese Names. In
John E. deYoung (Ed.), The use of names by Micronesians, Anthropological

Working Papers, No. 3, (2nd ed.), (pp. 99-111). Guam, Marianas Islands: Office of the Staff Anthropologist, Trust Territory of the Pacific Islands. Describes naming customs of the Marshall Islands. Most people have Christian names. There are also nicknames. Father's first name tends to be used as a surname although other patterns are used.

[8.50.3] Carucci, Laurence Marshall. (1984). Significance of change or change of significance: A consideration of Marshallese personal names. Ethnology, 23, 143-155.
Traces naming practices among the Enewetak people. Includes original names, names from periods of missionary, German, Japanese, and American influence and current naming practices. 24 refs.

[8.50.4] Defngin, Francis. (1960). Yapese names. In John E. deYoung (Ed.), The use of names by Micronesians, Anthropological Working Papers, No. 3, (2nd ed.), (pp. 1-15). Guam, Marianas Islands: Office of the Staff Anthropologist, Trust Territory of the Pacific Islands.
Naming customs of Yap, an island in the Carolines with a population of about 3000. Most of the younger people are now using Christian or baptismal names as a first name and their Yapese name as a last name when official procedures require. 1 ref.

[8.50.5] deYoung, John S. (Ed.). (1960). The use of names by Micronesians, Anthropological Working Papers, No. 3, (2nd ed.) 124 p. Guam, Marianas Islands: Office of the Staff Anthropologist, Trust Territory of the Pacific Islands.
Includes 6 articles on naming practices in Micronesia written by anthropologists to help government officials cope with a number of different practices and still keep records coherent. See other entries under this section--8.50. Oceania.

[8.50.6] deYoung, John S. (1960). Notes on use of names in the Marianas. In John E. deYoung (Ed.), The use of names by Micronesians, Anthropological Working Papers, No. 3, (2nd ed.), (pp. 112-124). Guam, Marianas Islands: Office of the Staff Anthropologist, Trust Territory of the Pacific Islands.
The Chamorros, the indigenous residents of the Marianas have been exposed to Spanish, German, and American influences and their names reflect this. Description of naming practices, nicknames, forms of address, and surnames. 5 refs.

[8.50.7] Feinberg, Richard. (1983). What's in a name? Personal identity and naming on Anuta. Central Issues in Anthropology, 5, 27-42.
Description and discussion of the naming system on Anuta, a Polynesian island in the Eastern Solomons. Anutans have personal names, baptismal names, and marital names (a marital name is a new name taken at marriage and shared by husband and wife, similar to Tikopia). Names are frequently changed. According to Feinberg "an Anutan identifies other people, groups, or objects through his name."

[8.50.8] Franklin, Karl J. (1967). Names and aliases in Kewa. Journal of the Polynesian Society, 76, 76-81.
Reports on a people living in the Southern Highlands of Papua. Each man has 2 names. The first name often describes an important event in the father's life. The second name, necessary because of taboos at marriage, is often chosen by the wife. 7 refs.

[8.50.9] Goodenough, Ward H. (1965). Personal names and modes of address. In Melford E. Spiro (Ed.), Context and meaning in cultural anthropology (pp. 265-276). New York: Free Pr.
Contrasts naming customs in 2 Pacific societies: Truk in the Caroline Islands and Lakalai (West Nakanai) on the N coast of New Britain. In Truk a person's name emphasizes uniqueness compensating for the suppression of individuality in the social system. Contrasts with Lakalai which emphasizes personal achievement but where naming (less unique) serves as a reminder of the social order. 14 refs.

[8.50.10] Grant, Jill & Zelenietz, Martin. (1983). Naming practices in Kilenge. Names, 31, 179-190.
Naming patterns of the Kilenge of NW New Britain, Papua New Guinea. In their system the type of name used represents a social statement. Among the types of name are: napasis (primary name), kuria (secondary identification marker), mourning name, nickname, insulting name, Catholic name, and government name. Some examples. 2 refs.

[8.50.11] Levy-Bruhl, Lucien. (1966). Primitive mentality (Lillian A. Clare, Trans.). Boston: Beacon Pr., pp. 205-207. (Originally published by George Allen & Unwin in London, 1923)
Describes examples of where a criminal can be detected among the Papuans by pronouncing his name. Anecdotal stories seem to be taken from other anthropologists. 19 refs on these pages.

[8.50.12] Lindstrom, Lamont. (1985). Personal names and social reproduction on Tanna, Vanuatu. Journal of the Polynesian Society, 94, 27-45.
Tanna is an island in the southern district of Vanuatu (formerly New Hebrides) and has a population of about 15,000. Description of naming customs; there are limited sets of male and female names. Groups composed of members of the same name-set bestow names by nomination. Names are recycled since there are a limited number of names available for the name-set. 37 refs.

[8.50.13] Lawrence, Pencile & deYoung, John E. (1960). In John E. deYoung (Ed.), The use of names by Micronesians, Anthropological Working Papers, No. 3, (2nd ed.), (pp. 57-79). Guam, Marianas Islands: Office of the Staff Anthropologist, Trust Territory of the Pacific Islands.
Naming customs on Ponape, an island in the Eastern Carolines with a population of about 10,000. An individual may be known by several different names, a personal name given by parents, a Christian name given by a clergyman, by title, by matrilineal clan, or in some cases, by matrilineal family name. There are also "joking" or nicknames. 5 refs.

[8.50.14] Mahoney, Frank. (1960), Trukese names. In John E. deYoung (Ed.), The use of names by Micronesians, Anthropological Working Papers, No. 3, (2nd ed.), (pp. 80-98). Guam, Marianas Islands: Office of the Staff Anthropologist, Trust Territory of the Pacific Islands.
Naming customs of the Truk group of islands in the East Carolines which has a population of about 20,000. In modern times, Christianity has had an effect on naming. The earliest missionaries were American Protestants, followed by German Protestants. These were followed by Spanish Catholic missionaries.

[8.50.15] McKnight, Robert K. (1960). Palauan names. In John E. deYoung
(Ed.), The use of names by Micronesians, Anthropological Working Papers,
No. 3, (2nd ed.), (pp. 16-54). Guam, Marianas Islands: Office of the Staff
Anthropologist, Trust Territory of the Pacific Islands.
Naming customs of the Palau Island group (about 9000 people) in the Western
Carolines. Effect of German, Japanese, Spanish, and American influences on
naming. Most common usage is birth name as a first name with father's
birth name as a second name. 1 ref.

[8.50.16] Needham, Rodney. (1954). The system of teknonyms and death
-names of the Penan. Southwestern Journal of Anthropology, 10, 416-431.
Field research on a tribe of forest nomads in NW Borneo, describes
teknonyms and death-names.

[8.50.17] Needham, Rodney. (1965). Death-names and social solidarity in
Penan society. Bijdragen tot de taal-, land- en volkenkunde, 121, 58-76.
Evaluation of 12 Penan groups concludes that the use of death-names
declines in proportion to contact with other ethnic groups. 9 refs. +
illus.

[8.50.18] Needham, Rodney. (1971). Penan friendship names. In T. O.
Beidelman (Ed.) The translation of cultures: Essays to E. E. Evans
Pritchard (pp. 203-230). London: Tavistock.
The Penan, a relatively small people of Central Borneo, use personal names,
teknonyms, mourning names (on the death of a relative), and also friendship
names (used exclusively between 2 individuals). 22 refs.

[8.50.19] Rivers, William Halsey Rivers. (1968). The history of
Melanesian society. Oosterhout, Netherlands: Anthropological Publications,
Vol. 1, 400 p. + plates, Vol. 2, 610 p. + map. (Originally published by
Cambridge University Pr. in 1914)
Comprehensive information on the peoples and cultures of a number of
islands in the South Pacific including Banks Islands, Torres Islands, and
Solomon Islands. There are a number of scattered references to naming
practices mostly with regard to forms of address. One unique practice
mentioned is that found on Tikopia where on marriage both parties
relinquish their former names for a new common name.

[8.50.20] Ryan, D'Arcy. (1958). Names and naming in Mendi. Oceania, 29,
109-116.
Naming customs of this tribe in the Southern Highlands of Papua. Short
list of birth names. Description of circumstances allowing change of name.
Friendship names.

[8.50.21] Strathern, Andrew. (1970). Wiru penthonyms. Bijdragen tot de
Taal-, Land- en Volkenkunde, 126, 59-77.
Research on the Wiru of the Southern Highlands of Papua/New Guinea shows
the use of penthonyms, sorrow names where a person expresses grief by
naming a child after a dead person. 14 items.

[8.50.22] Wormsley, William E. (1980). Tradition and change in Imbonggu
names and naming practices. Names, 28, 183-194.
The Imbonggu live in the mountains of Papua New Guinea. Their naming
system is described along with an evaluation of the effect of Australian
colonial influence. 6 refs.

8.51. Philippine

[8.51.1]   Eder, James. (1975). Naming practices and the definition of
affines among the Batak of the Philippines. Ethnology, 14, 59-70.
Describes the naming customs of the Batak, a small primitive group of the
Palawan Island.   All Batak possess at least 2 names, some possess five.
Batak have birth names, affinal names, and reciprocal (friendship) names.
9 refs.

[8.51.2]   Rosaldo, Renato.   (1984).   Ilongot   naming: The   play of
associations.   In Elisabeth Tooker (Ed.),   Harold C. Conklin (Symposium
Organizer), 1980 Proceedings of the American Ethnological Society (pp.
11-24).   Washington, DC: American Ethnological Society,
The Ilongot are a tribe of northern Luzon in the Philippines. Their naming
system has 5 types of name: (1) infant names, (2) childhood names, (3)
adult names, (4) in-law names, and (5) reciprocal names (used between same
sex individuals). 14 refs.

8.52. Polish

[8.52.1]   Borkowski, Thomas S. (1963). Some patterns in Polish surname
changes. Polish American Studies, 20, 14-16.
Examination of 2513 cases shows 6 patterns of change.   These are:
substitution (complete change as Czarnecki to Scott), 62%; combination
(keeping part of old name and adding a few letter(s) to the revised name as
Barzyk to Barr), 14%; and subtraction (Bolanowski to Bolan), 14%. The
other patterns are phonetic transcription (Gladysz to Gladys), 2%;
translation (Biskup to Bishop), 1%; and addition (Szabla to Szablack) less
than 1%.

[8.52.2] Brzezinski, Jerome A. (1963). History of Polish name changes in
America. Polish American Studies, 20, 4-7.
Poles first came to America in 1608 at Jamestown. Many Polish surnames
were changed.   Among them are Zabriskie which is traced to Albert
Zaborowski and Sandusky which is traced to Anthony Sadowski. 12 refs.

[8.52.3] Karpluk, Maria. (1981). Traces of the Slavonic rite in Poland
Proceedings of the 13th Congress of Onomastic Sciences, 1978, Cracow, 1,
pp. 593-598.
Connects Old Polish names such as Klimiont, Pawel and Toma to the Old
Slavonic rite introduced by SS. Cyril and Methodius in 867. 35 refs.

[8.52.4] Kotlarz, Robert J. (1963). Writings about the changing of Polish
names in America. Polish American Studies, 20, 1-4.
Description of some materials to aid research. 12 refs.

[8.52.5] Kowalik-Kaletowa, Zofia.   (1981). The properties of nomen
appellativum and nomen proprium within a category of names of inhabitants.
Proceedings of the 13th Congress of Onomastic Sciences, 1978, Cracow, 1,
pp. 677-681.
Using several examples from Poland and nearby areas, concludes that the
name of an inhabitant, i. e., a Cracovian ("one from Cracow"), can be
classified as a common name since its referent is not unique although it
functions closely to a proper name. 11 refs.

[8.52.6] Lyra, Franciszek. (1966). Polish surnames in the United States, American Speech, 41, 39-44.
Categorizes several patterns of Polish surname change including: transliteration, Dulac to Dulak; contraction, Kozlowski to Kozol; translation, Czarnecki to Black; and change, Urbanik to Michaels. Many examples. 2 refs.

[8.52.7] Magiera, Stanley A. (1963). Some reasons for first name changes. Polish American Studies, 20, 8-9.
Data from 383 individuals of Polish descent who changed their names indicate 3 chief reasons for the change: (1) grammatical (including spelling and pronunciation), 46%; (2) social, 39%; and (3) miscellaneous, 15%.

[8.52.8] Nalibow, Kenneth L. (1973). The opposition in Polish of genus and sexus in women's surnames. Names, 21, 78-81.
Traditional Polish surnames such as Fischer take suffixes to indicate a wife (Fischerow) or a daughter (Fischero'wna). With the rise in the number of working women there has been a pattern of women retaining the masculine form of the surname. 4 refs.

[8.52.9] Rzetelska-Feleszko, Ewa. (1975). A subsystem of family names in North Polish dialects. Berichte des XII. Internationaler Kongresses fuer Namenforschung, 1975, Bern, 3, 261-287.
Explanation of regional names have suffixes which indicate family relationship. 4 refs, in Polish.

[8.52.10] St. Mary's College Symposium. (1963). Changing of Polish names in America. Polish American Studies, 20, 1-16.
Contains abstracts of 7 papers presented by undergraduates at a symposium. See other entries in this section.

[8.52.11] Supranowicz, Elzbieta, (1981). Sources of inspiration for humanistic literarian pseudonyms ("pen-names"). Proceedings of the 13th Congress of Onomastic Sciences, 1978, Cracow, 2, 485-489.
Identification of 4 types of pseudonym used in Polish and other literature: (1) translation of family names into Latin, (2) linguistic hybrids using Latin and Polish, (3) metaphorical names, and (4) pseudo-Latin names. 7 refs.

[8.52.12] Szajna, Chester B. (1963). Some patterns in Polish first-name changes. Polish American Studies, 20, 10-12.
Examination of 383 first name changes shows several patterns. Most common is transformation (changing a name such as Piotr to Peter). A 2nd pattern is adaptation (changing a Polish or Slavic name into an English equivalent such as Wladyslaw to Walter). Some other patterns were also observed.

[8.52.13] Szymczak, Mieczylaw. (1981). Derivatives from proper names. Proceedings of the 13th Congress of Onomastic Sciences, 1978, Cracow, 2, 519-525. In Polish, there are 11 groups of derivatives from proper names. Of these 5 deal with personal names: surnames from placenames, surnames of wives from those of husbands, daughters from fathers, female names, and diminutive and hypocoristic names. Also considered, words from names.

[8.52.14] Zagraniczny, Stanley J. (1963). Some reasons for Polish surname changes. Polish American Studies, 20, 12-14.

Investigation of court records for 2513 changes of name shows 13 reasons
for change. Cited most often were: (1) spelling and punctuation errors,
31%; (2) business reasons, 20%; (3) legalization of name already in use,
15%; (4) desire to "Americanize" the surname, 6%; and (5) social advantage,
5%. Other reasons each had a frequency of less than 3%.

[8.52.15] Zand, Helen Stankiewicz. (1950). Polish given names in America.
Polish American Studies, 7, 34-38.
There are 3 trends in the changing of names: (1) simple translation, Piotr
to Peter, Jadwiga to Hedwig; (2) shift to international names, from Adam
and Boleslaw to Edward and Henry; and (3) shift to "American" names such as
Audrey, Donald, and Thomas. Examples.

Polynesian: See--8.50. Oceania
8.53. Portuguese

[8.53.1] Aman, Reinhold & Monteiro, George. (1979). Portuguese nicknames.
Maledicta, 3, 69-70.
Listing with meaning and derivation of about 50 colorful nicknames such as
Cabreiro ("goatherd"), Gago ("stutterer"), and Frangalha ("loose chicken").
1 ref.

[8.53.2] Fucilla, Joseph G. (1979). Portuguese office and occupational
surnames. Onoma, 23, 33-51.
Examination of Portuguese surnames indicates that occupational names are
relatively recent as compared to those in Britain and elsewhere. Many
examples. 12 refs.

[8.53.3] Fucilla, Joseph G. (1979). Portuguese nicknames as surnames.
Names, 27, 73-105.
The number of surnames apelidos derived from nicknames alcunhas has
increased. These new surnames come from several categories such as kinship
(Filho, "son"), anatomical (Casco, "skull"), metaphorical (Lobo, "wolf"),
desirable (Pio, "pious"), undesirable (Bregante, "bandit"), from
atmospheric phenomena (Orvalho, "mist"), from surnames (Ouro, "gold"), and
miscellaneous (Taumaturgo, "magician"). 26 refs.

[8.53.4] Monteiro, George. (1961). Alcunhas among the Portuguese in
Southern New England. Western Folklore, 20, 103-107.
The term alcunhas can refer to either nicknames or substitute surnames.
Examples are drawn from the Blackstone Valley area of Rhode Island. One
family was known as os Fumegas ("smokers"). Individuals had names such as
Gago ("stutterer"), Torto ("cockeye"), or Milhomens ("thousand men"). Many
further examples. 5 refs.

[8.53.5] Moser, Gerald M. (1960). Portuguese family names. Names, 8,
30-52.
Discusses various types of Portuguese names; where in the world Portuguese
names are found--Ceylon, England, South America, United States, Brazil,
Canada. Lists of Portuguese names from the 14th century and from current
telephone directories. 20 refs.

[8.53.6] Pap, Leo. (1949). Portuguese-American speech. New York: King's
Crown Pr., pp. 2-4; 124-138.
Describes the pattern of anglicization of Portuguese first names and

surnames in the United States, as Pereira to Perry, Barros to Barrows. A number of examples are listed. Some statistics on Portuguese names are given from telephone directories in New Bedford, Massachusetts and Oakland, California. Portuguese Jewish names are also covered very briefly. 26 refs.

Roman: See--Classical
8.54. Romanian

[8.54.1] Jiga, Caius T. (1976). The shepherd in Rumanian onomastics. Berichte des XII. Internationaler Kongresses fuer Namenforschung, 1975, Bern, 3, 522-533.
A whole series of surnames and variations are derived from various aspects of the shepherd's life. These include: Pastor ("shepherd"), Baci ("chief shepherd"), Barca ("shepherd of curly-haired sheep"), Cirlanaru ("shepherd of non-suckling kids"), and others. 44 refs.

[8.54.2] Jiga, Caius T. (1981). Some pastoral products and implements in Rumanian onomastics. Proceedings of the 13th Congress of Onomastic Sciences, 1978, Cracow, 1, pp. 543-551.
Uses documents from as far back as the 13th century to show how products such as cheese and implements such as the shepherd's caldron have influenced naming patterns. Cheese yields a number of names including the first names Brinzaru, Brinzea, and Brinzoi; surnames, Brinza, Brensa, Brenza; the caldron, surnames Caldarar, Caldare, Caldaruse, Caldarea, and others. Approx 55 refs.

[8.54.3] Vascenco, Victor. (1975). Concerning the standard system of Romanian surnames. Names, 23, 89-101.
Using a sample of 34,000, the top 100 surnames were analyzed in terms of type, surnames from first names, surnames ending in escu, surnames from appellatives, and borrowed names. The most common surnames were Ionescu, Popescu, and Dumitrescu. Table; 27 refs, mostly Romanian.

8.55. Russian

[8.55.1] Baecklund, Astrid. (1956). Could Old Russian feminine names end in -yata? Slavonic and East European Review, 35, 255-258.
In a dispute over the sex of a name (Gostyata) found in ancient writing on birch bark in Novgorod the Great, Baecklund agrees with Jakobson that it was masculine contrary to views of contemporary Russian experts. 7 refs, all in Russian.

[8.55.2] Baecklund, Astrid. (1959). Personal names in medieval Velikij Novgorod, I. Common names. Stockholm: Almqvist and Wiksell, 195 p.
Analysis of the 21 most frequent male names in various forms and spellings based upon legal documents of the 12th-15th centuries from this medieval Russian center. 100+ refs, mostly non-English, many footnotes.

[8.55.3] Benson, Morton. (1964). Dictionary of Russian personal names. Philadelphia: University of Pennsylvania Press, 175 p.
Covers 23,000 surnames and includes proper accentuation. Builds on the work of Unbegaun, Stankiewicz, and St. Clair Sobell. 35 refs, most in Russian.

[8.55.4] Benson, Morton. (1964). The stress of Russian surnames. Slavic and East European Journal, 8, 42-53.
Systematically discusses the patterns of stress in Russian surnames. Although there are many exceptions, most names have a penult stress. 11 refs.

[8.55.5] Case, Norman. (1969). The name Rasputin: A study in semantic complexity. Names, 17, 245-249.
Rasputin's original name was Vilkin ("fork-man"). Rasputin comes from rasputye ("fork in the road"). Further discussion of aspects of meaning of the name. 5 refs.

[8.55.6] Davis, Patricia Anne. (1968). Soviet Russian given names. Names, 16, 95-104.
Analysis of the names of 11,000 Muscovites taken from divorce notices published in a Russian newspaper in 1964. Only 4% of the names were saints' names. This 4% was analyzed in terms of pattern (borrowed from other languages, from writers such as Pushkin, new names, and others). Many examples. 9 refs, mostly Russian.

[8.55.7] Davis, Patricia Anne. (1970). Modern Russian given names: An historical and statistical study. Dissertation Abstracts, 26, 7313. (University Microfilms No. 66-4610)
Develops statistics on male and female names of 26,000 Russians (men from 1700-1956; women from 1856-1956), most of whom were intellectuals. Over 99% of pre-Revolutionary names and 96% of those born later are Church Calendar names. Some attention to Soviet-invented names.

[8.55.8] Deatherage, Melvin E. (1962). Soviet surnames: A handbook. Oberammergau, Germany: US Army Foreign Area Specialist Training Program (Russian), Part 1, 56 p., Part 2, 333 p.
Part 1 contains an extensive introduction to patterns of surnaming among the peoples of Russia and the Baltic areas. This includes Ukrainian, Georgian, Armenian, Jewish, Estonian, Latvian, and Lithuanian as well as Russian. Part 2 is a listing of 30,000 surnames in Cyrillic script in alphabetical order showing the pronunciation stress. The names are just listed. No meanings or derivations are shown. 13 refs.

[8.55.9] Frink, Orrin. (1983). American names in Russian. ANS Bulletin, No. 72, 25-35.
Discussion of how 15 American names such as P. T. Barnum, John Birch, and Allan Pinkerton are treated in a negative fashion in Russian dictionaries. 5 refs.

[8.55.10] Gerhart, Genevra. (1974). The Russian's world: Life and language. New York: Harcourt Brace Jovanovich, pp. 19-34.
Description and discussion of Russian first names in various forms as well as patronymics. Many examples. Even a short section on names for pets. 8 footnotes.

[8.55.11] Ktora, Alla. (1984). The migration of Russian pet names. ANS Bulletin, No. 94, pp. 46-49.
Comment and discussion on influence of foreign names, especially English, on personal names and names for pets. Some pet names are after people, Rasputin, Gromyko, or Portnoy.

[8.55.12]   Lederman,   Dov   B.   (1975).   Russian-English dictionary   of
suppositional names. Philadelphia: Guild of Professional Translators, 45 p.
This dictionary is designed to serve the needs of professional translators
working with scientific materials who wish to accurately convert names of
scientists (Russian and non-Russian) into the appropriate English form.
Approx 4500 names covered.

[8.55.13] Minns, Ellis H. (1948). Greek and Latin names in Russian dress.
Journal of Hellenic Studies, 66, 57-60.
Discussion of how Greek and Latin names have been modified through Slavonic
to modern Russian. Many examples. 4 refs.

[8.55.14]   Room, Adrian.   (1983).   Russian personal names   since the
Revolution: 1. Journal of Russian Studies, 45, 19-24.
The introduction to Russian first-naming is followed by a description of 2
major classes of modern names: (1) post-Revolutionary ideological names
(ex., Oktyabrina, Vladlen) and European imports (ex., Robert and Zhanna).
Many examples. 3 refs.

[8.55.15]   Room, Adrian.   (1983).   Russian personal names   since the
Revolution: 2. Journal of Russian Studies, 46, 13-18.
Continues the above article with many examples. 9 refs.

[8.55.16] Selishchev, A. M. (1979). Changes in surnames and given names.
Soviet Anthropology and Archeology, 17, 46-60.
A number of Russians have been changing their pre-Revolutionary surnames.
Many of these are considered insulting or ridiculing. Some are changing to
new surnames such as Leninskii (from Lenin), Stal' (from Stalin). Some
individuals are changing just the first name. 2 refs.

[8.55.17]   St. Clair-Sobell,   James. (1958).   Some remarks   on the
pronunciation of Russian surnames in the English-speaking world. Three
Papers in Slavonic Studies. Vancouver, BC: University of British Columbia,
pp. 23-34.
Evaluates the various categories of Russian surnames and the problems
encountered in pronunciation. Examples of names discussed include Molotov,
Pavlova, and Borodin. 6 refs.

[8.55.18] St. Clair-Sobell, James & Carlsen, Irina. (1959). The structure
of Russian surnames. Canadian Slavonic Papers, 4, 42-60.
Technical discussion on the variations in pronunciation of Russian
surnames. 14 refs, mostly non-English.

[8.55.19] Sosnowski, Jan. (1985). Names of Russian peasants in the 16th
century. XV, Internationaler Kongress fuer Namenforschung, 1984, Leipzig,
4, 301-306.
Data from 16th century tax registers of Moscovy provide information on the
naming system then in effect. Most common first names were: Ivan, Vasilij,
Fedor, Gregorij, Semen, and Mikhail. Further elaboration on diminutives,
hypocoristic, appellatives, and patronymics. Many examples. Some
attention to Ukrainian influence.

[8.55.20]   Stankiewicz, Edward. (1957). The expression of affection in
Russian proper names. Slavic and East European Journal, 25, 196-210.
Sets up categories to show expressive forms of proper names. These are:
(1) truncation of the full stem (hypocoristic formation) as Aleksander to

Sanja, (2) suffixation on full stems, as Pavel to Pavlik, and (3) a combination of (1) and (2) as Aleksandr to Al'ka. Several subcategories of each also included. Many examples. 6 refs.

[8.55.21] Throckmorton, Robert J. (1981). Origin and probable extinction of the Russian surname Ponafidine. Names, 29, 317-318.
Traces the name to a retainer of Sophia Paleologue in the 15th Century who had the motto, Bona in Fidem. 4 refs.

[8.55.22] Unbegaun, Boris O. (1972). Russian surnames. Clarendon Pr., 529 p.
Comprehensive description of thousands of Russian surnames. Includes non-Slavic and Jewish surnames. Indexing includes surname endings. 180 item bibliography, mostly non-English, many annotated.

8.56. Sardinian

[8.56.1] Rowland, Robert J., Jr. (1973). Onomastic remarks on Roman Sardinia. Names, 21, 82-102.
Sardinia was occupied by the Romans in 238 BC. Analysis of inscriptions and in Cicero shows influence of Libyans, Iberians, and Ligurians. Romanization was felt largely in the urban and coastal areas even through the Christian period. Greek names also included. 10 maps. 22 refs.

8.57. Scottish

[8.57.1] Baillie, Susan R. (1981). A surname analysis of two fishing communities in north-east Scotland. Annals of Human Biology, 72, 392.
Surnames used to measure inbreeding indicate that fishermen had more inbreeding than non-fisherman.

[8.57.2] Dorian, Nancy C. (1970). East Sutherland by-naming. Scottish Studies, 14, 59-65.
A summary of Dorian [8.57.3] below.

[8.57.3] Dorian, Nancy C. (1970). A substitute name system in the Scottish Highlands. American Anthropologist, 72, 303-319.
Field work in some small Gaelic-speaking communities shows the use of by-names (unofficial names) where there are many individuals with identical names. Both men and women have by-names and there are several varieties of by-name. 5 refs.

[8.57.4] Dorward, David. (1978). Scottish surnames. Edinburgh, Scotland: William Blackwood, 1978, 70 p.
Background and history of about 200 Scottish surnames plus variations. Listing of the most common surnames in Scotland.

[8.57.5] Dunkling, Leslie Alan. (1978). Scottish Christian names: An A-Z of first names. London: Johnston and Bacon, 151 p.
Introduction. Alphabetical listing of first names and origins; comments about current frequency; popular associations of the name. Index shows pet forms, i. e., Gail < Abigail; Sandy < Alexander. 49 refs.

[8.57.6] Hamp, Eric P. (1959). Proper names in Scottish Gaelic. Names, 7, 57-59.
In the dialect of Leurbost (Isle of Lewis) masculine names are defined by the occurrence of the genitive singular prefix. 3 refs.

[8.57.7] Nicolaisen, Wilhelm F. H. (1980). Tension and extension: Thought on Scottish surnames. Journal of Popular Culture, 14(1), 119-130.
One category of surnames, those derived from placenames (Colston, Fenwick) tells about population movement; a 2nd, tells about the occupations held by the original bearers (Barker, took bark off trees for tanning, Horner, made spoons out of horns); a 3rd category tells about kinship (Thomson, Macdonald). Naming patterns also show socioeconomic data. 19 refs.

[8.57.8] Walker, Maud Kimmel. (1974). Social constraints, individuals, and social decisions in a Scottish rural community. Dissertation Abstracts International, 34B, 5801B-5802B. (University Microfilms No. 74-12,232)
Includes description of naming decisions in a a Gaelic-speaking crofting community in the Hebrides.

8.58. Slavic

[8.58.1] Gerus-Tarnawecky, Iraida Irene. (1965). Anthroponymy in the Pomianyk of Horodysce of 1484, (2nd rev. ed.). Onomastica, No. 30, pp. 1-80.
According to the author this is a revision of the material listed under the same title by Tarnawecky [8.58.9] and [8.58.10].

[8.58.2] Jaszczun, Wasyl. (1965). The term and name "Brody." Onomastica, No. 29, Whole issue. 31 p.
Extensive discussion with examples of various meanings of Brody "ford" in the Slavic languages. Besides placenames there are three surnames that have the root. 70 refs.

[8.58.3] Klymasz, Robert B. (1961). A classified dictionary of Slavic surname changes in Canada. Onomastica, No.22, Whole issue, 64 p.
Listings of over 2000 surnames from the Manitoba Gazette followed by the new name, as Rogalski to Rogers. Part II gives the new name followed by the original name, as Sanford < Senchuk.

[8.58.4] Pauls, John P. (1960). Surnames of Soviet Russian and other communist celebrities. Names, 8, 220-239.
Gives surname meanings of 240 Eastern Bloc leaders who appear frequently in the press. Countries included are Russia, the Ukraine, Poland, Czechoslovakia, Bulgaria, and Yugoslavia. Examples include: Brezhnev ("cautious"), Shostakovich ("sixth male child" or "one who has six fingers"), and Lysenko ("bald-headed"). 8 refs.

[8.58.5] Rudnyckyj, Jaroslav Bohdan. (1960). Slaves or glorious ones. Names, 8, 65-74
Reviews the etymology of Slav. Concludes that the toponomic explanation is strongest, the root referring to people living on the shores of rivers, lakes, etc. Approx 30 refs.

[8.58.6] Rudnyckyj, Jaroslav Bohdan. (1964). Samo: The name of the first ruler of the Slavs. Names, 12, 215-219.

After examining available evidence, concludes that Samo was used as a Slavic name rather than Teutonic or any other nationality. 22 refs.

[8.58.7] Sotiroff, George. (1969). Slavonic names in Greek and Roman antiquities. Onomastica, No. 37, 23 p.
A selection of 22 names of Old Slavonic origin that have shown up in Ancient Greek and Roman sources. Includes some personal names: Zorina ("queen"), Vera ("faith"), Semele ("earth"), and Orolus ("eagle"). 19 refs.

[8.58.8] Struminskyj, Bohdan. (1977). Surnames in -kevic//-xevic//-gevic. Names, 25, 119-123.
Consideration of the presence of surnames ending in -kevic in Lithuania, White Ruthenia, Lithuanian Ukraine, and Polish settlements in the 15th and 16th centuries. 14 refs, all non-English.

[8.58.9] Tarnawecky, Iraida Irene. (1965). Anthroponymy in the Pomianyk Horodysce of 1484. Part I. Names, 13, 73-102.
The Pomianyk is a ms. from 1484-1737 found in a Ukrainian monastery. In this Cyrillic ms. there were 20,000 entries. Analysis of male and female Slavic first names. Explanation of the process by which foreign names, mostly Greek were slavicized. 50+ refs. See also: Gerus-Tarnawecky [8.58.1].

[8.58.10] Tarnawecky, Iraida Irene. (1965). Anthroponomy in the Pomianyk of Horodysce of 1484. Part II. Names, 13, 169-214.
Continuation of article above. There are 233 anthroponyms which are of Hebrew, Greek, Roman, and Slavic origin, ex., Ekaterina is derived from a virgin martyr of Alexandria. Each name has notes on its origin, pronunciation, and number of forms. Table of frequencies for each name. An additional A-tergo dictionary listing the names by ending. 105 refs.

8.59. South African

[8.59.1] Rosenthal, Eric. (1965). 8.59. South African surnames. Cape Town, South Africa: Howard Timmins, 262 p.
Histories are given of the families associated with the 60 most common European surnames followed by a listing of approximately 2600 European surnames with meaning in the original language. 40 refs.

8.60. South American

[8.60.1] Azevedo, Eliane S. (1980). The anthropological and cultural meaning of names in Bahia, Brazil. Current Anthropology, 21, 360-363.
This investigation focused on aspects of the racial ancestry of names. Black, Indian, and white surnames were evaluated. Results indicate that blacks tend to take devotional surnames; Indians, plant/animal surnames; whites, other types of name. Concludes that surnames are useful as racial and cultural markers. 23 refs.

[8.60.2] Bamberger, Joan. (1974). Naming and transmission of status in a Central Brazilian society. Ethnology, 1974, 14, 363-378.
Work among the Kayapo, a tribe of about 1400 in Central Brazil. Individuals possess ceremonial ("great names") and common ("little names").

Extensive   coverage   of   naming   customs,   rituals,   and   patterns   of
transmission.   21 refs.

[8.60.3] Gorden, Raymond L. (1968). Spanish personal names as barriers to
communication between Latin Americans and North Americans. Yellow Springs,
OH: Antioch College, 142 p.
Description of the Latin American naming system which involves a first name
(nombre), middle name (segundo nombre), and 2 surnames (primer apellido,
segundo apellido).   Anecdotes to show how lack of understanding of the
system can cause difficulties for North Americans. Origins of the 101 most
common first names. Several tables of the approximate frequency of first
names and surnames in 10 major Latin American cities. 13 refs.

[8.60.4] Holmberg, Allan. (1969). Nomads of the long bow: The Siriono of
Eastern Bolivia. Garden City, NY: Natural History Pr., 294 p.
Describes naming customs for children. A child can be named for the first
animal the father sees at the time of the birth, or a physical
characteristic of the child. There are no sex distinctions in names.
Nicknames, kinship names, and teknonyms are also used. 36 refs.

[8.60.5] Maybury-Lewis, David. (1984). Name, person, and ideology in
Central Brazil.   In Elisabeth Tooker (Ed.), Harold C. Conklin (Symposium
Organizer), 1980 Proceedings of the American Ethnological Society (pp.
1-10). Washington, DC: American Ethnological Society.
Description of the rationale for naming among the Northern Ge, Central Ge,
and Bororo tribes of Central Brazil. According to this rationale men enter
the world through the names given them; names represent the social self
since names transform the person. 14 refs.

[8.60.6] Price, Richard & Price, Sally. (1972). Saramaka onomastics: An
Afro-American naming system. Ethnology, 11, 341-367.
Thorough description and analysis of the naming of the Saramaka Maroons
("Bush Negroes") of Surinam, South America. Discussion of relevant
literature. 68 refs.

[8.60.7] Ramos, Alcida R. (1974). How the Sanuma acquire their names.
Ethnology, 13, 171-185.
The Sanuma are a small primitive society who live in a mountain range
between the Orinoco and the Amazon. Their language is a sub-group of the
Yanoama.   Two main groups of personal names are given.   One follows a
ritual hunt carried out by the father of the newborn. The slain animal
becomes the child's eponym. Other naming methods also used. 34 refs.

8.61. Spanish

[8.61.1] Brandes, Stanley. (1975). The structural and demographic
implications of nicknames in Navanogal, Spain. American Ethnologist, 2,
139-148.
Navanogal is a rural, mountain community of 800 people about 125 miles W of
Madrid. Concludes that nicknames thrive in communities which are small,
egalitarian, and traditional. Examples of nicknames include: Pinocho
(Pinochio, "has an enormous nose"), Carpanta (lazy), and Changarro (cow
bell, "he always chatters"). 15 refs.

[8.61.2] Buechley, Robert W. (1967). Characteristic name sets of Spanish populations. Names, 15, 53-69.
The use of Spanish surnames is important for demographic aspects of medical and other research. Different subsets are appropriately used in different parts of the United States. Examples of data are presented on the proportions of Spanish-surnamed persons in labor unions and in medicine. 5 refs.

[8.61.3] Buechley, Robert W. (1971). Spanish surnames among the 2000 most common United States surnames. Names, 19, 137-140.
Discussion of the 10 most frequent Spanish surnames in California and the United States as a whole. Further information on Spanish surnames in Puerto Rico, New Mexico, and South Texas. 3 refs.

[8.61.4] Duncan, Robert M. (1952-1953). Names in the Documentos linguisticos de Espana. New Mexico Folklore Record, 7, 1-12.
In 1919, Ramon Menendez Pidal published a collection of notarial documents showing the evolution of Spanish from the 11th to the 15th centuries. Among the documents are the names of 320 men and 410 women. First names and surnames are covered. Categories of names with examples are given. 1 ref.

[8.61.5] Fucilla, Joseph G. (1976). Office and occupational names in Spain. Names, 24, 144-164.
Analysis of telephone directories from Madrid and Barcelona plus other sources shows how several hundred surnames were derived from occupational associations. Categories include: noblemen and their entourage (Rey, "king;" Lancero, "lancer;"), churchmen (Perlado, "prelate;" Canonje, "canon:"), and trades (Ferrer, "smith;" Molinar, "miller") and others. 18 refs.

[8.61.6] Fucilla, Joseph G. (1978). Spanish nicknames as surnames. Names, 26, 139-176.
Comprehensive analysis showing the different categories of surnames developed from nicknames. The types include: kinship surnames (Padre, "father"), anatomical nickname surnames (Carillo, "cheek"), compound (Matalobos, "wolf hunter"), metaphorical (Gato, "cat"), desirable (Esperanza, "hope"), undesirable (Selvaje, "savage"), and miscellaneous (Aquado, "well-soaked"). Hundreds of examples. 11 refs.

[8.61.7] Hills, E. C. (1926). Spanish patronymics ending in -z. Revue Hispanique, 68, 161-173.
Description and analysis of a number of types of Spanish surname. The -z ending is derived from Latin genitive endings of -ci and -tii. Examples include Diaz, Ruiz, Sanz, and Ponz. 12 refs.

[8.61.8] Hinkle, Douglas P. (1980). Camacho: Curvature of the patronym In Pubs, place-names, and patronymics, Publications of the Names Institute, No. 1. Madison, NJ: Fairleigh Dickinson University, pp. 171-184.
Discussion and analysis of the origin of the surname Camacho, which seems related to crooked, lame, or bowlegged variants in other languages. 18 Refs.

[8.61.9] Madvell, Charles, R., Jr. (1967). The romance of Spanish names. New Orleans: Author, 233 p.
Includes a brief history of Spanish surnames. Most are patronymic or based

on location. Others are derived from occupations or nicknames. The main dictionary gives the etymology of approximately 1000 surnames. 17 refs.

[8.61.10] Woods, Richard D. (Compiler). (1984). Hispanic first names: A comprehensive dictionary of 250 years of Mexican-American usage. Westport, CT: Greenwood Pr., 222 p.
Lists approximately 90% of all Hispanic names in the United States. The listing was derived from: (1) baptismal records of the San Antonio Chancery, (2) telephone directories from over 750 locations, (3) New Mexico archives, and (4) other sources. There appears to be about 14,000 names covered although there are fewer main entries. Each main entry gives a transliteration of the name, the gender, English equivalent, descriptive material (meaning, origin), diminutives, and variants. Also included in the dictionary are an appendix with frequency tables and a glossary of English equivalent baptismal names. 92 refs plus a list of over 150 telephone directories.

[8.61.11] Woods, Richard D. & Alvarez-Altman, Grace. (1978). Spanish surnames in the Southwestern United States: A dictionary. Boston: G K Hall, 154 p.
Gives introduction to Hispanic surnames, etymology and meaning of approximately 1200 surnames. 119 endnotes. 21 refs.

8.62. Swedish

[8.62.1] Olson, Nils William. (1981). What's in a Swedish surname? Swedish American Genealogist, 1(1), 26-36.
Traces the development of Swedish surnames from the 15th and 16th centuries beginning with the aristocracy and spreading to the clergy in the 17th century. Then, citizens of towns and villages used a variety of nature names (Berg, "mountain;" Lind, "linden"). Other names covered are Walloon, military, and foreign.

[8.62.2] Person, Henry A. (1967). The Swedes and their family names. Scandinavian Studies, 39, 209-248.
Detailed description of the procedure for change of name in Sweden where those with common names or un-Swedish names are encouraged to change them. Several tables. 6 refs.

[8.62.3] Wiken, Erik. (1982). When did Swedish patronymics become surnames? Swedish American Genealogist, 2(1), 31-33.
Gives examples of Swedish immigrants in the 1st half of the 19th century who chose their own surnames on coming to the United States. 18 refs.

8.63. Swiss

[8.63.1] Dalcher, Peter. (1968). English names in Swiss-German usage. Onoma, 13, 333-342.
Comment and discussion on English names which have been incorporated into Swiss-German usage. Examples include Harry and Charlie. 15 refs. most in German.

[8.63.2] Richardson, Peter Nichols. (1974). German-Romance contact: Name-giving in Walser settlements, Amsterdamer Publikationem zur Sprache und Literatur (Amsterdam), 15, 372 p.

The Walser were a German people who had settled in the area of Valais, Switzerland. In the 13th century many of the Walser migrated to the Italian Piedmont and then E to Graubunden. This is the canton which is trilingual. Name-giving patterns and traditions are evaluated in both the German and Romance regions to show the effects of interpenetration of 2 cultures. 250+ refs, most in German.

[8.63.3] Richardson, Peter Nichols. (1974). Some notes on a Swiss bicultural onomasticon. Names, 22, 45-51.
The trilingual Swiss canton of Graubunden has 3 languages, German, Romansh, and Italian. A collection of 20,000 names from 1200 to 1700 was evaluated for cultural contact regarding first names. 9 refs.

[8.63.4] Senn, Alfred. (1962). Notes on Swiss personal names. Names, 10, 149-158.
Classification with examples of German-Swiss first names and surnames. Many examples. Some attention to transformation of Swiss names in the United States. 13 refs, most in German.

8.64. Turkish

[8.64.1] Spencer, Robert F. (1961). The social context of modern Turkish names. Southwestern Journal of Anthropology, 17, 205-218.
Description of modern Turkish first name and surname practices; the 1934 Turkish name law. 15 refs.

8.65. Ukrainian

[8.65.1] Bogdan, F. (1974). Dictionary of Ukrainian surnames in Canada. Winnipeg: Onomastic Commission of UVAN and Canadian Institute of Onomastic Sciences, 354 p.
Includes over 30,000 names with transliteration and stress. Has article by J. B. Rudnyckyj on name change. 50+ refs.

[8.65.2] Holutiak-Hallick, Stephen P., Jr. (1972). Orthographic variations of Ukrainian surnames in Western Pennsylvania. Names, 20, 193-199.
Evaluates 1100 Ukrainian surnames and their various American English transformations over a period of 3 generations (1907-1970). Many examples such as Strus becoming Struce, Struss, or Strus. 7 refs.

[8.65.3] Hursky, Jacob P. (1960). The origin of patronymic surnames in Ukrainian. Annals of the Ukrainian Academy of Arts and Sciences in the Ukrainian Academy of Arts and Sciences in the United States, 8, 169-190.
Systematic presentation of the various types of surname going back to the 10th century; also includes nicknames and explanations of suffixes. Map. 82 refs.

[8.65.4] Hursky, Jacob P. (1971). Phonetic peculiarities in Ukrainian patronynic surnames of the Fourteenth-Seventeenth centuries. Names, 19, 262-267.
Most of the changes associated with surnames conformed with those changes in the Ukrainian language system as a whole.

[8.65.5] Rudnyckyj, Jaroslav Bohdan. (1982). An entymological dictionary of the Ukrainian language, Vol. 1, 968 p., Vol. 2, 656 p. Ottawa, Ontario: University of Ottawa Press, distributors.
Includes many personal names such as Gregor and derivatives in various Slavic languages. Author estimates there are over 3,000 first names and surnames included. Hundreds of refs, most non-English.

[8.65.6] Slavutych, Yar. (1962). Ukrainian surnames in -enko. Names, 10, 181-186.
Historical background. Classification with copious examples, as Ivanenko, son of Ivan (patronymic); Kravcenko, son of Kravec, "tailor" (occupational); Usenko, son of a man with a long mustache (personal characteristics). 8 refs.

[8.65.7] Slavutych, Yar. (1966). The Russian deformation of Ukrainian surnames. Proceedings of the Eighth International Congress of Onomastic Sciences, Amsterdam, pp. 488-491.
Russian influence has deformed Ukrainian names in 2 ways, phonetic (Akimenko < Jakymenko), and morphological (Borodin < Borodyn, "son of a man with long beard"). 24 refs.

[8.65.8] Slavutych, Yar. (1966). Ukrainian onomastics II: The Ukrainia contribution to onomastic sciences 1954-1965. Names, 14, 161-168
Describes contributions of Ukrainian scholars after de-Stalinization. Among those discussed are: Burjacok, Humecka, and Rudnyckyj. 30 refs.

[8.65.9] Tarnawecka, Iraida. (1985). Canadian Ukrainian anthroponymy in language contact. XV, Internationaler Kongress fuer Namenforschung, 1984, Leipzig, 5, 223-226.
Patterns of name change by Ukrainian immigrants in Western Canada from 1972 to 1982. Some changes were voluntary; some involuntary. Voluntary changes show several patterns: entire, Yamchuk to Cooper; translation, Czornij to Black; hybridization, Baryliuk to Barlock; and others. An involuntary change is a distortion often by others (officials), as Onyschuk to Onyzsycuk. A new phenomenon is that of reverse name change where some people change their non-Ukrainian names back to Ukrainian, Jordan to Bayko. 3 refs.

[8.65.10] Wolnicz-Pawlowska, Ewa. (1980). 18th Century Ukrainian anthroponymy. Onoma, 24, 75-78.
Abstract of a Ph. D. thesis based on 7000 male personal names in Ruthenia, part of Poland. Fifty per cent of names were patronymics, Punio < Puniewicz, 34% were based on individual characteristics, Baran (lamb). Some Polish material. 6 refs.

[8.65.11] Zyla, Wolodymyr T. (1966). Ukrainian anthroponymy in the Kharkov Register of 1660. Proceedings of the Eighth International Congress of Onomastic Sciences, Amsterdam, pp. 596-604.
The Kharkhov Register included boiar (boyar) children, regimental Cossacks, townsfolk, and peasants. Their surnames are of 6 types: (1) relationship (patronyms), (2) local (geographical, nationality), (3) occupation or office, (4) nicknames, (5) foreign origin, and (6) doubtful or unexplained. 11 refs.

[8.65.12] Zyla, Wolodymyr T. (1966). Ukrainian onomastics I. Names, 14,
109-120.
Traces historically the work of a number of contributors to Ukrainian
onomastics.   Included are Miklosichm, Semeysysn, Franko, Simovye,
Rudnyckyj, and Cilujko. 28 refs, most non-English.

[8.65.13] Zyla, Wolodymyr T. (1970). Adjectival surnames in the Kharkov
Register of 1660. Names, 18, 89-96.
Indicates that by 1660 all classes had surnames. Considers the semantic
connection between names ending in -skyj and -ckyj and toponyms and
hydronyms. 14 refs.

[8.65.14] Zyla, Wolodymyr T. (1976). Kharkiv Register of 1660. Surname
derivative from placenames. Berichte des XII. Internationaler Kongresses
fuer Namenforschung, 1975, Bern, 3, 496-506.
The Kharkiv (Kharkov) Register shows that all classes of society had
surnames. These surnames were derived from many sources. Among them were
toponyms, hydronyms, and ethnonyms. Many examples. 21 refs.

8.66. Welsh

[8.66.1] Davies, Trefor Redall. (1952). A book of Welsh names. London:
Sheppard Pr., 72 p.
Has about 480 entries which include etymology, meaning, and prominent
bearers of the name. Included are: Glynis ("little valley"), Llewellyn
("leader"), and Selwyn (sel "ardor" + wyn "fair one").

[8.66.2] Faraday, M. A. (1979). Indexing late medieval personal names of
Wales and the Marches. Archives, 14, 11-15.
Explanation of some of the difficulties of indexing several categories of
Welsh names. Suggests that a name such as George ap Harry should be
indexed under George, under ap Harry, and probably under Parry as well. 5
refs.

[8.66.3] Fowkes, Robert A. (1981). Welsh naming practices, with a
comparative look at Cornish. Names, 29, 265-272.
Discussion of naming practices in Wales and Cornwall with some examples of
patronymics (Jones, Williams), descriptive names (Lloyd, "grey," Gwyn,
"white"), occupational names (Hughes the Carpenter), Jones the Draper),
location names (Mostyn the Grove, Evans the School), nicknames (Will Mouth,
Ned One-eye), and others. Numerous examples. 18 refs.

[8.66.4] Hamp, Eric P. (1969). Early Welsh names, suffixes and phonology.
Onoma, 14, 7-13.
Responding to a paper by Melville Richards on early Welsh territorial
suffixes, Hamp sets up alternative hypotheses of the phonological
development of British Keltic names. 9 refs.

[8.66.5] Hughes, Mark H. (1977-79). The distribution of Welsh surnames.
Genealogists' Magazine, 19, 61-62.
Comment on Leeson (1977-79) below.

[8.66.6] Leeson, Francis. (1977-79). The distribution of Welsh surnames.
Genealogists' Magazine, 19, 16-17, 62.

Shows the distribution of 26 common surnames in 13 counties in Wales. Among the names are: Davies, Edwards, Evans, and Griffiths. 2 refs.

[8.66.7] Powell, Anthony. (1977-79). The distribution of Welsh surnames. Genealogists' Magazine, 19, 61.
Comment on Leeson (1977-79) above.

[8.66.8] Raglan, Lord. (1961). Welsh surnames. Man, 61, 42.
A reply to Watkin (1960) below. Comments that names such as Jones, Richards, and Roberts are borne more by people of English rather than Welsh descent. 1 ref.

[8.66.9] Watkin, I. Morgan. (1960). A Viking settlement in Little England beyond Wales: ABO blood-group evidence. Man, 60, 148-153.
Along with other data on the area lists 40 surnames which are held to be characteristically Welsh. These names include:Bevan, Bowen, Richards, and Williams. 27 refs.

[8.66.10] Watkin, I. Morgan. (1961). Welsh surnames. Man, 61, 88-89.
This is a reply attacking Lord Raglan's comment above (1961) that the names Jones, Richards, Roberts, Walters, and Williams are borne by more people of English rather than Welsh origin. 9 refs.

9. FASHIONS AND TRENDS: See also--8.23. English Names

[9.1] Cumming, Elaine. (1967). The name is the message. Trans-Action, 4(July-August), 50-52.
Categories of popular names. Table of most popular names of children in New York City from 1898 to 1964. Also reports a survey from upstate New York.

[9.2] Dunkling, Leslie Alan. (1977). First names first. New York: Universe, 285 p. (also published as What's in a name? by Ventura in England and by Rigby in Australia)
General coverage of first names followed by information and tables on fashions and trends in names from the 17th-20th centuries. Extensive tables on the US (1875-1975), Canada (1950-1975), England (1850-1975), Scotland, and Australia. Also coverage of black names in the US. 27 refs.

[9.3] Thundy, Zacharias P. (1985). Name changes in America: A sign of the decline of religion? XV, Internationaler Kongress fuer Namenforschung, 1984, Leipzig, 3, 282-291.
Examination of recent first name bestowal in Marquette, Michigan and Sioux City, Iowa indicates that the increase of naming after TV stars is due to decline in church attendance and the decline of organized religion. 4 refs.

[9.4] Wright, F. Warren. (1954). Fashions in girls' names at Smith College. Names, 2, 166-168.
Pattern of women's first names at Smith College from pre-1900 to the 50s, Discussion.

10. FIRST NAMES

10.1. First Names: General: See also--10.3. First Names: Baby-Names

[10.1.1] Brown, Ivor. (1972). A charm of names. London: The Bodley
Head, 160 p.
Stories on the derivation, meaning, and famous personalities associated
with about 130 names.

[10.1.2] Busse, Thomas V. (1984). The professor's book of first names.
Elkins Park, PA: Green Ball Pr., 118 p.
A general work on first names. Among topics covered are: popularity of
names, trends, and gender ambiguous names. Integrates empirical research
of Busse and his coworkers. Approx 100 refs.

[10.1.3] Dunkling, Leslie Alan & Gosling, William. (1984). Facts on File
dictionary of first names. New York: Facts on File, 305 p.   (Published in
England by Dent as Everyman's dictionary of first names, 1983)
Contains 4500 main entries with additional names to a total of 10,000
giving background information on first names. 17 refs.

[10.1.4] Harder, Kelsie B. (1975). See Random House college dictionary
[10.1.6].

[10.1.5] Loughead, Flora Haines. (1958). Dictionary of given names (2nd
ed.). Glendale, CA: Arthur H. Clark, 248 p.
Entries are included for 3600 male and 4300 first names. Each entry
includes etymology, meaning, and, in some cases, distinguished bearers of
that name. Section on twin names. 154 refs.

[10.1.6] Random House college dictionary. (1975). New York: Random House,
pp. 1552-1558.
Contains brief entries on the pronunciation, derivation, and meaning of
about 500 male and 630 female first names.

[10.1.7] Stewart, George R. (1979). American given names. New York: Oxford
University Pr., 264 p.
Historical sketch of naming trends from the Colonial period followed by a
dictionary of approx 1200 male and female first names; scholarly. 18 refs.

10.2. First Names: Androgynous (Unisex)

[10.2.1] Barry, Herbert, III & Harper, Aylene. (1982). Evolution of unisex
names. Names, 30. 15-22.
Used 3 baby-naming books published before 1950 and 3 published after 1965
to test the hypothesis that names tend to evolve from masculine to unisex
and from unisex to feminine. Results support the prediction. 26 refs.

[10.2.2] Landman, Louis. (1974). Recent trends toward unisex. American
Journal of Psychoanalysis, 34, 27-31.
General discussion on unisex; sex role confusion arises for those who bear
androgynous (neutral) names such as Lynn, Leslie, or Dana. 4 refs.

[10.2.3] Rickel, Annette U., & Anderson, Lynn. (1981). Name ambiguity and androgyny. Sex Roles, 7, 1057-1066.
To test sex-role identification, men and women with gender ambiguous names or nicknames were compared on the Bem androgyny scale to those with common and those with unique names.   Both men and women with ambiguous nicknames were classified as androgynous; those with ambiguous first names were not. 20 refs.

[10.2.4] Winick, Charles. (1968). The new people: Desexualization in American life. New York: Pegasus, pp. 197-206, 370-372.
Describes naming patterns in the US with special attention to neutral names. 18 refs.

10.3. First Names: Baby-Names

[10.3.1] Ames, Winthrop, (Ed.). (1974). What shall we name the baby?. New York: Pocket Books, 207 p.
Brief entries on 2500 names.

[10.3.2] Browder, Sue. (1974). The New Age baby name book. New York: Warner, 270 p.
Has 3000+ names. Unusual in that it contains so many names from other cultures including, African, American Indian, Arab, Hindu, Hungarian, and Russian. Also includes astrological, numerological, and occult names.

[10.3.3] Cameron, Catherine. (1983). The name givers.   Englewood Cliffs, NJ: Prentice-Hall, 230 p.
Part I gives a general overview of factors associated with naming including: original meaning of a name, stereotypes, sound, fashions, and short forms. Part II explores the name-giver, the time of naming, and how it is done. Part III gives sketches of 14 name-givers. For information on name-give motives, parents in the US, England, Canada, Australia, and New Zealand were contacted. 67 refs.

[10.3.4] Four thousand and four baby names with origins and meanings (1985). Toronto: Royce, 173 p.
A popular listing of names.

[10.3.5] Kitchin, Moyna (Compiler). (1979). Choosing a name: An A to Z of first names and their meanings. London: Hamlyn, 255 p.
A 2000 item baby book. 15 refs.

[10.3.6] Lansky, Bruce & Lansky, Vicki. (1984). The best baby book in the whole wide world, (rev. ed.). Deephaven, MN: Meadowbrook Pr., 140 p. (Originally published in 1979)
Listing of 10,000 names. Some tables of popular names.

[10.3.7] McCue, Marion J. (1977). How to pick the right name for your baby. New York: Grosset & Dunlap, 167 p.
Brief entries on 7000 names. Includes a section on androgynous (unisex) names.

[10.3.8] Rule, Lareina. (1966). Name your baby. New York: Bantam, 206 p.
Lists and describes 6500 names.   Gives origins and names of famous people bearing that name. Includes a section on astrology. A very popular book.

[10.3.9] Schmidt, Jacob E. (1960). <u>Dr. Schmidt's baby name-finder</u>. Springfield, IL: Thomas, 390 p.
Has an unusual classification scheme. Gives the quality and shows the associated names. Thus, "abandoned infant" = Amelia; "abducted maiden" = Sabine; "protruding stomach" = Grosvenor. Approx 4200 names.

[10.3.10] Sleigh, Linwood & Johnson, Charles. (1971). <u>The Apollo book of boys' names</u>. New York: Crowell, 320 p. (orig. published by Harrap in London, 1962)
Approximately 1700 major entries give background information on first names including origin, variations, and important bearers of that name; an additional listing covers 1150 more names which are less common. Also, a Calendar of Saints. 25 refs.

[10.3.11] Sleigh, Linwood & Johnson, Charles. (1971). <u>The Apollo book of girls' names</u>. New York: Crowell, 256 p. (orig. published by Harrap in London, 1962)
Approximately 1400 major entries give background information on first names including origin, variations, and important bearers of that name; an additional listing covers 1300 more names which are less common. Also, a Calendar of Saints. 25 refs.

[10.3.12] Smith, Elsdon C. (1970). <u>Naming your baby</u> (2nd ed.). Philadelphia: Chilton, 94 p.
Gives 12 suggested rules for naming children followed by about 2500 first name entries giving language, derivation, and meaning.

[10.3.13] Tournier, Paul. (1975). <u>The naming of persons</u> (Edwin Hudson, Trans.). New York: Harper & Row, 118 p.
Somewhat informal thoughts on naming a child; possessiveness vs. naming a child for its own personality. Various meanings of names; implications of names from a mental health point of view.

[10.3.14] <u>Webster's dictionary of first names</u>. (1981). New York: Galahad, 255 p.
A popular alphabetical listing of male and female names with their meanings.

10.4. First Names: Foreign Equivalents

[10.4.1] Immigration and Naturalization Service. (1969). <u>Foreign versions, variations, and diminutives of English names: Foreign equivalents of United States military and civilian titles</u> (rev. ed.), M-131. Washington, DC: Government Printing Office, 53 p.
European language equivalents to about 500 common American first names. No index.

10.5. First Names: Specific

[10.5.1] Collins, Rowland L. & Collins, Sarah H. (1985). Yvonne and Juanita face the English language. Names, <u>33</u>, 207-209.
The name Yvonne has been modified in pronunciation to: ee-VAHN, ih-VONE, ee-VONE, EE-VONE, yuh-VAHN, yuh-VOHN, YAH-VONE, and WYE-VONE; Juanita to JEW-ah-NEE-tuh.

[10.5.2] Georgacas, Demetrius J. (1955). Melissa. Names, 3, 251-253.
Points out that the name Melissa has a meaning beyond that of "honey-bee"
that of "companion, courtesan, or concubine." 9 refs.

[10.5.3] Lawler, Lillian B. (1955). The name Melissa. Names, 3, 28-31.
Comment on the origin of the name (which means "bee") from Greek classical
times. Citation of ancient passages. 30 refs.

[10.5.4] Phillips, Hubert. (1951). Anne. London: P. Q. S., 62 p. + 2 p.
of photos.
Origin of the name, prominent women, novels with the name, lyrics.

[10.5.5] Phillips, Hubert. (1951). Charles.   London: P. Q. S., 76 p.   20
p. of photos.
Famous men and women from all walks of life who have borne the name of
Charles.

11. FOLKLORE AND NAMES

[11.1] Brunvand, Jan Harold. (1968). In Jan Harold Brunvand (Ed.), Special
issue on names in folklore, Names, 16, 197-206.
Review of research on names in folklore. Includes nicknames, ethnic names,
and in stories as well as others. 55 refs.

[11.2] Granger, Byrd Howell. (1961). Naming: In customs, beliefs, and folk
tales. Western Folklore, 20, 27-36.
Going back to Roman times, gives naming customs and traditions from many
cultures. Examples include the Apaches who were known as numbers by the
Army; that in England and Scotland a child with initials of the same letter
as, SSS, would die young. 26 refs.

[11.3] Hand, Wayland D.; Casetta, Anna; & Thiederman, Sondra B. (1981).
Popular beliefs and superstitions: A compendium of American Folklore 3
vols. Boston, MA: G K Hall, 1829 p.
Contains over 36,000 entries from the Ohio Collection of Newbell Niles
Puckett including a number dealing with aspects of names and naming as,
listing people's names cures hiccoughs; naming a child after a prominent
person helps to get rid of evil spirits; and that if on New Year's eve a
girl asks the first man she meets his name, that will be the name of the
man she marries. Hundreds of refs.

[11.4] Nicolaisen, Wilhelm F. H. (1984). Folklore and names.   In Murray
Heller (Ed.), Names, Northeast (pp. 14-21), Publications 3-4, Northeast
Regional Names Institute.   Saranac Lake, NY: North Country Community
College Pr.
Folk onomastics is valuable because it shows the creative side of naming.
This involves nicknames, private names, and other unofficial names. 34
refs.

12. GOD(S) AND NAMES

[12.1] Abba, Raymond. (1961). The divine name Yahweh. Journal of Biblical Literature, 80, 320-328.
Examination of the major explanations of the origin and significance of the name Yahweh. Many Bible passages cited. 500+ refs.

[12.2] Anderson, Bernhard W. (1962). Names of God. Interpreter's dictionary of the Bible, Vol. 2, pp. 407-417. New York: Abingdon Pr.
Examination of various names of God used in the Old Testament such as, Yahweh, The Shepherd, The Everlasting, and the Ancient of Days. 36 refs.

[12.3] Astour, Michael C. (1968). Semitic elements in the Kumarbi myth. Journal of Near Eastern Studies, 27, 172-177.
Develops arguments for assigning West Semites an important role in the rise of the Kumarbi myth. Approx 80 refs.

[12.4] Bailey, Lloyd R. (1968). Israelite 'El Sadday and Amorite Bel Sade. Journal of Biblical Literature, 87, 434-438.
The 2 gods are similar in that they are identified with Sin, the moon-god. Concludes "...if the biblical patriarchs were a part of the migration from the Balih-Harran region, there is good reason to believe that this epithet...was brought to Canaan...and eventually transferred to Yahweh..." 33 refs.

[12.5] Cross, Frank Moore. (1973). Canaanite myth and Hebrew epic. Cambridge, MA: Harvard University Pr., 376 p.
Systematic evaluation and comment on Yahweh and El based upon exhaustive research. Hundreds of refs and citations.

[12.6] Freedman, David Noel. (1960). The name of the God of Moses. Journal of Biblical Literature, 79, 151-156.
Evaluates a number of views on the name of the God of Moses. Believes that that the YHWH was pronounced yahwey and represents the hifil imperfect 3rd masculine singular form of the verb hyh and is translated, "He causes to be, he brings into existence; he brings to pass, he creates." 10 refs.

[12.7] Hyatt, J. Philip. (1967). Was Yahweh originally a creator deity? Journal of Biblical Literature, 86, 369-377.
After considering much scholarly work concludes that "the deity Yahweh...began as the patron deity of one of the ancestors of Moses, then became a god of his tribe, and eventually...the deity of the Israelite people." 33 refs.

[12.8] Kohl, Marvin. (1968). Ought God to be in Webster's Third? Names, 16, 134-145.
Concludes that the term God is a proper name, that the editor of Webster's Third excluded proper names. Therefore, God should not be in the dictionary. 5 refs.

[12.9] Lewis, I. M. (1959). The names of God in Northern Somali. Bulletin of the School of Oriental and African Studies, 22, 134-140.
Listing and discussion of 22 names in Somali which are, in some cases, equivalents of the 99 names of Allah in Arabic. 9 refs.

[12.10]   Oinas, Felix J. (1980). A Balto-Finnic and Baltic fertility spirit. Journal of Baltic Studies, 11, 119-214.
Develops material on a marriage divinity or being, Finnish Jumi, Estonian Jumm, Latvian Jumis, for which there is a number of customs. There is also a number of words in these languages that are traced to the name. 26 refs.

[12.11]   Smith, Elsdon C. (1954). The name of God in the Revised Standard Version. Names, 2, 101-105.
Criticizes the translators' use of Lord instead of Yahveh. 8 Bible refs; about 5 other general refs.

[12.12]   Sotiroff, George. (1986). The names of pagan divinities. In George Sotiroff, Elementa nova pro historia Macedono-Bulgarica (pp. 97-105). Regina, Saskatchewan: Lynn.
Discussion of the many cultural-ethnic forces in the Macedonian and Roman empires which lead to the suggestion that there are Slavic elements in the names of the gods: Vesta, Maia, Venus, Juno, Neptune, Jupiter, and Demeter. 8 refs.

[12.13]   Taylor, John. (1963). God: Names of. In James Hastings (Ed.) Dictionary of the Bible, (rev. ed.), Frederick C. Grant & H. H. Rowley, (Eds.), pp. 334-335. New York: Scribner's.
Brief examination of several names of God including: Elohim, El, El Shaddai, El Elyon, Adonai, and Yahweh.

Note--There are hundreds of additional items on this subject which can be found in the Religion Index.

13. GRAFFITI AND NAMES

[13.1] Grider, Sylvia Ann. (1975). Con safos; Mexican-Americans, names and graffiti. Journal of American Folklore, 88, 132-142.
Explains how Chicano youth use the symbolism of the expression con safos ("the same to you") abbreviated as CS, often along with names. About 40 refs + figures.

[13.2] Kohl, Herbert. (1969, April). Names, graffiti, and culture. Urban Review, 24-38.
Case history of a New York City 14-yr-old graffiti writer. General discussion of graffiti and naming.

[13.3] Kohl, Herbert & Hinton, James. (1972). Golden Boy as Anthony Cool: A photo essay on naming and graffiti. New York: Dial Pr., 177 p.
Description with comment of graffiti from several places including New York City and Chicago. Included is a number of nicknames such as Anthony Cool, 1/2 Pint, and Feo. 18 refs.

14. HOMOSEXUALITY AND NAMES

[14.1] Money, John. (1974). Two names, two wardrobes, two personalities.
Journal of Homosexuality, 1, 65-70.
"Applicants for sex reassignment can be placed on a spectrum of gender
role/identity transposition...." An example of this is the case of a man
who changed from Desmond to Desmarie. 2 refs.

15. HUMOR AND NAMES

[15.1] Aman, Reinhold. (1979). New improved dreck! Interlingual taboo in
personal names, and language learning. Maledicta, 3, 145-152.
Humorous article on how names take on different meanings in other
languages. 6 refs

[15.2] Aman, Reinhold. (1981). Interlingual taboos in advertising: Pshitt,
Fockink and other brand names. In Lawrence E. Seits (Ed.) The dangerous,
secret name of God, Fartley's compressed gas company; the barf'n
choke; and other matters onomastic.   Papers of the North Central Names
Institute, 2, 92-101.
Asserts that advertisers should be aware that a product with an innocuous
name in one culture or language might be a taboo in another. American
products that cause smiles abroad are Pet milk, Schlitz beer, and Coca
Cola.

[15.3] Casler, Lawrence. (1975). Put the blame on name. Psychological
Reports, 36, 467-472.
A lengthy listing, in a light vein, of individuals whose names seem to
reflect either their occupations or field of interest of their publications
as, "Forbidden Games" by Winn,

[15.4] Davis, Hank. (1974). On the names of animal behaviorists. Journal
of Biological Psychology, 16, 73-76.
A light article noting the number of individuals who study animal behavior
who have animal surnames. Examples are given of animal behaviorists named:
Swann, Finch, Heron, Crane, and Starling; of animal researchers named: Fox,
Wolf, Lyon, and Tiger. 44 refs.

[15.5] Davis, Hank. (1978). A further penetration into the deep and
enthralling mystery of names. Journal of Biological Psychology, 20,
101-104.
Continues the 1974 paper and expands into other areas: Reeder did a
monograph on school readers; papers in Science are by Wise, Yokel, and de
Wit; 2 scientists on urinary tract problems, Smellie and Leakey; etc.   39
refs.

[15.6] Grant, Mark. (1979, March 7). How doctors with funny names handle
it. Medical Tribune, p. 5.
Interviews with 2 people mentioned in Train's Remarkable names of real
people [46.20], Dr. Glen Bonecutter and Dr. Zoltan Ovary. 1 ref.

16. HYPOCORISTIC (SHORT) NAMES

[16.1] Heller, L. G., & Macris, James. (1968). A typology of shortening devices. American Speech, 1968, 43, 201-208.
Describes some of the mechanisms whereby a name may be modified or shortened, as Elizabeth to Liza (mesonym), to Beth (ouronym), to Lizabeth (mesouronym). 4 refs.

[16.2] Hughes, John P. (1972). Celtic lenition in English surnames. Names, 20, 101-105.
Theorizes that names such as Margaret, Mary, Martha, and William became Peg, Polly, Patty, and Bill due to Celtic lenition in bilingual Irish-English or Welsh-English territory. 8 refs.

[16.3] Holman, Winifred Lovering. (1963). Masculine nicknames (Introduction by Robert Leonard Reynolds). New England Historical and Genealogical Register, 117, 175-180.
Listing of about 130 "nicknames" derived from genealogical research. However, these appear to be either hypocoristic or affectionate name forms, ex., Alex from Alexander; Ozzy-Oswald, and Syd-Sydney. 5 refs.

[16.4] Holman, Winifred Lovering & Jacobus, Donald Lines. (1958). Female diminutives. American Genealogist, 34, 96-98.
Listing of over 70 names with associated diminutives from the period 1700-1800. Thus, Barbara can be found as Bab or Babbie, Antoinette as Nettie, and Christina as Kersty.

17. INFLUENCE OF NAMES (includes DESTINY, MAGIC, and SUPERSTITION): See also--34. PSYCHOLOGY AND NAMES

[17.1] Black, William George. (1883). Folk-medicine: A chapter in the history of culture. Publications of the Folk-Lore Society (London), 12, 228 p.
In medieval times, one custom was to attempt to make friends with evil spirits by ironically calling them Blessed and Good (p. 8).   Other practices involved the evoking of names to avoid various diseases (pp. 20, 58, 90, 138). There is even a listing of which saints to use for a specific disease. Thus, St. Lucy was for a toothache. About 15 refs. for these pages.

[17.2] Brown, P. W. F. (1954). Names magic. Names, 2, 21-27.
Describes a number of customs, taboos, and superstitions associated with names from Babylonian times to the recent king of Dahomey who refused to put his signature on an official paper lest it be bewitched. 27 items.

[17.3] Cavendish, Richard. (1967). The black arts. New York: Putnam, 408 p.
Chapter 2 (pp. 47-88) deals with names and numbers. Formulas are given for assigning numbers to names and birthdates to predict the future. Chapter 3 (pp. 89-107) concerns the names of power from the Cabala. About 50 refs for these chapters.

[17.4] Hand, Wayland. (Ed.). (1961;1964). The Frank C. Brown collection of North Carolina folklore: Popular beliefs and superstitions from North Carolina, Vol. 6, 664 p., Vol.7, 677 p.   Durham, NC: Duke University Press.
Index is in Volume 7.   There are about 50 entries that have to do with aspects of naming from folklore. Examples include No. 160, "If an unnamed baby falls ill, name it and it will get well" and No. 4585, "Plant a tree and name it for a person. If the one for whom it is named loves you, it will live." About 13 refs.

[17.5] Hand, Wayland D. (1984). Onomastic magic in the health, sickness, and death of man. Names. 32, 1–13.
Discussion, with a number of examples, of onomastic magic that is still (or recently has been) practiced in the US and Europe. Among these, that in Kentucky the belief that if a pregnant woman spoke the name she intended for her child, it would be born dead; in Cleveland, a Slovenian ritual for curing whooping cough was to put knots in a white ribbon and say, Jesus, Mary, and Joseph. 60+ refs.

[17.6] Knechtel, Lawrence A. (1973). Names and life roles.   Dissertation Abstracts International, 34, 396B. (University Microfilms No. 73-29, 190 p.)
Empirical research with secondary and junior college students on first names and (1) frequency, (2) stereotypes, (3) perceived success. Concludes that first names to some extent influence life roles.

[17.7] Moss, Leonard W., & Cappanari, Stephen C. (1976). Mal'occhio, ayin ha ra, oculus fascinus, Judenblick: The evil eye hovers above. In Clarence Maloney (Ed.), The evil eye. New York: Columbia University Press, 1–15.
Describes a custom among Jews (p. 7) that if a mother suspects that her child is ill from a disease due to the influence of the evil eye or some other source, the name of the child may be changed to fool the Angel of Death and to gain the strength of the lion, wolf, or bear for which it is named. 14 refs.

[17.8] Reik, Theodor. (1974). Of love and lust. New York: Jason Aronson, pp. 74-76, 594-597. (Originally published by Farrar Straus, 1949)
The 1st passage comments on the meaning of names illustrated by Romeo and Juliet. The 2nd describes African cultures such as the Kaffir and Zulu in which women may not pronounce the names of male relatives. This is also true of other cultures as the Kirghiz in Central Asia and the Waramungo in Central Australia.   Discussion of the magic influence implications of a name for Western man, rules for proper use of a name, nickname, or pet name.

[17.9] Roback, Abraham Aaron. (1954). Destiny and motivation in language. Cambridge, MA: Sci-Art, pp. 57-81.
This chapter deals with destiny and names. Drawing from Greek, Hebrew, Roman, Italian, and modern European names shows the Tacitus (a laconic writer), Justinian (known for his legal code), and Frescobaldi ("fresh and bold"). 1 ref.

[17.10] Shah, Sayed Idries. (1975). The secret lore of magic. Secaucus, NJ: Citadel Pr., 316 p.
This compilation of materials on magic and spells has a listing (pp. 299-300) of the names of 35 categories of magic power bestowed by spirits.

This listing is drawn from the Lemegeton of Solomon. Among the powers and the associated name are: fire by Halpas, alchemy by Berith, wisdom by Baal, and arts and sciences by Phoenix. 1 ref.

[17.11] Stuermann, 'Walter E. (1957). The name of Jesus: Word-magic in the Book of Acts. ETC: Review of General Semantics, 14, 262-266.
Use of the phrase "in the name of Jesus Christ" or some variant at baptism or at exorcism or healing as well as other situations suggests word-magic. Many biblical refs.

18. JUNIOR AND RELATED TYPES OF NAME
(includes child named after either parent)

[18.1] Busse, Thomas V., Busse, Kathleen, & Busse, Michael. (1979). Identical first names for parent and child. Journal of Psychology, 107, 293-294.
Reports that boys with same names as their fathers liked their names about as well as other children; girls with same names as their mothers, liked their names less. In writing their names, more boys with names like fathers wrote a different name doing the research. 2 refs.

[18.2] Edel, Leon. (1953). Henry James: 1843-1879, The untried years Philadelphia: Lippincott, citation on p. 56.
Describes the unhappiness of Henry James as being Henry James, Junior until the death of his father.

[18.3] Hunt, James G., & Jacobus, Donald Lines. (1960).   Brothers and sisters of the same name. American Genealogist, 36, 158-159.
Cites 8 examples of the same name given to 2 or more living children from 16th and 17th century England and from early American times. 7 refs.

[18.4] Jacobus, Donald Lines. (1961). Siblings of identical name. American Genealogist, 37, 62-63.
Several more examples of siblings with the same name in addition to those in Hunt & Lines above. 5 refs.

[18.5] Lenoski, Edward. (1981). The plight of the children. Toronto: Life Cycle Books, 5 p.
Reports an investigation in which children named after one of the parents showed a higher rate of being abused.

[18.6] Moriarty, G. Andres. (1961). Nomenclature. American Genealogist, 37, 72-76.
A follow-up to Hunt & Jacobus [18.3] describes cases of the same name in families in Colonial times. 7 refs.

[18.7] Plank, Robert. (1971). The use of "Jr" in relation to psychiatric treatment. Names, 19, 132-136.
Discussion and comment about the use of Junior in naming. Uses the Hamlet hypothesis (the notion that the father wants to perpetuate himself in his son) to suggest possible conflict over the name. Reports figures from a VA mental hospital that show a rate of 10% for Juniors, 3 times the rate for the general population. 7 refs.

[18.8] Taylor, Rex. (1974). John Doe, Jr.: A study of his distribution in space, time, and the social structure. Social Forces, 53, 11-21.
Telephone books of 20 cities were evaluated for use of Jr. and suffixes such as II, III, and IV. Analysis in terms of social structure. Blacks also included. 21 refs.

19. LANGUAGE AND NAMES

[19.1] Forrest, David V. (1973). On one's own onymy. Psychiatry, 36, 266-291.
Describes some of the metaphorical aspects of names as in Romeo and Juliet and unique aspects of graffiti writing (pp. 266-269) such as Rican 619 where name and number are included. 71 refs, mostly psychiatric.

20. LAW AND LEGAL ASPECTS OF NAMES: See also--7. CHANGE OF NAME

[20.1] Ashley, Leonard R. N. (1971). Changing times and changing names: Reasons, regulations, and rights. Names, 19, 167-187.
Review of British, French, and American legal precedents for name change. Many examples. Much documentation. 40+ refs.

[20.2] Bander, Edward J. (1973). Change of name and law of names. Dobbs Ferry, NY: Oceana, 116 p.
Publisher states this is a revision of How to change your name and the law of names by Lawrence G. Greene [20.6]. Provides a legal introduction to name changing. Appendix gives a summary of various state laws. 69 refs.

[20.3] Dannin, Ellen Jean. (1976). Proposal for a model name act. University of Michigan Journal of Law Reform, 10, 153-179.
Discusses the existing law on names, makes proposal for a model name act. 143 ref notes, some of which contain multiple legal citations.

[20.4] Eder, Phanor J. (1959). The right to choose a name. American Journal of Comparative Law, 8, 502-507.
Describes legal decisions involving change of name in Argentina, England, France, Switzerland, and the US. Indicates what some of the limitations are. 30+ refs.

[20.5] Goldberg, David. (1984). The right to choose one's own name in business. Names, 32, 156-169.
While the courts used to hold that if one man were in business and then a 2nd man with the same name (apparently surname) wanted to enter a similar business, it was legal. However, more recent rulings have indicated that the public has a right to be free from confusion and therefore the right of the second person may be restricted. Illustrative cases. About 100 refs.

[20.6] Greene, Lawrence G. (1954). How to change your name and the law of names. New York: Oceana, 96 p.
Rationale and procedures for change of name discussed. Topics include trade names, children's names, and married women's names. 16 biblio refs.

[20.7] Loeb, David Ventura & Brown, David W. (1985). How to change your name, (California 4th ed,). Berkeley, CA: Nolo Pr., 85 p.
Gives step-by-step procedure for the person who wishes a legal change of name without a lawyer. Copies of various legal forms are included.   18 refs.

[20.8] Lombard, Frederica K. (1984). The law and naming children: Past, present, and occasionally future. Names, 32, 129-137.
Discussion of the law with regard to names for legitimate children, illegitimate children, changing names for children, and for those being adopted.   Among a number of specific points made, it is noted that in Massachusetts a married couple is free to choose whatever surname they wish even if it is not either of theirs as long as they have no fraudulent intent.   36 refs.

[20.9] Rennick, Robert M. (1965). Judicial procedures for change-of-name in the United States. Names, 13, 145-168.
Comprehensive discussion of the differences in laws for change of name in federal and state jurisdictions; reasons for change of name; discussion of several cases including the bias of some judges. 39 refs.

[20.10] Rennick, Robert M. (1984). On the right of exclusive possession of a family name. Names, 32, 138-155.
Discussion of name changing (apparently mostly in reference to surname) under English common law, the right of property in a name, and appropriating the name of another. Several outstanding principles of law on name are described and discussed which generally seem to show that the courts are permissive about name change as long as there is no confusion on the part of the public.   Several illustrative cases including those of Samuel Goldwyn and Peter Lorre are given. 37 refs.

[20.11] Slovenko, Ralph.   (1980). On naming. American Journal of Psychotherapy, 34, 208-219.
Discussion of unusual names. Legal aspects of change of name. 39 refs.

[20.12] Slovenko, Ralph. (1981). The sexual revolution and the manner of naming. SIECUS Report, 9(4), p. 4.
Brief discussion of problems in naming especially from a legal view.   8 refs.

[20.13] Slovenko, Ralph. (1984). Overview: Names and the law. Names, 32, 107-113.
An adaptation of the author's article on law and legal aspects [20.11].

[20.14] Stannard, Una. (1973). Married women v. husbands' names. San Francisco: Germainbooks, 55 p.
Aspects of change of name for women.   Index by state of appropriate rulings.   10 refs.

[20.15] Stannard, Una. (1984). Manners make laws: Married women's names in the United States. Names, 32, 114-128.
Traces the fight for women to keep their surnames at marriage from Lucy Stone in 1856 to the present when most states now allow this right.   42 refs.

[20.16] Stevenson, Noel C. (1984). Names and the right of privacy. Names, 32, 170-176.
Discussion of the principles of law that define the right to privacy in the use of one's name; what ways this right is limited. Examples include a case where as a promotion stunt for a Hollywood film, suggestive letters were sent out to men on a mailing list. These letters were signed by an actress in the film but it turns out there was another actress in the town where the letters were sent who had the same name. The ensuing uproar caused the 2nd actress to sue for loss of privacy. She won her case. 10 refs.

21. LENGTH OF NAME

[21.1] Cabe, Patrick A. (1967). Name length as a factor in mate selection. Psychological Reports, 21, 678.
Assumed that since women are more dissatisfied with long surnames than men, that they would tend to marry men with shorter surnames. Results with 238 engaged couples were non-significant but in the expected direction. 3 refs.

[21.2] Cabe, Patrick A. (1968). Name length as a factor in mate selection: Age controlled. Psychological Reports, 22, 794.
A follow-up study of Cabe above. Again, there were no significant results but scores were still in the expected direction. 3 refs.

[21.3] Finch, M. D., & Mahoney, E. R. (1975). Name length as a factor in mate selection: An age-controlled replication. Psychological Reports, 37, 642.
In a follow-up study of Cabe [21.1],[21.2], names of engaged couples were evaluated to see if the man's name was shorter than the woman's. Couples in 4 age groups were used. No support was found for Cabe. 2 refs.

22. MEANING OF NAMES

[22.1] Algeo, John. (1973). On defining the proper name. University of Florida Humanities Monograph, No. 41. Gainesville: University of Florida Pr., 94 p.
Explores many of the complex aspects of the definition of a name. Evaluates the work of many scholars including: Russell, Gardiner, Feldman, J. S. Mill, and Pulgram. 145 refs.

[22.2] Algeo, John. (1985). Is a theory of names possible? Names, 33, 136-144.
After introductory material on the theory of names, sets up 7 aims for a theory of names. Included are: (1) meaning of names, (2) a taxonomy of names, and (3) a capacity to distinguish between synchronic and diachronic aspects. 4 refs.

[22.3] Bean, Susan S. (1980). Ethnology and the study of proper names.
Anthropological Linguistics, 22, 305-316.
Solid theoretical presentation on the philosophical basis of meaning and
function of names applied to several cultures. 27 Refs.

[22.4] Brown, Roger. (1958). Words and things. Glencoe, IL: Free Pr., pp.
110-131.
Describes meaning from the point of view of a psycholinguist. Discusses
phonetic symbolism especially the role of the sound of words in various
cultures. Onomasticians may see applications here for understanding the
meaning of names.

[22.5] Evans, Gareth. (1977). The causal theory of names. In Stephen
Schwartz (Ed.), Naming, necessity, and natural kinds (pp. 192-215).
Ithaca, NY: Cornell University Pr.
Discussion and analysis of Kripke's Description theory of names.
Presentation of Evans' Causal Theory of names. 15 refs.

[22.6] Gardiner, Sir Alan. (1954). The theory of proper names (2nd ed.).
London: Oxford University Pr., 77 p.
A philosophical discussion of the meaning of proper names. Criticism of
Russell, Stebbing, Keynes, Bertelsen, and others. Concludes that a proper
name has identification for a specific situation without regard for other
situations. 26 authors cited with references.

[22.7] Hymes, Dell. (1966). Two types of linguistic relativity (with
examples from Amerindian ethnography). In William Bright (Ed.),
Sociolinguistics (pp. 131-158). The Hague, Netherlands: Mouton.
Describes the complex naming customs of the Wishram Chinook of the Columbia
River in Washington in relation to the Whorfian hypothesis of linguistic
relativity. 4 refs.

[22.8] Kowalik-Kaleta, Zofia. (1982). The plural of proper names and in
semantic interpretation. Onoma, 26, 34-44.
Deals systematically with various meanings of plurals in proper names, ex.,
"There are five Marys in the office" is semantically different from
"Napoleons are not needed." 7 refs.

[22.9] Kripke, Saul A. (1980). Naming and necessity. Cambridge, MA:
Harvard University Pr., 172 p.
Transcripts of 3 lectures given at Princeton University on naming.
Contains Kripke's Description theory of proper names as well as comments on
many of the leading name theorists.

[22.10] Lassiter, Mary. (1983). Our names, our selves: The meaning of
names in everyday life. London: Heinemann, 163 p.
An introduction to names and naming. Includes first names, nicknames, pet
names, and surnames. Raises questions about the custom of women changing
their names at marriage. 150+ refs.

[22.11] Linsky, Leonard. (1977). Names and descriptions.   Chicago:
University of Chicago Pr., 184 p.
Philosophical approach to the theory of names; criticisms of Russell,
Frege, Kripke, Quine, and others. Chapt notes. Approx 57 refs.

[22.12]   Long, Ralph B. (1969). The grammar of English proper names.
Names, 17, 107-16.
Discussion and evaluation of how several grammarians, including Lamb,
Trager, Smith, and Chomsky, define proper names. 16 refs.

[22.13]   Pamp, Bengt. (1985). Ten theses on proper names. Names, 33,
111-118.
Calls for a theory to be developed in which: (1) the semantic similarities
and differences between names and definite non-onomastic nouns should be
further investigated, (2) integrates the transition of monoreferential
non-onomastic nouns to names, and (3) that this be begun with the grammars
and lexica of individuals. 7 refs.

[22.14]   Pulgram, Ernst. (1954). Theory of names. Berkeley, CA: American
Name Society, 49 p. (First published in Beitraege zur Namenforschung,
1953, 5(2))
Scholarly description and analysis of naming from early times.   149
footnotes.

[22.15]   Schwartz, David S. (1979). Naming and referring: The semantics
and pragmatics of singular terms. Berlin: de Gruyter, 196 p.
An exposition on referring with some attention to proper names. Schwartz's
views are related to Gottlob Frege, Bertrand Russell, Peter Strawson, Saul
Kripke, and Paul Grice as well as others. 53 refs

[22.16]   Searle, John R. (1969). Speech acts: An essay in the philosophy
of language. Cambridge, England: University Pr., pp. 162-174.
Philosophical discussion of the properties of proper names with special
reference to J. S. Mill and Frege. 9 refs.

[22.17]   Sorensen, Holger Steen. (1963). The meaning of proper names
Copenhagen: G. E. C. Gad, 117 p.
A philosophical analysis of the problems of proper names.   Concludes that
proper names are "signs, just signs."

[22.18]   Van Langendonck, Willy. (1985). Pragmatics and iconicity as
factors explaining the paradox of quantified proper names. Names, 33,
119-126.
Develops a system of distinguishing differences between proper names and
common nouns in the light of psycholinguistic evidence. 10 refs.

[22.19]   Zabeeh, Farhang. (1968). What is in a name? The Hague,
Netherlands: Martinus Nijhoff, 78 p.
Reviews theories of logicians, Mill, Frege, Russell, and others; of
linguists, Gardiner, Sorensen, and others. Offers a system of analyzing a
name based on meaning, the bearer, unique properties in the bearer, and
connotation of the name. 35 refs.

MEMORY OF NAMES: See--34.6. Psychology, Learning, Memory, and
Cognition and Names

23. MIDDLE NAMES

[23.1] Adamson, Thaire (Henry). (1978). Middle names. Rhode Island Roots, 4(1), pp. 1, 3-5.
Middle names can furnish important clues to ancestors. Sometimes they represent surnames of earlier generations. Mention of some early New England middle names. 11 refs.

[23.2]   McCracken, G. E. (1978).   Early middle   names. American Genealogist, 54, 108.
Evidence for the earliest record of a New England child having 2 first names. She was Martha Johanna Winthrop, born May 9, 1630 in England and a granddaughter of Governor Winthrop. 2 refs.

24. MISCELLANEOUS

[24.1] Ames, Jay. (1982). Names from membership list. ANS Bulletin, No. 68, 20-35.
Gives the origin and meaning of the names of over 300 American Name Society members.

[24.2] Borkowski, Casimir G. (1966). A system for automatic recognition of names of persons in newspaper texts. Yorktown Heights, NY: IBM Watson Research Center, 62 p.
Systematic description of a computer approach to recognition of personal names; advantages and problems discussed. 70 refs.

[24.3] Borkowski, Casimir G. (1967). An experimental system for automatic identification of personal names and personal titles in newspaper texts. American Documentation, 18, 131-138.
A briefer presentation than in Borkowski above.

[24.4] Borys, Robert & Pike, Jennifer. (1985). A note on name signs for deaf people. ANS Bulletin, No. 76, 32-33.
Describes how deaf people usually have a sign name which is a handshape typically representing one of the letters of the alphabet. This handshape is made at some location at, or in front of, the body. The handshape may move.

[24.5] Cameron, Catherine. (1983). What's in a name society? ANS Bulletin, No.73, 3-7.
Results of a mail survey of American Name Society members. Questions dealt with occupation, interest in names, report of meaningful experience with onomastics, and areas of investigation. 1 ref.

[24.6]   Carnog, Martha. (1981). Tom, Dick, and Hairy: Notes on genital names. Maladicta, 11, 31-40.
Reports from men and women. Use of such names implies a more intimate relationship. 27 footnotes, most with refs.

[24.7] Diament, Henri. (1981). Ethnonyms in American usage: The story of a partial breakdown in communication. Names, 29, 197-215.

Discussion of some of the ambiguities of ethnonyms (an ethnonym is a term which generally refers to a person who is a citizen of a country, as French, meaning the person is from France). In some usage (French, Spanish) the term may refer to an individual who is only of that descent but has no direct connection with the country. 6 refs.

[24.8]   Georgia. (1980). What's wrong with one name? The Name Gleaner (Canada), 6(3), 5. (originally published in the Ottawa Citizen, May 23, 1980)
Description of the experiences of Georgia who insists on using only one name and has brushes with government officials.

[24.9] Kolin, Philip C. (1981). Names in business and technical writing textbooks. Names, 29, 285-295.
Analysis of the naming examples used in texts. Examples in letters and problems show a number of humorous or punning names, such as D. C. Scrivener, copy editor; or Rob N. Hood, Commissioner of Transportation. Ethnic names such as William Chang, Carlos Montoya, and Pincus Berkowitz are also used, as well as names of women in responsible positions. 33 refs.

[24.10]   Landau, Robert M. (1967). Name or number--Which shall it be? Names, 15, 12-20.
Description of some new approaches for classification and retrieval of names in a large data bank through use of computers. One technique is the soundex system, a combination of letters and numbers.

[24.11] Macnamara, John. (1982). Names for things: A study of human learning, Cambridge, MA: MIT Pr., 287 p.
A presentation by a psychologist directed at developing a theory of name learning. One part focuses on how children develop a sense of proper names as Spot vs. dog. Experimental evidence is presented on children's development of naming ability. Organization of names and other semantic aspects of names also covered. 200+ refs.

[24.12]   Prince, Walter Franklin. (1917). Psychological tests for the authorship of the Book of Mormon. American Journal of Psychology, 28, 373-389.
Name analysis was used to attribute the Book of Mormon to Joseph Smith. 8 refs.

[24.13] Reirdon, Suzanne. (1978). "How 'bout you, Bullshipper? Ya' got'cha ears on?" In Fred Tarpley (Ed.), Ethnic names (pp. 97-103) Publication 6, South Central Names Institute. Commerce, TX: Names Institute Pr.
Description of terms employed by those using citizens' band radios on the highways. Included are the distinctive "handles" such as Shorty, Trouble-Shooter, Georgia Peach, River Rat, and Tinker Belle by which users are identified. Many examples.

[24.14] Smallman, Mary H. (1984). Acclaim to fame: The name's the same. In Murray Heller (Ed.), Names, Northeast (pp. 91-100), Publications 3-4, Northeast Regional Names Institute. Saranac Lake, NY: North Country Community College Pr..
A study of namesakes from the 19th century in the North Country of New York state shows a variety of people were commemorated. Among these were Presidents Martin Van Buren and Millard Fillmore, Governor DeWitt Clinton, ministers, physicians, and others. 3 refs.

[24.15] Stewart, George R. (1960, April 9). Murder and onomatology. The Nation, 313-316.
Description by an author (and former president of the American Name Society) of his role as an expert witness at a murder trial which involved an unusual surname, D'Avious. Also describes how a writer creates surnames for his characters.

[24.16] Tarpley, Fred. (1982). Presidential address. ANS Bulletin, No. 68, 4-16.
The 1981 presidential address for the American Name Society. Description of past, present, and future trends in personal names, placenames, and literary names. Numerous examples included one being a female student named T-9-C Ponder. 10 refs.

[24.17] van Oss, Rosine G. (1983). Names of European diplomats in July of 1914. ANS Bulletin, No. 72, 22-24.
Lists the names of 13 key diplomats assigned to European countries at the time of the outbreak of WWI. None of the names listed could be linguistically thought to come from the countries represented. Discussion with reference to names in the US Foreign Service. 3 refs.

25. NAMING PROCESS

25.1 Theoretical and Linguistic Aspects: See also--22. MEANING OF NAMES

[25.1.1] Ackerman, Diana. (1979). Proper names, propositional attitudes and non-descriptive connotations. Philosophical Studies, 35, 55-69.
Points out limitations of the view of Frege on naming. Incorporates some views of Kripke and Donnellan into a new position. 13 refs.

[25.1.2] Campbell, Richard. (1968). Proper names. Mind, 77, 326-350.
Argues against the doctrine that proper names are marks that bear a relationship to some existing, or once-existing, bearer. 10 refs.

[25.1.3] Canfield, John V. (1979). Names and causes. Philosophical Studies, 35, 71-80.
Criticism of the view of Kripke on naming as well as those of others. Concludes that a name refers to an object but not to a specific causal history in the use of that name. 9 refs.

[25.1.4] Canfield, John V. (1980). Note on names and causes. Philosophical Studies, 37, 91-92.
Note to Canfield above. 1 ref.

[25.1.5] Clark, Cecily. (1979). Clark's first three laws of applied anthroponymics. Nomina, 3, 13-19.
Develops 3 "laws" of naming for homogeneous, or originally homogeneous communities in England from Anglo-Norman times. 26 refs.

[25.1.6] Devitt, Michael. (1981). Designation. New York: Columbia University Pr., 311 p.
Oriented toward developing a causal theory of proper names. Contributions of a number of scholars (J. S. Mill, Bertrand Russell, J. R. Searle, K. S.

Donnellan, and others) are evaluated. Many examples. Approx 144 refs.

[25.1.7] Grodzinski, Eugeniusz. (1980). Proper names, common names and singular descriptions. Onoma, 24, 10-15.
Discussion of the premise that although both proper names and common names designate singular objects, the categories are essentially different.

[25.1.8] Grodzinski, Eugeniusz. (1981). Proper names, common names and singular descriptions. Proceedings of the 13th Congress of Onomastic Sciences, 1978, Cracow, 1, pp. 477-481.
Essentially the same as the article above.

[25.1.9] Kowalik-Kaleta, Zofia. (1985). Tracing surname patterns by means of structuralistic methods in various languages. XV, Internationaler Kongress fuer Namenforschung, 1984, Leipzig, 2, 223-230.
Examination and analysis of the surname structure in several European languages from the 8th to the 14th centuries indicates existence of a protosurname as an intermediate stage between the one- and two-element naming systems. The 2 patterns identified show an attachment either to a definite locality or a definite person.

[25.1.10] Markey, Thomas L. (1981).   Indo-European theophoric personal names and social structure. Journal of Indo-European Studies, 9. 227-243.
Also appears in Proceedings of the 13th Congress of Onomastic Sciences, 1978, Cracow, 2, 107-119.
Discussion of the contributions of Levi-Strauss and Georges Dumezil to the formation of Indo-European personal names. Presentation of a model for theophoric and personal names involving the presence or absence of deity and totem names. 42 refs.

[25.1.11] Markey, Thomas L. (1982). Crisis and cognition in onomastics. Names, 30, 129-142.
Considers onomastics relevant to formal linguistics, philosophy of language, and ethnography but considers the mainstream of onomasticians outside of the mainstream of linguistics and has little to contribute. Considers that settlement history placename research by onomasticians has made a contribution and then raises the question of why original placenames persisted but personal names did not. Onomastics in its current stage of development is now more open to the New Philology of Alton L. Becker than the formalisms of current linguistic theory. 21 refs.

[25.1.12] McKay, Tom. (1981). On proper names in belief ascriptions. Philosophical Studies, 39, 287-303.
Argues that proper names have many of the characteristics of demonstratives. Discussion of the position of Kripke. 13 refs.

[25.1.13] Nicolaisen, William F. H. (1976). Words as names. Onoma, 20, 142-163.
Discussion of the process of how words become names and the lexical, associative, and onomastic aspects involved. 19 refs.

[25.1.14] Nicolaisen, Wilhelm F. H. (1984). What crisis in onomastics? Names, 32, 14-25.
Gives a rebuttal to 7 arguments raised by Markey [25.1.11] about the contemporary state of onomastics and disputes the alleged crisis. 67 refs.

[25.1.15]   Pulgram, Ernst. (1960). New evidence on Indo-European names.
Language, 36, 198-202.
Argues on the basis of new research from Mycenae and other places that
Indo-European names are not typically and originally dithematic. 8 refs.

[25.1.16]   Schwartz, Stephen P. (Ed.). (1977). Naming, necessity, and
natural kinds. Ithaca, NY: Cornell University Pr., 277 p.
A collection of 10 previously published articles on naming and meaning by
Keith S. Donnellan, Saul Kripke, Hilary Putnam, William K. Goosens, W. V.
Quine, Irving M. Copi, Gareth Evans, and Alvin Plantinga. Approx 85 refs.

[25.1.17] Van Langendonck, Willy. (1981). On the theory of proper names.
Proceedings of the 13th Congress of Onomastic Sciences, 1978, Cracow, 1,
pp. 63-78.
After evaluation of the shortcomings of several theories of naming,
develops a 6 part approach with a number of examples. 64 refs.

[25.1.18] Vygotsky, Lev Semenovich. (1962). Thought and language (Eugenia
Hanfmann & Gertrude Vakar, Trans.). Cambridge, MA: MIT Pr., 168 p.
Some thoughts on the development of the naming process in children by a
famous Russian psychologist (pp. 43, 49, 61-62, 72-74, 81).   About 5
specific refs to this material.

[25.1.19]   Zareba, Alfred. (1981). Anthroponyms and their place in the
system of language. Proceedings of the 13th Congress of Onomastic
Sciences, 1978, Cracow, 1, pp. 51-61.
Comment on the development of the personal naming process in history.
Names show 2 powerful factors: the individualizing and the emotive.
Nicknames have a special influence because of their emotive factor. 19
refs.

[25.1.20] Zink, Sydney. (1963). The meaning of proper names. Mind, 72,
481-499.
Systematic presentation on proper names with some attention to personal
names. Zink's emphasis seems to be on the importance of location in time.
1 ref.

25.2 Patterns and Practices

[25.2.1] Bonnet, Clairelise & Tamine, Joelle. (1983). Names constructed by
children: Description and symbolic representation. Archives de
Psychologie, 51, 229-259. (In English)
Interviews with 150 children under 9 from the Marseilles area in France and
Neuchatel in Switzerland furnished 280 examples of names created by
children to identify relatives, friends, toys, and sex. These names have
been put into a system.   Tables show the entries, many with English
equivalents.   Examples include Poufere from petit frere (Lillbrudda in
English) and Tantanette from Tante Antoinette (an English equivalent would
be Antagret from Aunt Margaret).   13 refs. all in French. French and
German summaries.

[25.2.2] Brown, Roger. (1958). How shall a thing be called? Psychological
Review, 65, 14-21.
Brown deals with the question of how adults teach children to name objects
(or people). He concludes that adults prefer shorter to longer expressions

and those most common, i. e. dog to quadraped. There is also further
discussion of categories and hierarchies. 10 refs.

[25.2.3] Brender, Myron. (1963). Some hypotheses about the psychodynamic
significance of infant name selection. Names, 11, 1-9.
Description and analysis of the various motivational factors in the naming
process. Topics include: family tradition, religious customs, current
fashions, desire for uniqueness, and others. 17 refs.

[25.2.4] Friedman, Favius Louis. (1975). What's in a name: Meanings and
origins of first and last names. New York: Scholastic Book Services, 152
p.
Popular presentation on meaning and background of approximately 600, mostly
first, names.

[25.2.5] Gaffney, Wilbur G. (1971). Tell me your name and your business:
Or some considerations upon the purposeful naming of children.   Names, 19,
34-42.
Develops 2 principles of naming: (1) one's name determines one's character
and hence career, (2) children with unusual names become bookish early and
frequently end up as professors. Discussion and examples.

[25.2.6] Harre, Rom. (1976). Living up to one's name. In Rom Harre (Ed.),
Personality (pp. 44-60). Oxford: Basil Blackwell.
General discussion of the naming process, attention to nicknames. 6 refs.

[25.2.7] Levi-Strauss, Claude. (1966). The savage mind.   Chicago:
University of Chicago Pr. (Also published in French as La Pensee sauvage
by Plon, Paris, 1962)
Review of literature on naming practices among North and South American
Indians as well as societies in other parts of the world. Develops a
cultural theory of naming which is widely quoted. 20 refs.

[25.2.8] Levy-Bruhl, Lucien. (1982). How natives think (Lilian A. Clare,
Trans.). New York: Knopf, 392 p. (First published in English by Allen &
Unwin in 1926 in London; in French as Les fonctions mentales dans les
societes inferieures, 1910)
Describes (pp. 50-54) several primitive groups such as the Cherokees, the
Warramunga of Australia, and the Kwakiutl of British Columbia that believe
in the magic power of a name. Other mentions of naming are on pp. 346-347,
356-357. 19 refs to these pages.

[25.2.9] Lieberson, Stanley. (1984). What's in a name?...some
sociolinguistic possibilities. International Journal of the Sociology of
Language, 45, 77-87.
Parents name children according to the image or stereotype suggested by the
name and what the parents are at ease with in terms of the ethnic origins
of the name. However, there are processes of social change by which other
names rise in popularity and later fade out. The processes of change in
the distribution of names are of interest to the sociolinguist. 5 refs.

[25.2.10] Nicolaisen, Wilhelm F. H. (1985).   Socio-onomastics. XV,
Internationaler Kongress fuer Namenforschung, 1984, Leipzig, 1, 118-132.
Makes the case for sociolinguistics which deals not with the original
naming process but rather the changes that take place in usage. Examples
are given from placenames and surnames. Attention also devoted to

translated placenames such as the Gaelic Inbhir-nis, which is in English, Inverness; Branbh, Banff. 42 refs.

[25.2.11] Pearce, T. M. (1963). The lure of names. New Mexico Quarterly, 32, 160-177.
Wide-ranging description of naming practices from biblical times through Roman, Early Germanic, and modern times. Includes attention to American Indian and Spanish naming practices as well as eponyms, space missiles, and satellites. 28 refs.

[25.2.12] Rossi, Alice. (1965). Naming children in middle class families. American Sociological Review, 30, 499-513.
Interviews with middle class mothers show a trend over the past 40 years from naming sons for paternal kin and daughters for maternal kin. This suggests that an effective social symmetry is only now in the making. Extensive discussion. 18 refs.

[25.2.13] Seeman, Mary V. (1972). Psycho-cultural aspects of naming children. Canadian Psychiatric Association Journal, 17, 149-151.
Short discussion of psychological and cultural aspects of naming children. Touches on popularity, astronaut names, names beginning with letter "J", phonemes, and other factors. 7 refs.

[25.2.14] Starnes, D. T. (1962). The Geneva Bible on names for children. Names, 10, 53-57.
The 1560 and subsequent editions of the Geneva Bible in English listed about 1000 personal names considered appropriate for naming children. This list was quite influential. 6 refs.

25.3. Historical and Geographical Aspects in the United States

[25.3.1] Anderson, Robert C. (1984).   Siblings of the same name in colonial New England.   In Murray Heller (Ed.), Names, Northeast (pp. 31-40), Publications 3-4, Northeast Regional Names Institute.   Saranac Lake, NY: North Country Community College Pr.
Deals with families where siblings of the same name reached maturity.   Of the 16 situations where this occurred, 4 were born after the death of the older sibling, 12 were born to different mothers.   Extensive documentation of the families. 32+ refs.

[25.3.2] Ashley, Leonard R. N. (1984). Names in reports of common soldiers of the American Revolution. In Murray Heller (Ed.), Names, Northeast (pp. 22-30), Publications 3-4, Northeast Regional Names Institute.   Saranac Lake, NY: North Country Community College Pr.
Describes the problems Revolutionary soldiers had in trying to recall names such as in applying for a pension in the 1830s.   Nicknames serve to distinguish individuals as Old Put for Israel Putnam. 5 refs.

[25.3.3] Bailey, Rosalie Fellows. (1954). Dutch systems in family naming: New York-New Jersey.   Genealogical Publications of the National Genealogical Society, (Washington, DC), No. 12, 21 p.
The Dutch system of naming in America was different than that of the English.   The dominant system was the patronymic (Jansen, "Jan's son," Abrahamszen, "Abraham's son").   Other surname origins were placename (Opdyck, "on the dike," Hoogland, "highland"), occupation (Bleecker,

"bleacher," Cuyler, "archer"), and personal characteristics (de Groot, "big man," Vroom, "pious"). 51 refs.

[25.3.4] Barry, Herbert, III. (1979). Birth order and paternal namesake as predictors of affiliation with predecessor by Presidents of the United States, Political Psychology, 1, 61-66.
Most presidents, 31 (82%), came from a family where one son was named after the father. Of these, 7 out of 8 who were also the first-born were affiliated with their predecessor in office (i. e., of the same political party). Of those who were later born and who had a brother with the same name as the father only 1 out 9 was of the same party as the predecessor. The interpretation is that paternal identification and identification with authority are enhanced by birth order and being a namesake. 19 refs.

[25.3.5] Barry, Herbert, III. (1979). Psychological analysis for parental namesakes in colonial New England. In Murray Heller (Ed.), Names, Northeast (pp. 67-77), Publications 1, Northeast Regional Names Institute. Saranac Lake, NY: North Country Community College Pr.
Using a sample of 349 families in which the oldest child was born before 1700 found that 77% of families with a son had a father's namesake; of families with daughters, 65% had a mother's namesake. 13 refs.

[25.3.6] Barry, Herbert, III. (1984). Predictors of longevity of United States presidents. Omega, 14(4), 315-321.
Reports that presidents with the same first name as their fathers were more likely to be affiliated with their predecessors in office and to have long lives. This is interpreted as being related to identification with authority figures. 11 refs.

[25.3.7] Baumann, Klaus-Dieter. (1985). Proper names and personal group names in the historiographical special text. XV, Internationaler Kongress fuer Namenforschung, 1984, Leipzig, 3, 13-20.
Analysis of 7 different types of educational material, such as texts, scientific reviews, and historical essays, indicates that some appellatives such as "Good Queen Bess" (Queen Elizabeth) and "The Wisest Fool" (James I) indicate evaluative connotations. Group names also discussed, i. e., Marxists, Luddites. 6 refs.

[25.3.8] Droege, Geart B. (1979). Czech and German background material from Moravia on first Pennsylvania Herrnhuters and their family names. The Palatine Immigrant/Quarterly Journal of Palatines to America, 5, 15-21.
Herrnhuters take their name from Herrnhut ("the Lord's Lookout") mountain in NE Moravia. Concludes that their Slavic family names show more East Middle High German influence than Czech. Many names listed including Neisser, Demuth, and Quitt. 2 refs.

[25.3.9] Dumas, David W. (1978). The naming of children in New England 1780-1850. New England Historical and Genealogical Register, 132, 196-210.
Used a sample of records in Charlemont, Massachusetts to show trends of shift in naming practices from biblical to English names. About 16 refs.

[25.3.10] Dumas, David W. (1982). Roxana Matteson alias Sweet. American Genealogist, 58, 229-230.
Defoe wrote his Roxana in 1724. The earliest recorded use of that name in Colonial America was in West Greenwich, Rhode Island in 1727. 6 refs.

[25.3.11] Filby, P. William & Meyer, Mary K. (1981). <u>Passenger and</u>
<u>immigration lists index:A guide to published arrival records of</u>
<u>500,000 passengers who came to the United States and Canada in the</u>
<u>seventeenth, eighteenth, and nineteenth centuries,</u> 3 vols.
Detroit: Gale Research, 2339 p.
Extensive data based upon passenger lists with name, age, place, and year
of arrival where known for each person. 300+ refs.

[25.3.12]   Filby, P. William & Meyer, Mary K. (1983).   <u>Passenger and</u>
<u>immigration lists index: 1982 supplement.</u> Detroit: Gale Research, 950 p.
Covers 200,000 additional records to those of Filby and Meyer above. 360+
refs.

[25.3.13] Fischer, Daniel Hackett. (1986). Forenames and the family in New
England: An exercise in historical onomastics. In Robert M.   Taylor, Jr.,
& Ralph J. Crandall (Eds.), <u>Generations of change</u> (pp. 217-241). Macon,
GA: Mercer University. Pr.,
Examination of the naming practices of 1000 Concord, Massachusetts families
from the 17th to the 19th centuries.   Description of 3 great naming
systems: Puritan, Victorian, and the current.   Several tables, many
examples. 24 refs.

[25.3.14] Frazer, Timothy C. (1980). Regionalism and naming practices in
1860. In Lawrence E. Seits (Ed.), in <u>What's in a name</u> (pp. 38-45), Vol. 1,
Papers of the North Central Names Institute.   Sugar Grove, IL: Waubansee
Community College.
Analysis of the patterns for first names in different regions of Illinois
which were settled by: (1) Southerners, (2) Yankees from New York and New
England, and (3) people from Pennsylania and Ohio. The sample included 822
males and 862 females. The most popular boy's name for those from the
North was John; from the Midland, James; from the South, William.   For the
women, Mary was the most highly chosen name. 10 refs.

[25.3.15] Grise, George C. (1959). Patterns of child naming in Tennessee
during the Depression years. <u>Southern Folklore Quarterly</u>, <u>23</u>, 150-154.
Investigation of 700 white children born between 1935 and 1940 concludes
that 35% of the boys and 21% of the girls did not know for whom they had
been named. Of the remaining boys, 35% were named after their fathers; 15%
of the girls after their mothers. Other sources of names were relatives,
politicians, religious leaders, and movie stars.

[25.3.16] Henretta, James A. (1978). Families and farms: <u>Mentalite</u> in
pre-industrial America. <u>William and Mary Quarterly</u>, Third Series, <u>35</u>,
3-31.
Brief description of naming patterns in Hingham, Massachusetts in the 19th
century including necronyms; also, sons were given the same first names as
fathers, but different middle names. 1 relevant ref.

[25.3.17]   Jacobus, Donald Lines. (1968). <u>Genealogy as pastime and</u>
<u>profession</u> (2nd ed. rev.). Baltimore: Genealogical Publ., pp. 28-32.
Naming patterns in New England in the 17th and 18th centuries: religious,
biblical, classical, and political.

[25.3.18]   Marshall, Martha L. (1925).   A pronouncing dictionary of California names in English and Spanish. San Francisco: French Bookstore, 41 p.
Lists about 1000 names of Spanish origin.   Most are placenames but there are approximately 200 surnames included such as Duarte, Nervo, and Pacheco. Meanings of most surnames are not given.

[25.3.19]   Mockler, William E. (1973).   West Virginia surnames: The pioneers.   Parsons, WV: McClain Printing; for West Virginia Dialect Society, 197 p.
The introduction gives background material on history of the region, transitions of names, and their pronunciation. The main section is devoted to entries concerning about 500 surnames plus variants which were recorded in West Virginia during the period 1750-1800 of individuals who were from English, Irish, Scottish, or other European stock. A few of the names are Claypool, Lefevors, Lewis, and Stirling. 100+ refs.

[25.3.20]   Nall, Kline A. (1973). Love and Wrestling, Butch and O. K.   In Fred Tarpley (Ed.), Love and Wrestling, Butch and O. K. (pp. 1-6), Publication 2, South Central Names Institute.   Commerce,   TX: Names Institute Pr.
After evaluation of Puritan names and contemporary Lubbock, Texas names, concludes that names such as Butch, Hoot, Skinny, and O. K. as opposed to Bible-oriented Puritan names such as Ezekiel, Nathan, Abishag, and Patience demonstrate a faith away from divinity. Numerous examples. 8 refs.

[25.3.21]   Pyles, Thomas. (1959). Bible Belt onomastics or some curiosities of anti-pedobaptist nomenclature. Names, 7, 84-100.
In those areas of the South where infant baptism is not practiced, there is a decline of the use of formal first names such as Robert and James. Instead, there is wide use of affectionate names (Bobby, Jimmy), short names (Don, Bert), and nicknames (Buddy, Buck). Other names are also given.   Many   examples, women's names   also   included.   Widely-cited investigation. 4 refs.

[25.3.22] Rutman, Darrett B., & Rutman, Anita H. (1984). A place in time: Explicatus. New York: Norton, 207 p.
This book is concerned with Middlesex, Virginia between 1650 and 1750. Chapter 7 (pp. 83-106) is concerned with child-naming patterns.   In contrast to data reported by Daniel Smith [25.3.24], shows that 27% of the first children shared their names with the same-sex parent as compared with 60% in Hingham, Mass. Additional analyses of slave names show that only 4.4% had African names. 30 refs.

[25.3.23] Rutman, Darrett B., & Rutman, Anita H. (1986). "In nomine avi": Child-naming patterns in a Chesapeake County, 1650-1750. In Robert M. Taylor, Jr., & Ralph J. Crandall (Eds.), Generations and change (pp. 243-265). Macon, GA: Mercer University Pr.
Systematic description of the naming practices for first names in this area of Maryland. Patterns show a high percentage of name-sharing with parents, grandparents, aunts, and uncles for both boys and girls. A section on black names comments on the significance of white influence on the naming of black children. 33 refs. Several tables.

[25.3.24] Smith, Daniel Scott. (1977). Child-naming patterns and structure change: Hingham, Massachusetts, 1640-1880. Newberry Papers in Family and

Community History, No. 76-5, 37 p.
Indentification of patterns of naming. Among several patterns: children
named after a deceased child, first children named after relatives. 10
tables showing various patterns. 30 refs.

[25.3.25] Smith, Daniel Scott. (1984). Child-naming practices as cultural
and familial indicators. Local Population Studies, 15, 17-27.
Comparison of English naming practices in 1700 with those in Hingham, Mass.
and York County, Va. at roughly the same time. Attention to naming after a
relative and godparents. 3 refs.

[25.3.26] Smith, Daniel Scott. (1985). Child-naming practices, kinship
ties, and change in family attitudes in Hingham, Massachusetts, 1641-1880.
Journal of Social History, 18, 541-566.
Comprehensive systematic analysis of the naming trends of this community
near Boston based upon the records of 7520 children. Among the trends
covered are the strong influence of biblical names until the 19th century,
naming after parents, and necronymic naming for siblings. Several tables.
Comparisons with other studies in Massachusetts and Virginia. 69 refs.

[25.3.27] Smith, Elmer Lewis; Stewart, John G., & Kyger, M. Ellsworth.
(1964). The Pennsylvania Germans of the Shenandoah Valley, Vol. 26,
Pennsylvania Folklore Society, 278 p.
The book focuses on the German settlements which began in 1732 in the
Shenandoah Valley in Virginia. A number of German pioneers are mentioned by
name. There is also some linguistic analysis of family names. Estimated
50+ refs. No index.

[25.3.28] Stoudemire, Sterling. (1980). Names of girls (and boys) in
Colonial Virginia. Names, 28, 98-100.
Listing of first names of 1300 men and women by sex and frequency from a
publication of the Virginia Colonial Dames of America. The most common
girls' names are Elizabeth (214), Mary (187), Sarah (86), and Anne (76);
boys' names, John (207), William (176), Thomas (125), and Robert (57). 1
ref.

[25.3.29] Tebbenhoff, Edward H. (1985). Tacit rules and hidden family
structure: Naming practices and godparentage in Schenectady, New York,
1680-1800, Journal of Social History, 18, 567-585.
A comprehensive analysis of the naming system of this predominantly Dutch
community shows differences in comparison to the results found in Hingham,
Massachusetts by Daniel Smith [25.3.26]. Among several other differences,
it was found that between 1781 and 1800 that 8 out of 10 first sons or
daughters were named after grandparents in comparison with 2 out of 10 in
Hingham. 27 refs.

[25.3.30] Waters, John J. (1984). Naming and kinship in New England;
Guilford patterns and usage 1693-1759. New England Historical and
Genealogical Register, 138, 161-181.
Evaluation of the naming pattern in East Guilford, Connecticut which drew
"upon a pool of scriptural names with a new Israel identification and a
Christological focus." There are 108 male first names representing 394
individuals, and 73 female first names representing 354. Reasons are
discussed for the popularity of specific names such as John, Nathaniel,
Sarah, and Mary. There was a bilateral naming system such that 82% of the
fathers with a male child named a son after themselves; 72% of mothers with

female children named a daughter after themselves. Additionally, 1st sons
tended to be named after father or paternal grandfather, 2nd sons after
maternal grandfathers or fathers. First and 2nd daughters had equal
chances of being named after their grandmothers or mothers. The tables
indicate the Guilford names, their frequency, and origin (Old Testament,
New Testament, Puritan, and others). Additional comparison tables from
England, Virginia, and Hingham, Massachusetts are given. 49 refs.

[25.3.31] Zelinsky, Wilbur. (1970). Cultural variation in personal name
patterns in the Eastern United States. Annals, Association of American
Geographers, 60, 743-769.
Factor analyzed male first names in 16 counties in 1790 and 1968.   Found 3
early basic culture areas: New England, the Midland, and the South.   44
refs. 2 figs. 7 tables.

26. NICKNAMES

26.1. Nicknames: Individuals

[26.1.1] Ames, Jay. (1981). The nicknames of Jay Ames. Nomina, 5, 80-81.
Also appeared with the title of Nicknames in The Name Gleaner (Canada),
7(2), 7-8 in 1982.
Anecdotal report of the large variety of nicknames borne by the Canadian
author (apparently red-haired).

[26.1.2] Boyet, Aggie. (1973). What siblings call each other.   In Fred
Tarpley (Ed.), Love and Wrestling, Butch and O. K. (pp. 21-27), Publication
2, South Central Names Institute. Commerce, TX: Names Institute Pr.
Results of a questionnaire administered to students at 4 colleges as to
what they called their siblings. For Brother, there were 25 variations
(ex., Brother, Bubba, Buddy); for Sister, 17 variations (Sister, Sis,
Sissy). Other appellations are from animals (Beaver, Pig, Mouse, Kitty,
Fat Cat, and Hen); from insects (Bug, Termite); from birds (Crow, Crane);
foods (Punkin, Candy), and others.

[26.1.3] Brown, P. W. F. (1956). Some semantics on onomancy. Names, 4,
39-45.
Discusses the development of nicknames with examples of nick-surnames from
Wales. Further discussion of common nicknames such as Topper Brown and
Nobby Clark and their derivation. 12 refs.

[26.1.4] Busse, Thomas V. (1983). Nickname usage in an American high
school. Names, 31, 300-306.
At a high school in the NE, 114 boys and 149 girls responded to a nickname
questionnaire. Of the boys, 58% reported having a nickname; of the girls,
40%. The largest category for the boys was the one that had variations or
short forms of the last name (19%), as Mort for Moriarty. The next
category was those nicknames based upon physical characteristics, 8%, as
Torch or Shorty. The remaining boys had names of varied origins.   For
girls, physical characteristics ranked 1st; last name variations, 5%.   Of
the boys, 13% did not know why they received their nicknames; of the girls,
6%. A number of examples are given. 6 refs. German abstract.

[26.1.5]   Costa, Frank   Joseph & Radcliff-Umstead, Douglas.   (1975).
Nicknaming among the Calabrese. Onoma, 17, 492-503.
Nicknames acquired in a town in Calabria, Italy survive as social
identification in Pittsburgh. Among the 26 examples are: Pinnatu
("hairless"), Ziggaru ("cigar"), and Cagnolinu ("puppy"). 3 refs.

[26.1.6]   Dexter. Emily S. (1949). Three items related to personality:
popularity, nicknames, and homesickness. Journal of Social Psychology, 30,
155-158.
Students at 3 colleges were evaluated on a questionnaire on the
relationship between their popularity and their: (1) nicknames, (2)
abbreviation names (probably short names such as Pat for Patricia), and (3)
first names. Popularity was rated by the social dean's office. Results
indicate that those with nicknames were rated significantly more popular.

[26.1.7]   Franklyn, Julian. (1962). A dictionary of nicknames. London:
Hamish Hamilton, 132 p.
Lists over 2000 nicknames mostly from England but including others from
Scotland, Ireland, Australia, Canada, and the United States. Among
American entries are Kicky ("hard to please, petulant girl"), Joe Doakes
("average American"), and Rackensack ("a native of Arkansas"). 14 refs.

[26.1.8]   Habbe, Stephen. (1937). Nicknames of adolescent boys. American
Journal of Orthopsychiatry, 7, 371-377.
Nicknames were investigated with New York City schoolboys between 12 and
16. Concludes that nicknames most frequently "are simply--name adaptations
without significance as caricatures or condensations of outstanding
characteristics...." Special attention to hearing handicapped in the
sample. 3 refs, tables.

[26.1.9]   Harre, Rom. (1980, Jan.). What's in a nickname. Psychology
Today, 13(8), 78-79, 81, 84.
Summary of a 4 year study of children's nicknames in Britain and other
countries. Names such as Four Eyes, Grasshopper, and Concorde establish
status and norms of behavior. 3 refs.

[26.1.10] Hendley, W. Clark.(1979). What's your handle, Good Buddy? Names
of citizen band users. American Speech, 54, 307-310.
The use of handles allows the CBer to select his/her own nickname. Most
male CBers select names with a macho spirit (Magic Man, Tom Cat). Female
CBers have names such as Lucky Lady or Motor Mouth.

[26.1.11] Jackson, Bruce. (1967). Prison nicknames. Western Folklore, 26,
48-54.
Based upon a visit to a prison near Houston, Texas, lists and describes 16
guard nicknames such as Two Bone and Capt. Easy; and 15 white inmate names
such as Cat Man and Blanket Ass. There is also a listing over 80 black
nicknames such as Bear, Fat Cat, and Foot. 6 refs.

[26.1.12] James, Allison. (1979, June 14). The game of the name: Nicknames
in the child's world. New Society, 48, 632-634.
A semi-popular description and discussion of nicknames of British
schoolchildren. Includes a large number of nicknames, description of their
origins, and impact on others.

[26.1.13] Lomax, Ruby Terrill. (1943). Negro nicknames. In J. Frank Dobie (Ed.), Backwoods to border (pp. 163-171), Publications of the Texas Folklore Society, No. 18. Dallas: Southern Methodist University Pr.
Collection with some discussion and explanation of about 200 nicknames mostly from black convicts. Some categories and examples are: color (Red, Blue, Midnight), physical appearance (Peewee, Lighthouse, Macaroni), deformity (Wing, Crab-Finger), and crime (Porch-Climber, Confidence).

[26.1.14] Manning, Frank C. (1974). Nicknames and number plates in the British West Indies. Journal of American Folklore, 87, 123-132.
Nicknames such as Froggie, Cracker, and Kingfisher are common among West Indian men and to a lesser extent, women. License plate numbers such as J2415 (standing for Book of Joshua, Chapter, 24, Verse 15) are also used widely as identifiers as in dance announcements and death notices. Both types of names are functional where only a few surnames are shared by the majority of the population. 16 refs.

[26.1.15] Maurer, David W. & Futrell, Allan W. (1982). Criminal monickers. American Speech, 57, 243-255.
Discussion of origin and development of monickers (names used in criminal subcultures). Listing of over 80 monickers such as Gold-Tooth Kelly and Whitey Reno. 7 refs.

[26.1.16] Morgan, Jane; Oneill, Christopher, & Harre, Rom. (1979). Nicknames: Their origins and social consequences. London: Routledge & Kegan Paul, 151 p.
The nicknaming of a child is important in understanding social development and entry into the adult world. The authors discuss the definition of nicknames (ekenames) and petnames, nicknaming in school, lack of a nickname, as a norm, as a form of social control, and as an insult. Accounts are also given of nicknaming in other cultures as, Japan, the Arab world, Spain, and Ceylon. 48 refs.

[26.1.17] Moses, Rafael & Freedman, Daniel X. (1958). 'Trademark' function of symptoms in a mental hospital. Journal of Nervous and Mental Disease, 127, 448-457.
Nicknames may also serve the magical function of inducing certain desired qualities. Nicknames based on behavioral traits (Sunny, Chief) seem often to act as prescriptions for a role the child is to follow. 5 refs.

[26.1.18] Opie, Iona & Opie, Peter. (1961). Lore and language of schoolchildren. Oxford: Oxford University Press (3rd impression), 417 p.
Some verses of British schoolchildren associated with nicknames as "What's your name? Baldy Bain; What's your ither? Ask ma mither" (pp. 156-160); epithets, "bag o' bones" (pp. 167-172); onomancy, divination of the future on the basis of a name in children's games (pp. 336-337). 4 specific refs + sources of the verses.

[26.1.19] Orgel, Samuel Z., & Tuckman, Jacob. (1935). Nicknames of institutional children. American Journal of Orthopsychiatry, 5, 276-285.
Study of nicknames of 235 boys and 75 girls in an institutional setting. Nicknames serve 5 functions: approval, punishment, depreciation, revenge, and therapy. Children classified in the normal group use affectionate nicknames and less objectionable names more than those in the problem group. Except for the affectionate nicknames, the nickname is a source of much unhappiness. 1 ref.

[26.1.20] Payton, Geoffrey. (1970). Webster's dictionary of proper names. Springfield, MA: G. & C. Merriam, 752 p.
Covers Aircraft (Jumbo jet, MiG) to Nicknames (Vinegar Joe, Sultan of Swat) to University (Ivy League, Seven Sisters); items which might not be found in the usual dictionary. Hundreds of citations. Approx. 12,000 entries.

[26.1.21] Peterson, Robert. (1970). Only the ball was white. New York: Prentice-Hall, 406 p.
About black baseball players between 1884 and 1950. Appendix C (pp. 310-399) gives an all-time register of black players and officials along with nicknames. Included are: Georgia Rabbit Ball, Cool Papa Bell, Plunk Drake, and Bullet Rogan. No specific refs.

[26.1.22] Reichler, Joseph L. (Ed.). (1982). The baseball encyclopedia (5th ed., rev. & expanded). New York: Macmillan, 2248 p.
Has information on all players and managers in the major leagues. Entries include full name, name under which the man played, and nicknames. Thus, Henry Benjamin Greenberg played under the name of Hank Greenberg and his nickname was Hammerin' Hank. Approx 3000 entries.

[26.1.23] Schmidt, Herbert, Mrs. (1961). Nicknames among the Mennonites from Russia. Mennonite Life, 16(July), 132.
Provides background information on over 50 Low German Mennonite names. Included are: Eadschocke Schmett ("potato Smith"), Schinke ("ham") Hiebat, and Peta hingarem Bosch ("Peter behind a big beard which he refused to trim")

[26.1.24] Shankle, George E. (1955). American nicknames: Their origin and significance, (2nd. ed.). New York: Wilson, 524 p.
Contains nicknames of all types including individuals. Among these are: P. T. Barnum (Prince of Humbug), W. T. Sherman (Old Tecumseh), and Horace Greeley (Old White Hat). Most items appear to be historical. Each entry has its sources.

[26.1.25] Sifakis, Carl. (1984). The dictionary of historic nicknames: A treasury of more than 7,500 famous and infamous nicknames from world history. New York: Facts on File, 566 p.
Contains short descriptive entries such as Will Rogers (the Cowboy Philosopher), Jack London (the American Kipling), Francis Marion (the Swamp Fox), and Otto von Bismarck (the Iron Chancellor).

[26.1.26] Skipper, James K., Jr. (1981). An analysis of baseball nicknames. Baseball Research Journal, 10, 112-119.
Analyzes the nicknames (often colorful) of 2851 major league players over a 100 year period in terms of popularity and category. The pattern shows a peaking in the 1910-1919 period and a decline thereafter. The most common names are Lefty (153), Red (120), and Doc (61). 1 ref.

[26.1.27] Skipper, James K., Jr. (1982). Feminine nicknames: 'Oh You Kid,' from Tilly to Minnie to Sis. Baseball Research Journal, 11, 92-96.
Identification of 53 major league players who had feminine nicknames including Grandma (Johnny Murphy), Little Eva (William Lange), and Minnie (Saturnino Minoso). 1 ref.

[26.1.28] Skipper, James K., Jr. (1984). Baseball's 'Babes" —Ruth and others. Baseball Research Journal, 13, 24-26.
Reports several anecdotes about how George Herman Ruth got his nickname. Also gives names of 24 other players who were named Babe. 8 refs.

[26.1.29] Skipper, James K., Jr. (1984). The sociological significance of nicknames: The case of baseball players. Journal of Sport Behavior, 7, 28-38.
Evidence presented for the decline in nicknaming of baseball players. This is explained as due to the public's change in perception of players from folk heroes to entrepreneurs, or part of a general cultural shift from a gemeinschaft society to a gesellschaft type. 28 refs. French abstract.

[26.1.30] Skipper, James K., Jr. (1985). Nicknames of notorious American Twentieth Century deviants: The decline of the folk hero syndrome. Deviant Behavior, 6, 99-114.
Evaluates the decline of public nicknames by deviants (gangsters, racketeers, bootleggers, murderers et al.) over the past 7 decades. While the decline is noted for men, this is not found for women. Influence of Prohibition and the Depression are evaluated. 25 refs.

[26.1.31] Skipper, James K., Jr. (1985). Nicknames, folk heroes, and assimilation: Black League baseball players, 1884-1950. Journal of Sport Behavior, 8, 100-114.
Discussion and analysis of the pattern of nicknames for black players which shows a similarity to that of white players. Among the 30 most popular white player nicknames, 20 had counterparts among black players. Among these are: Lefty, Red, Bud-Buddy, Doc, Mickey, Chick, and Tex. Many examples. 34 refs.

[26.1.32] Smith, H. Allen. (1966, Oct). The nature of nicknames. Holiday, 40, pp. 24, 26, 28, 29, 31-32.
Stories of how some prominent people got their nicknames such as Whizzer White, Preacher Roe, and Spike Fowler. 1 ref.

[26.1.33] Spears, James E. (1972). Folk children's pejorative nicknames and epithets. Kentucky Folklore Record, 18, 70-74.
Listing of 83 nicknames used by children. Some are used in one-to-one encounters, some to describe an unpopular person held in contempt by the entire group. Examples include: Battle Axe (defensively aggressive), Chisel Chin (sharp chin), and Spider (long-legged).

[26.1.34] Sullivan, Edward J. (1985). The pseudonyms of artists. XV, Internationaler Kongress fuer Namenforschung, 1984, Leipzig, 3, 239-245.
Discussion of a number of names artists were known by beginning with the Middle Ages. Included are: Master of the Middle Rhein, Duccio, Giotto, Donatello, Tintoretto, Coravaggio, up to Jackson Pollock. 1 ref.

[26.1.35] Urdang, Laurence. (Ed.)., Kidney, Walter C., & Kohn, George C. (Compilers). (1979). Twentieth century American nicknames, New York: Wilson, 398 p.
Contains about 13,000 entries including individuals, cities, and athletic teams. Users can search by either nickname or regular name. Entries for Ronald Reagan list: Mr. Clean, The Most Happy Fellow, and The Not-So-Favorite Son; for Armand Hammer: The Russian Connection; for Hubert Humphrey: HHH, Happy Warrior, The Hump, and Pinky.

[26.1.36] Van Buren, H. (1974). The American way with names. In Richard
Brislin (Ed.), Topics in Culture Learning, Vol. 2, pp. 67-86. Honolulu:
East-West Culture Learning Institute. Also ERIC Documentation Service No.
ED 006 497.
Patterns of development and usage of nicknames and affectionate nicknames.
Many examples. 5 refs in notes.

[26.1.37]   Williams, Mary E. (1959). Welsh nicknames, Malad, Idaho.
Western Folklore, 18, 165-166.
Lists 14 nicknames for this Welsh community. Examples include: Tom Goose
("his father had a large flock of geese"), Sparrow Bill ("he shot sparrows
with a slingshot"), and Creamery Bill ("president of the creamery").

[26.1.38]   Winslow, David J. (1959). Children's derogatory epithets.
Journal of American Folklore, 82, 255-263.
Classification and discussion of about 40 children's nicknames such as
Mooseface, Bubble Head, and Lester Fester which are used in a derogatory
way. 13 refs.

26.2 Nicknames: Group

Note: For additional items on nicknames, See-- [6.1] Allen, Irving Lewis.
(1983). The language of ethnic conflict: Social organization and lexical
culture.

[26.2.1] Adler, Jacob. (1975). The etymology of Canuck.   American Speech,
1975, 50, 158-159.
Speculates that the name Canuck is derived from a Polynesian word meaning
native, referring to the dark complexion of French-Canadians.

[26.2.2] Algeo, John. (1977). Xenophobic ethnica. Maledicta, 1, 133-140.
Comment and discussion of a number of ethnic terms which have extended
meanings. Examples include corinthians, bohemians, and amazons. Many
others. 2 refs.

[26.2.3] Allen, Harold B. (1958). Pejorative terms for Midwest farmers.
American Speech, 33, 260-265.
Listing of the negative terms (hayseed, farmer, country jake) used to
describe rural dwellers. Data were collected in 5 upper Midwest states.

[26.2.4] Allen, Irving Lewis. (1983). Personal names that became ethnic
epithets. Names, 31, 307-317.
A systematic description and evaluation of how personal names became ethnic
epithets as a function of conflict in the cultural differences between
groups in America. Begins with ethnic epithets as Mike and Murphy for
Irishmen, to Ivan for Russian men. Then, goes on to the social origins of
the name vocabulary, loanwords from other cultures, cultural allusions, and
stereotyping (calling black men George, James, Leroy). 17 refs. Dutch
abstract.

[26.2.5]   Aman, Reinhold. (1983). Bavarian terms of abuse derived from
common names. Maledicta, 7, 212-217.
Origin of about 40 common Bavarian names used in a deprecatory manner, ex.,
Efal: a young, simpleminded woman < Eva; Hansdampf: a simpleminded man; a
foolish, silly jerk < Hans Jack + Dampf "steam." 1 ref.

[26.2.6] Appel, John J. (1963). 'Betzemer': A Nineteenth-Century cognomen
for the Irish, 38, 307-308.
The term Betzemer, was used by Jews in the 1890s to refer to the Irish in
an apparently neutral manner. The etymology is explained in that the sound
of the word Irish in English is similar to the German Eier (eggs in
German). The Hebrew word for eggs is Betz (pl. Betzim). Most Jews of that
time were Yiddish speaking. Thus, the derivation. 1 ref.

[26.2.7] Ashley, Leonard R. N. (1967). Pomp and its circumstances. Names,
15, 85-110.
Explains titles and epithets to describe rulers (mostly English) from 800
on. Examples include: Henry VIII (Defender of the Faith), Elizabeth I
(Virgin Queen), and William IV (Silly Billy). 8 refs.

[26.2.8] Ashley, Leonard R. N. (1980). "Lovely, blooming, fresh, and gay":
The onomastics of camp. Maledicta, 4, 223-248.
Listing and discussion of a number of sexual slang names in the US and
Britain, ex., Abigail: a conservative auntie; Adam: one's first trick. 12
refs.

[26.2.9] Ashley, Leonard R. N. (1982). Every Tom, Dick and Harry. Word
Ways, 15(May 2), 94-95.
20-item quiz (with answers) on meaning of slang names such as Holy Joe
(chaplain in the armed forces).

[26.2.10] Berrey, Lester V. & Van den Bark, Melvin. (1953). The American
thesaurus of slang: A complete reference book, (2nd. (ed.). New York:
Crowell, pp. 342-399.
These pages contain hundreds of slang/epithet terms for people including:
Joe, Tom, Brother Jonathan, Vanishing American, Sweeney, and alfalfa
grower.

[26.2.11] Boggs, R. S. (1972). From what areas of vocabulary does the folk
choose group names? In Issachar Ben-Ami (Ed.), Folklore Research Center
Studies-Jerusalem, Vol. 3, pp. 107-118.
Examination of 54 ethnic names from Spanish America shows 10 categories
including: color (Albino, "white"), animal (Lobo, "wolf"), and geography
(Cimmaron, "highest point of a hill"). Most names are from Spanish but
other languages included are: Mexican, Quechua, Cuna, Carib, Taino, and
Dutch. 16 refs.

[26.2.12] Bradley, Frances. (1964). Sandlappers and clayeaters. North
Carolina Folklore, 12(December), 27-28.
Notes on the origin of the terms sandlapper and clayeater applied to people
from North Carolina. 9 refs.

[26.2.13] Cassidy, Frederic G. & DeCamp, David. (1966). Names for an
albino among Jamaican Negroes. Names, 14, 129-133.
Discussion of a number of terms such as Come-between, Whitey-Whitey,
White-Eboe, and White-labor that are used to describe albino blacks. 7
refs.

[26.2.14] Gordon, David Paul. (1983). Hospital slang for patients: Crocks,
gomers, gorks, and others. Language in Society, 12, 173-185.
Systematic explanation of categories of hospital slang; how it is used and
what need(s) it fulfills. A crock demands more attention than is warranted;

a gomer is a socially stigmatized patient; a gork is a comotose patient.
Many examples are given. These include: Beached Whale, Dying Swan, and
Lazarus. 3 refs.

[26.2.15] Halaby, Raouf & Long, Carolyn. (1975). Future shout: Name
calling in the future. In Fred Tarpley (Ed.), Naughty names (pp. 51-59),
Publication 4, South Central Names Institute. Commerce, TX: Names Institute
Pr.
Results of a questionnaire on name-calling. Included are terms such as
nixonitis, Wallace-white, dolphin-lips, (someone who talks a lot) and Molly
Polly (a girl who takes drugs known as black mollies).

[26.2.16] Kantrowitz, Nathan. (1969). The vocabulary of race relations in
a prison. Publication of the American Dialect Society, 51, 23-34.
Classification of 100+ names used by whites and blacks in an inmate
culture. Includes names used by both groups such as stoolpigeon, names
used by blacks only such as free thinker, and those used by whites only
such as nigger lover. 18 refs.

[26.2.17] Kleinke, Chris L. (1974). Knowledge and favorability of
descriptive sex names for males and females. Perceptual and Motor Skills,
39, 419-422.
Grade school and junior college respondents listed and rated descriptive
sex names such as Kid, Guy, Chick, and Broad under the categories of Male
and Female. The hypothesis was confirmed that there would be more listings
under Female and also less favorable ratings. 8 refs.

[26.2.18] Malone, Kemp. (1954). Epithet and eponym. Names, 2, 109-112.
Discussion and analysis of several old European names such as King Scyld of
the Danes, Brundingas, and Helmingas as having patronymic rather than
epithet roots.

[26.2.19] McDavid, Raven I., Jr. & McDavid, Virginia. (1973). Cracker and
Hoosier. Names, 21, 161-167.
The term cracker is found in several Atlantic states and has overtones of
the comic and loutish; hoosier, in the North and Middle West, is a more
neutral term. 6 refs.

[26.2.20] McDavid, Raven I., Jr. & Witham, Sarah Ann. (1974). Poor whites
and rustics. Names, 22, 93-103.
Results of a survey of 19 Eastern states and 2 Canadian provinces indicate
that the most common terms for poor whites and rustics are backwoodsman,
countryman, and hayseed. Appendix shows 200 terms as used by whites and
blacks. 11 refs.

[26.2.21] Moe, Albert F. (1965). Leatherneck: A borrowed nickname. Names,
13, 225-257.
American soldiers and American marines wore black leather stocks during
most of the eighteenth century (presumably to assure that the chin was held
high giving a more military appearance). However, the term leatherneck
seems to have been more associated with the marines, especially since WWI.
The term in British usage has a separate derivation. Approx 100 refs.

[26.2.22] Opie, Peter. (1970). Children's derogatory epithets. Journal of
American Folklore, 83, 354-355.
Comment on Winslow [26.1.39].

[26.2.23] Palmore, Erdman B. (1962). Ethnophaulisms and ethnocentrism. American Journal of Sociology, 67, 442-445.
An ethnophaulism is a derogatory nickname applied to one ethnic group by another. Palmore gives a set of 5 generalizations about the use of such names, ex., "All racial and ethnic groups use ethnophaulisms to refer to other groups." 7 refs.

[26.2.24] Taylor, Jo Beth. (1973). Names behind bars. In Fred Tarpley (Ed.), Love and Wrestling, Butch and O. K. (pp. 28-34), Publication 2, South Central Names Institute. Commerce, TX: Names Institute Pr.
An investigation of group nickname terms used in three Texas prisons. Confirms many terms found in Eric Partridge's Dictionary of the underworld and identifies some terms with newer meanings such as old lady (prison wife), and queen (female impersonator). Identifies some new terms such as pill head (hypochondriac) and rapo (rapist). Many examples. 1 ref.

[26.2.25] Wentworth, Harold & Flexner, Stuart Berg. (1957). Dictionary of American slang (suppl. ed.). New York: Crowell, 718 p.
Included are 2 categories of onomastic interest, (1) individual words/names such as a Jasper (a theological student), an Annie Oakley (a meal ticket), a Holy Joe (chaplain), and a Huey (helicopter); (2) group/ethnic, a Boche (German) a flange-head (Chinese), and Litvak (Lithuanian). The appendix has an extensive list of group (ethnic) names. Over 1000 refs.

27. NUMBERS AS NAMES

[27.1] Campbell, John. (1980). Hello! My name is 1069. The Futurist, 14(5), 45-47.
In a light vein describes the possibilities open for a society in which individuals are free to select a number as a name.

[27.2] Lockney, Thomas M. & Ames, Karl. (1981). Is 1069 a name? Names, 29, 1-35.
Discussion of the case of Michael Herbert Dengler who wanted to be known as 1069 and tried to change his name legally. His petitions were carried through 5 courts and denied. Arguments pro and con for such a type of name change discussed and evaluated. 76 refs.

[27.3] Read, Allen Walker. (1977). The numerical naming of people. In M. Paradis (Ed.), The Fourth Lacus Forum, 1977, Linguistics Association of Canada and the United States (pp. 615-624). Columbia, SC: Hornbeam Pr.
Background of assignment of numbers to individuals as names in the American West as Three Stickney and R-14 and also in Europe. Discussion of current controversies involving Social Security and other numbers assigned to individuals. Over 35 refs many from newspapers.

28. OBSCENITY AND NAMES

[28.1]   Rennick,   Robert   M. (1968).   Obscene   names   and naming   in   folk
tradition. Names, 16, 207-229.
Definition and classification of obscene names. Listing with derivations a
number   of   names   perceived as   offensive such   as   Backhouse   < bakehouse,
Fokker < cattle breeder, Raper < roper. Anecdotal reports on names such as
Wannamaker, Glasscock, and Sexauer. 24 refs.

29. POPULAR NAMES
(includes Common Names, Frequency of Names, Desirability of Names, and
Liking for Names)

[29.1]   Boltinghouse,   Llyle.   (1962).   Tabulation   of   common   names and
surnames.   Baltimore, MD: Llyle   Boltinghouse,   Room 315,   Administration
Building, Social Security Administration, 12 p.
Lists the frequencies of the 10 most common surnames and the 10 most common
first   names (male,   female, and   both) associated   with each   of these   10
surnames   as   found   in Social   Security   records.   These 10   most   common
surnames account for 6,634,000 records out of a total of 117,358,000. 40+
tables.

[29.2]   Busse,   Thomas V.,   & Helfrich,   James. (1975). Changes in   first name
popularity across grades. Journal of Psychology, 89, 281-283.
Schoolchildren in   grades 2-11 (N   = 2212) rated   179 male   and   246 female
first   names.   Correlations   between   the   sexes was   high at   all   levels.
However, adolescent girls showed variation from adolescent boys and younger
children of both sexes. 5 refs.

[29.3] Busse,   Thomas V. &   Seraydarian, Louisa.   (1977).   Desirability of
first names, ethnicity and parental education. Psychological   Reports, 40,
739-742.
The study first showed the relationship between parental education and name
desirability in elementary and high   school students.   The 2nd part of   the
study evaluated name desirability in 8 ethnic groups.   Afro-American names
for both boys and girls   were liked significantly less than those   of other
groups.

[29.4]   Busse, Thomas V.,   & Seraydarian, Louisa. (1978). The   relationship
between first name   desirability and school readiness,   IQ, and   school
achievement. Psychology in the Schools, 15, 297-302.
Girls showed significant relationships with 5 criterion measures, boys with
3.   When partial correlations were done controlling for   parental education
and ethnicity, 4 of the 5 correlations for the girls   remained significant,
none for the boys did. 14 refs.

[29.5] Busse,   Thomas V. &   Seraydarian, Louisa. (1979).   First   names and
popularity in   grade school children.   Psychology   in   the Schools,   16,
149-153.
Girls' popularity   as measured by   sociometric choice   was   correlated with
desirability of first   names.   Boys' popularity with   girls was   related to
attractiveness of their first names. 19 refs.

[29.6] Cento, Sydney Swanson. (1983). Current infants' names in Geneva, Illinois--1981. Bulletin of the Illinois Name Society, 1(1), 4-10.
Tallies from newspapers indicate that in 1981 there were 316 boys born who had 105 different names. The most common were Matthew, 6.3%; Michael, 5.3%, and Jason, 3.5.%. There were 307 girls with 125 different names. The most common were: Sarah, 5.8%; Jennifer and Amanda, both 4.2%. Several tables also show middle names and comparisons with other samples including Illinois in 1860. 5 refs.

[29.7] Colman, Andrew M., Hargreaves, David J., & Sluckin, Wladyslaw. (1981). Preferences for Christian names as a function of their experienced familiarity. British Journal of Social Psychology, 20, 3-5.
Four samples of 20 men and women rated male and female first names for familiarity and liking. A similar investigation was done in Australia. Linear correlations in England between familiarity and liking were: English men, .82; English women, .67; for Australian men, .66; for Australian women, .57. Results interpreted in terms of monotonic (Zajonc-type) and non-monotonic (inverted U-type) functions. 13 refs.

[29.8] Crisp, Debra R., Apostal, Robert A., & Luessenheide, H. Duane. (1984). The relationship of frequency and social desirability of first names with academic and sex-role variables. Journal of Social Psychology, 123, 143-144.
Used several measures on 1094 students who entered the University of North Dakota in 1974 to conclude that while social desirability of names and frequency were related, other factors such as academic success, sex-role orientations, or sex-appropriate goals were not. 5 refs.

[29.9] Davis, Patricia Anne. (1973). Current infants' names in Charlottesville, Virginia. ANS Bulletin, No. 38, 1-4.
Birth announcements and names of high school graduates were used to indicate naming patterns. Women's names showed the greatest shift. Cathy and Mary, among the most popular names in 1955, did not appear at all in the 1973 sample. Several tables including names of twins.

[29.10] de Silva, Guido Gomez. (1972). The linguistics of personal names. Onoma, 17, 92-136.
Used telephone directories in 154 cities world-wide to compile lists of the 5 most frequent male first names, female first names, and surnames. Some variations in procedure were made due to local conditions. Etymology given for most of the names. 2 refs.

[29.11] Evans, Cleveland Kent. (1975). Current infants' names in Ann Arbor, Michigan. ANS Bulletin, No. 42, 12-17.
A survey of first names from birth notices in Ann Arbor from September 1973-August 1974. There were 1733 boys and 1589 girls reported. The top names for boys were: Michael, Matthew, Jason, Christopher, and John; for girls, Jennifer, Amy, Sarah, Kimberly, and Michelle. Results were compared to a similar survey by Davis [29.9] in Charlottesville, Virginia. 1 ref. Tables.

[29.12] Evans, Cleveland Kent. (1984). Births in Washtenaw County, Michigan, U. S. A., 1983. Bulletin of the Illinois Name Society, 2(3), 9-17.
Gives tables of frequencies for birth names of 2794 boys and 2777 girls (Ann Arbor is located in Washtenaw County). Leading boys' names were:

Michael,   Christopher, David,   and Matthew;   girls'   names   were: Jennifer,
Sarah, Elizabeth, and Jessica.

[29.13] Hargreaves, David J., Colman, Andrew M., & Sluckin, Wladyslaw.
(1983). The attractiveness of names. Human Relations, 36, 393-401.
Summarizes previous work by the authors on the relationship between
familiarity and liking for first names and surnames. Proposes the
preference-feedback hypothesis for names.   First names are voluntarily
chosen so that when they are overexposed, they drop in popularity.
Surnames, not as much voluntarily chosen, do demonstrate the inverted U
phenomenon (most and least familiar are least attractive). 15 refs.

[29.14] Harrison, Albert A.   (1969). Exposure and popularity. Journal of
Personality, 37, 359-377.
Four studies were carried out with students at the University of
California, Davis.   In the 1st, 200 public figures were rated for affect
and familiarity.   In the 2nd, religious political, ethnic, and occupational
groups were rated on affective and curiosity scales.   In the 3rd,
familiarity and likability of 50 male and 50 female names randomly drawn
from a telephone directory were rated.   The final study replicated Study 1
in a following year. Among the results reported are: a strong relationship
occurs between familiarity and exposure and liking; subjective estimates of
the familiarity of a person or name and an objective index of exposure tend
to be highly correlated; subjective estimates of familiarity tend to
predict the liking ratings. 9 refs.

[29.15] Koulos, Betty Kay. (1984). Current infant (1983) names in Northern
Illinois. Bulletin of the Illinois Name Society, 2(4), 5-12.
The birth announcements of over 40 communities in Northern Illinois which
appeared in the Daily Surburban Trib were tabulated for 732 boys and 662
girls.   Several tables indicate frequencies for first names and middle
names. For boys, the most widely chosen names were Mat(t)hew and Michael;
for girls, Sara(h) and Jennifer. 4 refs.

[29.16]   Stephens, J. C. (1978).   What did Hiawatha call his son? An
analysis of given names of 1,271 junior high school students in Richardson,
Texas. In Fred Tarpley (Ed.), Ethnic names (pp. 105-114), Publication 6,
South Central Names Institute. Commerce, TX: Names Institute Pr.
Presentation and discussion of 6 tables for both sexes on most frequent
names (John, William, Robert, Lisa, Susan), variant spellings (Geffery,
Marq, Audri, Lynda), short names (Al, Bert, Pam, Beth), nicknames
(affectionate names) (Jack, Danny, Cindi, Vicky). Stephens accounts for
the large number of variants in girls' names (but not for boys) as due to
"the drugged stupor of post-parturition." 2 refs.

[29.17] Tompkins, Richard C. & Boor, Myron. (1980). Effects of students'
physical attractiveness and name popularity on student teachers'
perceptions of social and academic attributes. Journal of Psychology, 106,
37-42.
Followed the work of Harari and McDavid [41.25].   Results show a
nonsignificant relationship between name and peer popularity; those with
unpopular first names were rated as higher status. Other predicted name
effects were nonsignificant. 6 refs.

[29.18] West, Stephen G., & Shults, Thomas. (1976). Liking for common and uncommon names. Personality and Social Psychology Bulletin, 2, 299-302.
Men and women in university rated common (popular) and uncommon names. Common names were liked > uncommon; male commons > female commons; female uncommons > male uncommons. 7 refs.

30. POPULATION STRUCTURE AND NAMES

Note: An additional source of further references on this subject may be found in: [30.8] Lasker, Gabriel W. (1985).

[30.1] Chakraborty, Ranajit; Weiss, Kenneth M., Rossmann, David L., & Norton, Susan L. (1980). Distribution of last names: A stochastic model for likelihood determination in record linking. In Bennett Dyke & Warren T. Merrill (Eds.), Genealogical demography (63-69). New York: Academic Pr. Abstract in American Journal of Physical Anthropology, 1979, 50, 426-427.
Develops a statistical model for the distribution of surnames from records in Laredo, Texas and Guam from 1829-1977. 10 refs.

[30.2] Kaplan, Bernice; Lasker, Gabriel W., & Chiarelli, Brunetto. (1978). Communality of surnames: A measure of biological interrelationships among thirty-one settlements in Upper Val Varaita in the Italian Alps. American Journal of Physical Anthropology, 49, 251-256.
A study of surname relationships in house clusters in 3 nearby communities in the Alps. The coefficient of relationship is highest between clusters close or contiguous and is highest in those communities least affected by tourism and migration. 9 refs. & map.

[30.3] Kaplan, Bernice A., & Lasker, Gabriel. (1981). English place names as surnames: Do such surnames tend to cluster near the place named? American Journal of Physical Anthropology, 54, 238-239.
Results in a large British sample confirm that surnames derived from places are more common near their place of origin than elsewhere.

[30.4] Kitano, Harry H.; Yeung, Wai-Tsang; Chai, Lynn; & Hatanaka, Herbert. (1984). Asian-American interracial marriage. Journal of Marriage and the Family, 46, 179-190.
Surnames were used to measure the frequency of in- and outmarriages for Chinese, Japanese, and Koreans in Los Angeles and Hawaii. In Los Angeles, Japanese rates of outmarriage were highest, followed by Chinese. These positions were reversed in Hawaii. 36 refs.

[30.5] Lange, Kenneth. (1981). Minimum extinction probability for surnames and favorable mutations. Mathematical Biosciences, 54, 71-78.
Uses mathematical proofs to develop extinction probabilities for surnames. Minimum probability is attained when the variance in the number of offspring is smallest. 17 refs.

[30.6] Lasker, Gabriel W. (1978). Relationships between English villages. American Journal of Physical Anthropology, 48, 413-414.
Brief summary of a study done on 17 villages near Oxford using the coefficient of relationship by isonymy (people with the same surname).

[30.7] Lasker, Gabriel W. (1978). Relationships among the Otmoor villages and surrounding communities as inferred from surnames contained in the current register of electors. Annals of Human Biology, 5, 105-111.
Reports on population interrelationships that can be determined through isonomy. 12 refs.

[30.8] Lasker, Gabriel W. (1980). Surnames in the study of human biology. American Anthropologist, 82, 525-538.
Surnames can be useful in studies of human genetics. 42 refs.

[30.9] Lasker, Gabriel W. (1985). Surnames and genetic structure. Cambridge, England: Cambridge University Pr., 1985. 148 p.
Begins with a comprehensive review of the use of surnames in studying inbreeding from the time of Darwin and describes a number of investigations all over the world using isonymy to measure inbreeding. Of major interest is the appendix which contains maps and diagrams of 100 surnames from England and Wales showing the dispersions of 1975 isonymous marriages. This information throws light on the migration pattern of those name bearers. These 100 names comprise 20% of the total population. About 160 refs.

[30.10] Lasker, Gabriel W., & Kaplan, Bernice. (1983). English placename surnames tend to cluster near the place named. Names, 31, 167-177.
Using 272 surnames selected from the list of individuals getting married in England, during a selected period in 1975, leads to the conclusion that despite internal migration in England and Wales, surnames are more common near places of the same name than would be expected by chance. Tables. 12 refs.

[30.11] McClure, Peter. (1979). Patterns of migration in the Late Middle Ages: The evidence of English placename surnames. Economic History Review, Second Series, 32, 167-182.
Suggests that placename surnames give an indication of the patterns of migration for social betterment. 7 refs.

[30.12] Raspe, Pamela D., & Lasker, Gabriel W. (1980). The structure of the human population of the Isles of Scilly: Inferences from surnames and birthplaces listed in census and marriage records. Annals of Human Biology, 7, 401-410.
Surnames were used to study the structure of the population of the Islands of Scilly (off the SW coast of England). Isonomy (people with the same surname) statistics were computed for the period 1726-1975. Coefficients of relationship by marital isonymy show a decrease and a slight tendency to avoid marriage between close relatives. No relationship was found between random isonymy and marital migration. 19 refs. German & French abstracts.

[30.13] Weiss, Kenneth M., Rossmann, David L., Chakraborty, Ranajit & Norton, Susan L. (1980). Wherefore art thou, Romio? Name frequency patterns and their use in automated genealogy assembly. In Bennett Dyke & Warren T. Merrill (Eds.), Genealogical demography (41-61). New York: Academic Pr.
Utilization of computer techniques to plot patterns of Spanish first names in Laredo, Texas, 1897-1977. These are contrasted with those in Guam and England. 10 refs.

31. PROVERBS AND POPULAR SAYINGS AND NAMES

[31.1] Straubinger, O. Paul. (1953). Der wahre Jakob. Names, 1, 112-114.
Traces the old German proverb "This is the real Jacob." 12 refs.

[31.2] Straubinger, O. Paul. (1955). Names in popular sayings.   Names 3,
157-164.
Background of about 25 common sayings many of which refer to biblical
characters as "We are all Adam's children," "As chaste as Susanna," as well
as others such as "Let George do it" and "All work and no play makes Jack a
dull boy."

[31.3] Taylor, Archer. (1958). "Tom, Dick, and Harry." Names, 6, 51-54.
Background material and derivation of the expression; comment.   About 30
refs.

32. PRONUNCIATION OF NAMES

[32.1] Dunlap, Arthur R. (1974). The replacement of /schwa/ and /i/ in the
English pronunciation of names. Names, 22, 85-92.
Evaluation of the various types of vowel change in names. Although mostly
dealing with placenames, several examples of first names and surnames are
included, ex., for Maurice, MOR-iss and mor-EESE. 15 refs.

[32.2] Ehrlich, Eugene & Hand, Raymond, Jr. (1984). NBC handbook of
pronunciation (4th ed.). New York: Harper & Row, 539 p.
Contains over 21,000 entries using a simple system for pronunciation.
Thus, Mikhail Suslov is pronounced as mi kah EEL SOOS lahf. A number of
personal names are included.

[32.3] Metcalf, Allan. (1985). A reason for Reagan. Names, 33, 259-267.
Gives background of President Reagan's preference for pronunciation of his
name as RAY-gan rather than REE-gan. Comments on the preferred form as
connoting greater size.   Mention of some political opponents using the
non-preferred pronunciation. 32 refs.

[32.4] Metcalf, George J. (1985).   Translation pronunciation: A note on
adaptation of foreign names in the United States, Names, 33, 268-270.
Description of several instances in which names were spelled in one way
(usually German) but pronounced in another, more American(?) way. Examples
include Schmidt as Smith, Freitag as Friday, and Albrecht as Albright.   2
refs.

[32.5] Miller, G. M. (1971). BBC pronouncing dictionary of British names:
With an appendix of Channel Islands names. London: Oxford University Pr.,
170 p.
Introduction; alphabetical listing of over 17,000 names with pronunciation.
18 refs.

[32.6] Neuffer, Claude & Neuffer, Irene. (1983). Correct
mispronunciations of some South Carolina names. Columbia: University of
South Carolina Pr., 182 p.

Listing of about 450 names with pronunciation and background information. Over half appear to be surnames as well as placenames. Names included with correct pronunciation are: Fenwick (FEN-ik), Moise (moe-EEZ), and Neuffer (NIFE-uh). Huguenot names are well-represented.

[32.7] Pointon, G. E. (Ed.). (1983). BBC pronouncing dictionary of British names, (2nd ed.). Oxford: Oxford University Pr., 274 p.
Introduction, pronunciation key, and listing of approx 23,000 names, many of which are personal names. Special attention to Welsh names. 23 refs.

33. PSEUDONYMS
(includes Pen-Names and Fictitious Names)

[33.1] Ashley, Leonard R. N. (1966). Classical pseudonyms in Europe at the time of the Reformation. Names, 14, 193-196.
Many leaders of the Reformation chose classical pseudonyms. These include theologians (Johannes Agricola, Osiander) and scientists (Copernicus, Fallopius), and others.

[33.2] Atkinson, Frank. (1975;1977;1982). Dictionary of pseudonyms and pen-names: A selection of popular modern writers in English. London: Clive Bingley; also Hamden, CT: Shoe String Pr., 1975, 166 p; 2nd ed., 1977, 248 p., published under the title of Dictionary of literary pseudonyms: A selection of popular modern writers in English; 3rd ed., 1982, 305 p., same title as 2nd ed.
Lists 2500 real names along with pseudonyms, then a listing of pseudonyms and real names. Seems to be mostly British. has 1500 additional names and synonyms, mostly North American.

[33.3] Bauer, Andrew (Compiler). (1971). The Hawthorne dictionary of pseudonyms. New York: Hawthorne, 312 p.
10,000 entries. Each person listed under real name and pseudonym (or other variation). All fields, world-wide.

[33.4] Clarke, Joseph F. (1977). Pseudonyms: The names behind the names. Nashville: Nelson, 252 p.
Includes 3400 pseudonyms and pen-names. Half are stage names. 30 item bib, 25 names quotes.

[33.5] Felton, Gary S. (1972). Who is the real John Doe? Names, 20, 297-300.
The use of fictional names such as, John Doe, Jane Doe, Richard Roe et al., goes back to early Roman and British law. In contemporary law, fictitious names are used for anonymity and as a straw man; in psychiatry, as a temporary identity; in literature, as anonymity for authors; in advertising, to represent the common man. 23 refs.

[33.6] Kassman, Deborah N. (1977). What's in a pen name. In A. S. Burack (Ed.), The writer's handbook (pp. 593-601). Boston: The Writer.
Develops reasons for and against the use of pseudonyms. Number of mentions of pseudonyms and real names.

[33.7] Loomis, C. Grant. (1955). About American pseudonymity. Names, 3, 236-238.
Classifies types of pseudonyms used by American writers during the period 1850-1980, such as word play (P. Q. Lyre) and learned reference (Fides).

[33.8]   Mossman, Jennifer (Ed.). (1980). Pseudonyms and nicknames, (2nd ed.). Detroit: Gale, 627 p.
According to the author, the work contains 17,000 original names and 22,000 assumed names. Authors account for 40%; entertainers, 55%. Entries give original name, birth date, and where appropriate, death date, nationality, and occupation. 15 refs.

[33.9] Sharp, Harold S. (Compiler). (1972;1975;1982).   Handbook of pseudonyms and personal nicknames, 1104 p. (2 vols.); First Supplement, 1975, 1395 p. (2 vols.); Second Supplement, 1982, 289 p. Metuchen, NJ: Scarecrow Pr.
In the first 4 volumes, there are about 30,000 main entry names and about 50,000 pseudonyms. Entries can be located by real name, nickname, or pseudonym. The 2nd supplement contains 7000 main entries and 10,000 nicknames and/or pseudonyms.

34. PSYCHOLOGY AND NAMES

34.1. General Psychology

[34.1.1] Albott, William L. & Bruning, James L. (1970). Given names: A neglected social variable. Psychological Record, 20, 527-533.
Survey of the social science literature on names. Focuses on how first names are chosen, effect of name on personality. Calls for further research. 27 refs.

[34.1.2]   Carroll, John M. (1985).   What's in a name? An essay in the psychology of reference. New York: Freeman, 204 p.
A presentation of laboratory and field research in naming strategies from a psychological point of view incorporated into a theoretical position. Emphasizes the role of context and isomorphism in naming. Approx 130 refs.

[34.1.3]   Dion, Kenneth L. (1983). The psychology of names. In E. B. Wolman (Ed.). International Encyclopedia of Psychiatry, Psychology, Psychoanalysis & Neurology (pp. 361-363). New York: Aesculapius.
A survey of recent research on names in the field of psychology. Topics included are stereotyping, correlates of name, achievement, sociometric popularity, personality, identity, and cognitive processes. 8 refs.

[34.1.4]   Holt, Robert R. (1939).   Studies in the psychology of names. Unpublished bachelor's thesis, Princeton University, 307 p.
Comprehensive and critical review of the literature on names in the fields of history, religion, anthropology, psychology, and psychoanalysis. Empirical investigation of stereotypes with undergraduates rating potential members of an eating club. An investigation of ethnic name stereotypes using jury judgments. Discussion of name-changing which includes interviews with name-changers. 129 refs and notes.

[34.1.5]   Seeman, Mary V. (1983). The unconscious meaning of personal names. Names, 31, 237-244.
Systematic discussion of the psychological purposes (conscious and unconscious) that names serve. Among these purposes are: commemorative (after a dead ancestor), connotative (where the name gives information about genealogy and social standing), induction (wished-for qualities), nicknames, and pseudonyms. Also discussed are name changes and rites of passage. Examples given of each type of name. 19 refs. French abstract.

34.2. Abnormal Psychology
(includes Clinical Psychology, Psychiatry, Psychoanalysis, and Psychosis)

[34.2.1]   Bagley, Christopher & Evan-Wong, Louise. (1970). Psychiatric disorder and adult and peer group rejection of the child's name.   Journal of Child Psychology and Psychiatry, 11, 19-27.
First names and surnames of 83 children in a London, England clinic and the names of normal controls were rated in a randomized pattern by adults, and in sociometric situations by 7-yr-olds and 11 yr-olds.   Results indicate that the adults clearly chose more of the names of the clinical group as odd, as did the children. Further work with 11-yr-olds indicated the surname rather the first name that was the basis of rejection. Analysis of the clinical children supports the conclusion that the name is an important factor in psychiatric disorder. 9 refs

[34.2.2] Burnham, Donald L., Gladstone, Arthur I., & Gibson, Robert W. (1974). Schizophrenia and the need-fear dilemma. New York: International Universities Pr., pp. 190-217.
Describes the clinical history of William Gabriel Alberto Richter who had serious difficulties over his names. He was called Bill by his father with whom he was ambivalent at best; Alberto, Al, and Gabriel by his mother. This latter association developed a linkage which contributed to his urge to save the world.

[34.2.3] Drake, David. (1957). On pet names. American Imago, 14, 41-43.
The pet name involves less of the total self than does the first name but allows more libidinal intensity. Examples from 3 clinical cases: Couple 1, a highly phallic couple both refer to each other as "Thing," Couple 2 has a highly oral relationship and refer to each other as "Honeybear." Couple 3 is unmarried. The man refers to the woman as "Squirrel." The woman calls the man "Acrane."

[34.2.4]   Fast, Irene.   (1974). Multiple identities in borderline personality organization. British Journal of Medical Psychology, 47, 291-300.
Describes patients with multiple identities (and names) and describes similar work of other investigators. 21 refs.

[34.2.5]   Feldman, Harold. (1959). The problem of personal names as a universal element in culture. American Imago, 16, 237-250.
Review and discussion of naming practices in various cultures. Suggests that names are an expression of the antagonism people feel toward the objects they name. 41 refs. and notes

[34.2.6] Fenischel, Otto. (1945). Psychoanalytic theory of neurosis. New York: Norton, pp. 14, 46, 295.
References to names by a famous psychoanalyst. One (p. 14) deals with the aspect of consciousness-unconsciousness where a person knows that he knows a name but cannot immediately recall it. The other references deal with the magic quality of names, that one has control or mastery over what one can name. The example is given of Rumpelstilzchen. 2 refs on these pages.

[34.2.7] Fisher, Charles. (1945). Amnesic states in war neuroses. Psychoanalytic Quarterly, 14, 437-468.
Description of several cases of amnesic servicemen in fugue states who could not remember their identities. Discussion of underlying motivations. 16 refs.

[34.2.8] Flugel, John Carl. (1939). Psychoanalytic study of the family. London: Hogarth, pp. 106-107.
Describes individuals who unconsciously select as love objects those with a specific name, Schiller with women who were Charlottes; Shelley with Harriets.

[34.2.9] Fodor, Nandor. (1956). Nomen est omen. Samiksa, 10, 9-45.
Solid discussion of the effects of names on personality from a psychoanalytic point of view. The name is an important aspect of the self. Amnesiacs forget their names. Many examples of interesting aspects of names. 41 refs.

[34.2.10] Forrest, David V. (1983). Language as object--and subject. Journal of the American Academy of Psychoanalysis, 11, 513-529.
Brief discussion of proper names through psychoanalytic interpretation similar to Forrest [19.1]. 38 refs.

[34.2.11] Freud, Sigmund. (1954). The origins of psychoanalysis: Letters to Wilhelm Fliess, drafts and notes: 1887-1902, (Marie Bonaparte, Anna Freud, Ernst Kris, Eds., Eric Mosbacher, James Strachey, Trans.). New York: Basic, pp. 261-262, 264-265, 302-303.
Freud describes some of his own experiences in forgetting. Shows how he took simple everyday situations and incorporated them into his theories. These excerpts deal with forgetting, repression, and displacement of names. 4 footnotes.

[34.2.12] Freud, Sigmund. (1955). Totem and taboo and other works, Vol. 13 (1913-1914), The standard edition of the complete psychological works of Sigmund Freud, (James Strachey, Ed. and Trans.). London: Hogarth, pp. 54-59, 81-82, 112-113.
Analysis of the taboos in various cultures about pronouncing a name; the fear than an enemy's knowledge of one's name can bring harm. Much of the material is from Frazer. 12 ref. notes.

[34.2.13] Freud, Sigmund. (1960). The psychopathology of everyday life, Vol. 6 (1901), The standard edition of the complete psychological works of Sigmund Freud, (James Strachey, Ed. and Trans.). London: Hogarth, pp. 1-8, 15-42, 84.
Discussion of repression and forgetting of names; slips of the tongue involving names, displacement of names. 8 ref. notes.

[34.2.14] Freud, Sigmund. (1962). Early psychological associations, Vol. 3 (1883-1899), The standard edition of the complete psychological works of Sigmund Freud, (James Strachey, Ed. and Trans.). London: Hogarth, pp. 289-297.
Discussion of repression and memory. 5 ref notes.

[34.2.15] Freud, Sigmund. (1964). Moses and monotheism, Vol. 23 (1937-1939), The standard edition of the complete psychological works of Sigmund Freud, (James Strachey, Ed. and Trans.). London: Hogarth, pp. 7-9.
Derivation of name of Moses from non-Hebrew sources. 1 ref. note.

[34.2.16] Jones, Ernest. (1938). Papers on psychoanalysis, (4th ed. Baltimore: William Wood, pp. 29-30, 64-73. (Originally published in 1913)
Comments and expounds on Freud's work on the memory of names. Gives examples. 4 ref. notes.

[34.2.17] Jones, Ernest. (1955). The life and work of Sigmund Freud, p. 349.
A short passage on the sequence of vowels in dreams. Although the name in a dream may change, the order of the vowels remains the same. 1 ref.

[34.2.18] Kros, Erih. (1966). Names, (Lovett F. Edwards, Trans.). New York: Harcourt, Brace & World, 152 p. (Original work published in Yugoslavia in 1966 under the title Imena)
A novella about names set in Yugoslavia concerning a man who lost his memory for the names of people. He was treated by a therapist and regained his memory for the names of people but then lost memory for his own name.

[34.2.19] Laffal, Julius. (1965). Psychological and normal language New York: Atherton, pp. 101-109.
Describes a paranoid patient whose fantasies included being possessed by others by means of his and his mother's names. 2 refs.

[34.2.20] Murphy, William F. (1957). A note on the significance of names. Psychoanalytic Quarterly, 26, 91-106.
Discussion of names from a psychoanalytic view. Murphy draws from a number of case histories involving fantasy, rejection, and inferiority regarding names. His mention of patient surnames such as Small, Little, Short, and Paine and their symptoms is widely quoted as showing the influence of name on personality. 12 refs.

[34.2.21] Plank, Robert. (1977). Selective attacks on people whose names begin with B. Names, 25, 1-4.
The Austrian writer Karl Kraus, editor of Die Fackel, selectively attacked people whose surnames began with B. This is an example of how one's surname can affect another person. 18 refs.

[34.2.22] Schacter, Daniel L., Wang, Paul L., Tulving, Endel; & Freedman, Morris. (1982). Functional retrograde amnesia: A quantitative case study. Neuropsychologia, 20, 523-532.
Description of a patient whose amnesia involving loss of memory of his name can be understood as being in an affective (emotional) as opposed to a temporal dimension. 17 refs. French & German abstracts.

[34.2.23] Seeman, Mary V. (1976). The psychopathology of everyday names.
British Journal of Medical Psychology, 49, 89-95.
Systematic coverage from a psychoanalytic view of   name-giving, its
denotative, connotative, magical, and commemorative aspects.   Further
coverage is on the same aspects of name-changing. Discussion follows. 45
refs.

[34.2.24] Seeman, Mary V. (1979). Names and dream work.   Canadian Journal
of Psychiatry, 24, 243-246.
Analysis of 4 dreams. Discussion of dynamic processes involving names and
dreams, nicknames, surname-associated nicknames, metonymic nicknames. 3
refs.

[34.2.25] Stekel, Wilhelm. (1949). Compulsion and doubt, Vol. 1, (Emil A.
Gutheil, Trans.). New York: Liveright, pp. 319-323.
Description of 4 patients whose names bore some relationship to their
symptoms, ex., a man named Haft (German for "custody") who was afraid of
being held responsible for other people's crimes. 3 refs.

[34.2.26] Stoller, R. J. (1966). The mother and infant transvestic
behaviour. International Journal of Psychoanalysis, 47, 384-395.
Describes a trans-sexual boy patient who was named after his mother's
younger brother who was a transvestite. 32 refs.

[34.2.27] Tarachow, Sidney. (1963). Psychotherapy. New York: Universities
Pr., p. 102.
Description and analysis of a male psychotic who called all men by the same
first name; all women with another same first name.

34.3 Developmental Psychology

[34.3.1] Davis, E. A. (1937). Development in the use of proper names.
Child Development, 8, 270-272.
When asked to name, the younger child is more likely to name friends,
teachers, and family members; the older child, historical and fictional
characters.

34.4. Hostility and Names

[34.4.1] Berkowitz, Leonard & Knurek, Dennis A. (1969).   Label-mediated
hostility generation. Journal of Personality and Social Psychology, 13,
200-206.
Men were first given association training to have a negative attitude
toward either of the names, Ed or George. Then, they were angered by the
trainer. A further situation tested how they would react to a discussion
partner with the critical name. Results show displacement of hostility in
the direction of the critical name. 18 refs.

34.5. Identity, Self-Concept, and Names

[34.5.1]   Adelson,   Daniel.   (1957).   Attitudes   toward   first   names: An
investigation   of   the   relation   between   self-acceptance,   self-identity and
group and individual attitudes toward first names.   Dissertation Abstracts,
8, 1831. (University Microfilms No.   57-2945, 135 p.)
College   and   high   school   students   (181   in   all) completed   the   Berger
Self-Acceptance Scale, a questionnaire on attitudes toward one's   own name,
and ratings on first names.   Results from both groups show that: (1) people
like their own   first names, (2) a   name liked by the   group   increases its
attractiveness, (3) those who dislike their own first name tend to   be less
self-accepting,   (4)   unique   names   that   are   liked   have   higher
self-acceptance. 135 pp. 28 refs.

[34.5.2]   Allport,   Gordon   W.   (1937).   Personality: A   psychological
interpretation. New York: Holt, pp. 163-164.
Short passage   that   the name   is the most   important anchor   point   for the
concept of self.

[34.5.3] Allport, Gordon W. (1961).   Pattern and growth   in personality.
New York: Holt, Rinehart and Winston, p. 117.
Short passage   that the name   is the most   important anchor   point   for the
concept of self.

[34.5.4]   Allport, Gordon W.,   &   Schanck, R.   L. (1936).   Are   attitudes
biological or cultural in origin? Character and Personality, 4, 195-205.
In an attitude study of Harvard and Radcliffe undergraduates, it   was found
that   either   due   to   civilized   codes   or   to   "the   traditional   'magic'
associated with one's name and reputation, situations involving   honor take
precedence over situations in which property is an issue."   This means that
people will fight more for their name than for property.   5 refs.

[34.5.5]   Boshier, Roger. (1968). Self-esteem and first names   in children.
Psychological Reports, 22, 762.
The Coopersmith Self Esteem Inventory along with the question "Do   you like
your first   name?"   was administered   to intermediate   schoolchildren   in New
Zealand.   Results   with boys indicate   a correlation of   .81 between the   2
measures; for girls, .77.   The correlations indicate a relationship between
liking one's name and attitude toward self.   6 refs.

[34.5.6]   Boshier,   Roger. (1968). Attitudes   toward self and   one's proper
name. Journal of Individual Psychology, 24, 63-66.
A sample of 40 women   and 10 men indicated attitudes toward   first, middle,
and last   names.   A week   later, they completed   a modified   version   of the
Bills Index of Adjustment   and Values.   Results indicate a   tendency toward
higher score on adjustment though not significantly so.   However,   there is
a significant   relationship with the   combined samples between   middle name
and self-esteem.   10 refs.

[34.5.7]   Bugental,   James   F.   T.,   &   Zelen,   Seymour   L.   (1950).
Investigations into the 'self-concept' I.   The W-A-Y technique.   Journal of
Personality, 18, 483-498.
The   question "Who   are   you?"   was asked   of 63   men   and 71 women.   The
investigators   conclude   that   the   response   with   the   individual's   name
demonstrates that   the name is   a central aspect   of   self-perception.   The
name occurred on 63% of all responses in the core group category.   9 refs.

[34.5.8] Calvello, Angelo A. (1983). Lived body and personal name: A philosophic description of the constitutive structures of a person's sense of identity. Dissertation Abstracts International, 43, 3935-A (University Microfilms Order No. DA8310645)
This philosophical approach asserts that a person's sense of identity is founded on the experiences of his/her body and name.

[34.5.9] Gordon, Chad. (1968). Self-conceptions: Configurations of content. In Chad Gordon and Kenneth J. Gergen, The self in social interaction, vol. 1: Classic and contemporary perspectives, pp. 115-136.
Reports the results of the Who Am I? test to samples of high school students and college students from Los Angeles City College and from Harvard-Radcliffe. In the high school sample, 17% gave name as one of 20 answers ranking 3rd after age, 82%, and sex, 74% (p. 124). In the college sample, 30% mentioned name as part of identity but several other variables had higher frequencies (pp. 133-134). 60+ refs.

[34.5.10] Dion, Kenneth L. (1983). Names identity, and self. Names, 31, 245-257.
Presents evidence from several areas of research in psychology (personal identity, self-acceptance, and attention and memory) that demonstrate the psychological connections between names, identity, and self. 29 refs. French abstract.

[34.5.11] Guardo, Carol J., & Bohan, Janis Beebe. (1971). Development of a sense of self-identity in children. Child Development, 42, 1909-1921.
In a suburb of Rochester, New York, 116 Caucasian children, ages 6-9 were interviewed in a study of self-identity. Among the results was the finding that when asked about the future, children replied that the name gave a sense of continuity, of sameness. 18 refs.

[34.5.12] Jourard, Sidney M. (1974). Healthy personality: An approach from the viewpoint of humanistic psychology. New York: Macmillan, pp. 150-151.
Describes how various aspects of name and title give the individual a sense of identity. 1 ref.

[34.5.13] Lewis, Michael & Brooks-Gunn, Jeanne. (1979). Social cognition and the acquisition of self. New York: Plenum, pp. 141-160.
Reports a series of investigations of the development of self-identity in verbal infants 15-22 months old. Half of the 15-month-olds correctly labeled pictures of themselves with their own names. This percentage increased with age. 5 refs for this section.

[34.5.14] Leyens, Jacques-Philippe & Picus, Steve. (1973). Identification with the winner of a fight and name mediation: Their differential effects upon subsequent aggressive behavior. British Journal of Social and Clinical Psychology, 12, 374-377.
In an attempt to determine whether name identification would transfer to a subsequent situation, subjects were first angered by the experimenter, then watched an aggressive film clip. Then, they were given an opportunity to give an electric shock to another participant. The name aspect of the experiment was not confirmed. 7 refs.

[34.5.15]   Lynd, Helen Merrell. (1958).   On shame and the search for
identity. New York: Harcourt, Brace, pp. 65, 174.
Mentions that a name gives security and protection along with structure (of
society), norms, and rituals. Refers to Through the looking glass where no
creature has a name and hence is a place of terror.   Also refers to an
essay by Anselm Strauss on identity. Points out that naming tells how one
feels about a person, object, or institution. 2 refs.

[34.5.16] McGee, Thomas F. (1984).   Names and lawyering: A psychodynamic
approach. Names, 32, 177-189.
An exploration of the psychodynamic aspects of names linked to some kind of
identification with the individual, surnames (Beers, Short, and Kreep),
reverse identification where the individual's personality is the opposite
of the first name (Joy, Felix) or surname (Freud), similar first, middle,
and last names (Judge Judge, Sirhan Sirhan), and names which make a
statement (Carrie A. Nation, Thurgood Marshall). Other dynamic aspects of
names also considered. Many examples. 15 refs.

[34.5.17]   Plottke, Paul. (1950). The child and his name.   Individual
Psychology Bulletin, 8, 150-157.
Reports on interview with 10 adults on their names. Also, an analysis of
50 compositions written by pupils at a senior school near Paris on "Myself
and My Name." Among other results the data show that more liked their
first name (64%) than their last name (32%). Reasons for like/dislike are
tabulated. Included are some extracts from the papers. 6 refs.

[34.5.18] Seeman, Mary V. (1980). Name and identity. Canadian Journal of
Psychiatry, 25, 129-137.
The naming of a child has close associations with its identity. This shows
up in the naming traditions of different ethnic or cultural groups such as,
Canadian Indians, Inuit, Chinese-Canadians; and those with Hebrew, French,
European, and black North American backgrounds. The structure and form of
the name is also important. Finally, the meaning of the name is important.
There is also some coverage of clinical aspects of names and the influence
of a name in twinning. 35 refs.

[34.5.19] Snyder, C. R., & Fromkin, Howard L. (1980).   Uniqueness: The
human pursuit of difference. New York: Plenum, pp. 129-143.
Discusses uniqueness and names as symbols of uniqueness. Included in the
discussion are maiden names, names for adopted children, nicknames and
their roots, and graffiti names.   Studies by Zweigenhaft and others on
unusual (unique) names are briefly described. There is also a brief
section on signature size. 26 refs.

[34.5.20] Stampfer, Judah. (1974, Aug. 31). The hunger for namelessness.
The Nation, 152-155.
Surnames give the individual a sense of historical-cultural identity and
destiny, but in the United States many individuals have striven to get away
from that name and identity.

[34.5.21]   Strumpfer. D. J. W. (1978). Relationship between attitudes
toward one's name and self-esteem. Psychological Reports, 43, 699-702.
Ninety-three men and 73 women at a white South African university rated
first, second, and last names and also took 3 scales dealing with
self-esteem: the Ziller, the Bills, and the Coopersmith. Men liked last
names significantly more than middles; women liked last names more than

either first or middles. First name attitude was somewhat related to Bills and Coopersmith scores but not to Ziller. With women, attitude toward last name showed a relationship to self-esteem in a social context. 11 refs.

[34.5.22] Strunk, Orlo, Jr. (1958). Attitudes toward own name and one's self. Journal of Individual Psychology, 14, 64-67.
In an investigation between the relationship between liking for one's name and self-satisfaction (self-esteem), 100 men and 20 women college students rated their first, middle, and last names. The students also completed the Brownfain Self-Rating Inventory. First names were found most important. Those who liked their names showed a significantly higher score on the Brownfain (indicating higher self-satisfaction) than those who disliked theirs. 15 refs.

34.6. Learning, Memory, Cognition, and Names

[34.6.1] Alexander, William Hardy. (1954). The purposive study of names. Names, 2, 169-174.
Reacting to the article by McCartney [34.6.12], on memory and names, reports the case of a senator reputed to have a phenomenal memory for names being found to prepare for meetings by first studying 3 x 5 cards with relevant information. 5 refs.

[34.6.2] Bahrick, H. P., Bahrick, P. O., & Wittlinger, R. P. (1975). Fifty years of memory for names and faces. Journal of Experimental Psychology: General, 104, 54-75.
Complex investigation of the ability to identify and match names and faces. Respondents ranged from recent high school graduates to those who had been out 57 years. Results appear to indicate that there is ability to match names and faces for at least 15 years. Free recall of class names is independent of class size and declines with negative acceleration by 60% during 48 years. 32 refs.

[34.6.3] Bjorklund, David F. & Zeman, Barbara R. (1983). The development of organizational strategies in children's recall of familiar information: Using social organization to recall the names of classmates. International Journal of Behavioral Development, 6, 341-353.
Reports of a project in which 1st, 3rd, and 5th graders were tested to determine what strategies are used in the recall of names. 10 refs.

[34.6.4] Blandford, Donald H., & Sampson, Edward D. (1964). Induction of prestige suggestion through classical conditioning. Journal of Abnormal and Social Psychology, 69, 332-337.
College students participated in an experiment in classical learning in which conditioned stimuli (nonsense syllables such as YOF, LAJ, and WUH) were associated with unconditioned stimuli (names of people). Some of the names were positive such as Winston Churchill, Admiral Rickover, and John F. Kennedy; some were negative such as Joseph Stalin, Jimmy Hoffa, and Adolph Hitler. The results indicate that evaluative meaning responses were conditioned to the nonsense syllables without the participant's awareness. 15 refs.

[34.6.5] Bruning, James L. (1972). The effects of connotative meaning on the learning of names. Journal of Social Psychology, 86, 105-110.
Three experiments were performed on the connotative meaning of first names.

In the 1st, it was demonstrated that liked names were learned a bit easier than disliked. In the 2nd, it was shown that a disliked name, <u>Cecil</u>, was easily learned when it was imbedded within a list of liked names. The isolation effect showed that it was easier to learn. In the 3rd experiment, photographs accompanied names. The names were learned easier than in Experiment 2. Again, <u>Cecil</u> was learned very easily.

[34.6.6] Clarke, H. W. (1934). <u>Journal of Applied Psychology</u>, <u>18</u>, 757-763.
Use of the Moss Social Intelligence Test to measure recall and recognition value for names and faces showed that names are easier to recognize than faces. Recall tests show a similar trend. 18 refs.

[34.6.7] Cromwell, Rue L. (1956). Factors in the serial recall of names of acquaintances. <u>Journal of Abnormal and Social Psychology</u>, <u>53</u>, 63-67.
Two experiments were conducted at Ohio State University. In the 1st, recall of names and factors of liking (pleasure), frequency of contact, recency, acquaintance, and construction were evaluated. Ranking on the first 4 variables was correlated with the order in which the names were recalled. In the 2nd experiment, a greater relationship was found between recall of name and liking than between recall and height of the person. 3 refs.

[34.6.8] Early, C. Joan. (1968). Attitude learning in children. <u>Journal of Educational Psychology</u>, <u>59</u>, 176-180.
In an experiment with 4th and 5th grade schoolchildren on classical conditioning and attitudes, it was shown associating a name such as KAREN with a word such as NEAT could bring classmates to show more approach behavior to isolates with those names.

[34.6.9] Hanley-Dunn, Patricia & McIntosh, John L. (1984). Meaningfulness and recall of names by young and old adults. <u>Journal of Gerontology</u>, <u>39</u>, 583-585.
Contrary to other investigations, this research indicates that in free recall of some types of list, elderly adults recall as well as young adults. 5 refs.

[34.6.10] Kaess, Walter A., & Witryol, Sam L. (1955). Memory for names and faces: A characteristic of social intelligence? <u>Journal of Applied Psychology</u>, <u>39</u>, 457-462.
On the premise that memory for names and faces is an important aspect of social intelligence, 2 measures were used: the Names and Faces picture subtest of the George Washington University Social Intelligence Test and a miniature social situation. Results indicate that women are better on both types of social recall tests. Set, as defined by preparatory instructions, does not significantly influence performance. 12 refs.

[34.6.11] Katz, Nancy; Baker, Erica, & Macnamara, John. (1974). What's in a name? A study of how children learn common and proper names. <u>Child Development</u>, <u>45</u>, 469-473.
To learn how naming processes develop, 80 children aged 17-24 mos. were tested in 2 experiments. Results confirm the hypothesis that with a class of objects such as people, individuals are first discriminated. Then, names are learned for them. However, with a class of objects such as children's blocks, there is no discrimination of individual items, only for the class. 4 refs.

[34.6.12] Mason, Susan E. & Reid, Howard M. (1984).   Remembering people's names. In Murray Heller (Ed.), Names, Northeast (pp. 84-90), Publications 3-4, Northeast Regional Names Institute. Saranac Lake, NY: North Country Community College Pr.
Reports 2 studies using men and women college students.   Results showed that women were better than men at associating names and faces and that women's names were remembered better than men's. 11 refs.

[34.6.13] McCartney, Eugene S. (1953). On remembering names in antiquity, Names, 1, 192-195.
Even the ancients such as Cyrus the Great, Themisticles, and Cicero were concerned with remembering names and tried hard to do so. 10 refs.

[34.6.14] McCarty, David L. (1980). Investigation of a visual mnemonic device for the use of mediators in paired-associate learning. Journal of Experimental Psychology: Human Learning and Memory, 6, 145-155.
Two experiments were performed using face-name mnemonics involving: (1) a prominent facial feature, (2) high imagery transformation of the person's name (Bryant to "bride ant'), and an interactive visual image of these 2 components. 12 refs.

[34.6.15] Mulhall, Edith F. (1915). Experimental studies in recall and recognition. American Journal of Psychology, 26, 217-228.
A pioneer study on memory and retention.   Part of the investigation centered on names and photographs. Results indicate that intent to recall in an important factor in retention. 1 ref.

[34.6.16] Neely, James H. & Payne, David G. (1983). A direct comparison of recognition failure rates for recallable names in episodic and semantic memory tests. Memory & Cognition, 11, 161-171.
To evaluate the Tulving-Wiseman episodic-semantic (episodic = materials from a studied list, semantic = materials known without study), pairs of lower case cues and uppercase targets involving famous names (ex., betsy ROSS), nonfamous names (edwin CONWAY), related words, and unrelated words were studied. Results support Tulving-Wiseman for famous names. 22 refs.

[34.6.17] Payne, David G., & Neely, James H. (1983). Recognition failure of recallable famous names in a hybrid semantic-episodic memory task. Bulletin of the Psychonomic Society, 21, 85-88.
A further study related to Neely & Payne above provides some support for the distinction between semantic and episodic memory. 8 refs.

[34.6.18] Ramirez, Manuel & Castenada, Alfred. (1967).   Paired-associate learning of sociometrically ranked children's names. Child Development, 38, 171-179.
In a learning experiment with children in elementary school, first names were initially ranked on the basis of sociometric scores.   Then, paired associate lists composed of 8 of the names and consonants were presented to the children.   Results indicate that the names of high sociometric rank children facilitated learning more than names of low sociometric rank. A 2nd experiment seems to confirm this. 6 refs.

[34.6.19] Rychlak, Joseph F., & Saluri, Rosemary. (1973). Affective assessment in the learning of names by 5th and 6th grade children. Journal of Genetic Psychology, 123, 251-261.
As a preliminary task, all the children rated 50 male and 50 female names

on a like-dislike scale. Then the children were tested in a memory experiment. High self-esteem children rated liked names more rapidly than low self-esteem children. Discussion of results and implications. 22 refs.

[34.6.20] Staats, Arthur W., Higa, William R., & Reid, Ian. (1970). Names as reinforcers: The social value of verbal stimuli (Technical Report No. 9). Honolulu: University of Hawaii, 19 p.
Association with a positive name vs. a neutral name increased desired frequency of response in a conditioning situation. 32 refs.

[34.6.21] Yesavage, Jerome A., & Rose, Terrence L. (1984). The effects of a face-name mnemonic in young, middle-aged, and elderly adults. Experimental Aging Research, 10, 55-57.
All groups with mnemonic training improved memory for names. The young improved the most, followed by the middle-aged, and the elderly. 7 refs.

[34.6.22] Yesavage, Jerome A; Rose, Terrence L.; & Bower, Gordon H. (1983). Interactive imagery and affective judgments improve face-name learning in the elderly. Journal of Gerontology, 38, 197-203.
Elderly adults were taught to associate surnames with faces under various conditions. Those who associated a prominent feature of the face and judged the pleasantness of that feature learned surnames best. 16 refs.

34.7. Miscellaneous Aspects of Names

[34.7.1] Kleinke, Chris L., & Staneski, Richard A. (1972). Evaluation of a person who uses another's name in ingratiating and noningratiating situations. Journal of Experimental Social Psychology, 8, 457-466.
Three types of laboratory situation were set up: (1), an applicant for a job, (2) an attractive woman interviewing 2 men simultaneously, and (3) a man and woman alone. These situations were presented under conditions of ingratiation where the name was used in a dependent sense (as by the job applicant) or an independent sense (woman in Situation 2), or not at all. Along with other results, the experiments suggest that using another's name was perceived more favorably in Situation 2, than in either Situation 1 or Situation 3. 9 refs.

34.8 Perception and Names

[34.8.1] Howarth, C. I. & Ellis, K. (1961). The relative intelligibility threshold of one's own name compared to other names. Quarterly Journal of Experimental Psychology, 13, 236-239.
Experimental confirmation that one's own name is perceived at a lower threshold (more easily) than other names. 5 refs.

[34.8.2] Moray, Neville. (1959). Attention in dichotic listening: Affective cues and the influence of instructions. Quarterly Journal of Experimental Psychology, 11, 56-60.
In experiments where 2 messages are simultaneously presented dichotically (one to each ear), participants are unable to report the content of the rejected message. The only stimulus which was able to break the barrier is the subject's own name. 7 refs.

[34.8.3] Oswald, Ian; Taylor, Anne M., & Treisman, Michel. (1960).
Discrimination responses to stimulation during human sleep. Brain, 83,
440-453.
Complex experiments under appropriate controls with men and women indicate
that during sleep individuals are more likely to awaken at the sound of
their own own names rather than to other stimuli. Measurements of brain
waves and galvanic skin responses to sound of names were also done. 21
refs.

35. PUBLIC HEALTH AND NAMES

[35.1]   Duncan, Burris; Smith, Ann N., & Briese, Franklin W. (1979).
American Journal of Public Health, 69, 903-907.
Shows how ethnic surnames can be used to differentiate public health
populations. 10 refs.

[35.2]   Enstrom, J. E., & Operskalski, E. A. (1978). Cancer and other
mortality among Spanish-surnamed Californians. American Journal of
Epidemiology, 108, 235.
Use of surnames to develop comparisons on standardized mortality ratios.
(Abstract).

[35.3] Schoen, Robert & Nelson, Verne E. (1981). Mortality by cause among
Spanish surnamed Californians. Social Science Quarterly, 62, 259-274.
Surnames were used to examine the demographic characteristics of Mexican
Americans by using Spanish surnames for comparisons with other whites and
blacks in California. 33 refs.

[35.4] Selby, Maija L.; Lee, Eun Sul; Tuttle, Dorothy M., & Loe, Hardy D.,
Jr. (1984). Validity of the Spanish surname infant-mortality rate as a
health status indicator for the Mexican-American population. American
Journal of Public Health, 74, 998-1002.
Indicates that in Harris County, Texas the Spanish surname mortality rate
is not a valid indicator for the Mexican-American population. 16 refs.

36. SIGNATURE SIZE

[36.1]   Hendrick, Clyde; Vincenzo, Joe; & Nelson, Cheryl A. (1973).
Formality of signature as an index of subject motivation in the
psychological experiment. Social Behavior and Personality, 3, 1-4. 1973,
3, 1-4.
Signup signatures were compared with those in a later experiment. Results
confirm that a more formal setting leads to a formal signature. 3 refs.

[36.2] Mahoney, E. R. (1973). Signature size and self-estimation: A brief
note. Journal of Psychology, 84, 223-224.
Attempting to replicate Zweigenhaft [36.6] on the relationship of
self-esteem to signature size, 227 students were tested on signature size,
the Who Am I scale, and the Marlowe-Crowne Social Desirability Scale.
Results fail to confirm Zweigenhaft. 4 refs.

[36.3] Snyder, C. R., & Fromkin, Howard L. (1977). Abnormality as a
positive characteristic: The development and validation of a scale
measuring need for uniqueness. Journal of Abnormal Psychology, 86,
518-527.
Assumes that a person's name may have importance in striving for
uniqueness. Results from high scorers on a uniqueness scale show that they
tended to write their signatures larger. 29 refs.

[36.4] Stewart, Robert A. C. (1977). Effects of self-esteem and status on
size of signature. Perceptual and Motor Skills, 44, 185-186.
Found a relationship between signature size and conditions of high and low
self-esteem. No significant relationship between signature size and
status. 8 refs.

[36.5] Swanson, Blair R., & Price, Raymond L. (1972). Signature size and
status. Journal of Social Psychology, 87, 319.
Confirms Zweigenhaft below that as social status awareness increases, so
does signature size. 1 ref.

[36.6] Zweigenhaft, Richard L. (1970). Signature size: A key to status
awareness. Journal of Social Psychology, 81, 49-54.
Three studies were performed testing perception of status and size of
signature confirming the basic hypothesis that signature size and status
correlated. 2 refs.

[36.7] Zweigenhaft, Richard L. (1977). The empirical study of signature
size. Social Behavior and Personality, 5, 177-185.
Summarizes a series of studies which have related signature size to
situational and personality characteristics. Results indicate a
correlation between signature size and feeling of status and self-esteem.
20 refs.

[36.8] Zweigenhaft, Richard L., & Marlowe, David. (1973). Signature size:
Studies in expressive movement. Journal of Consulting and Clinical
Psychology, 40, 469-473.
Four studies report the positive relationship between signature size and
self-esteem. 3 refs.

37. SOCIOLOGY AND NAMES

[37.1] Raper, Paul E. (1982). Sociology and the study of names. Onoma,
26, 63-74.
Drawing from data from all over the world, discusses several
sociolinguistic parameters of naming such as the sex distinction, family
relationships, and official vs. non-official. Gives a number of
suggestions for future research. 28 refs.

38. SOUND OF NAMES

[38.1] Butters, Donald H. (1967, July 8). Phonetic name searching: A new
technique. Insurance Management Review, pp. 19, 26.
Development of a system by an IBM engineer to search for surnames
phonetically. Thus Shaffer could be found as well with that spelling as
with Schaeffer; Smith with Smyth.

[38.2] Marcus, Leonard. (1962, August). What's in a name? High Fidelity,
pp. 48-49, 117.
Maintains that there is a relationship between the sound of a composer's
name and the sound of that person's music. Examples include Humperdinck
(Hansel and Gretel), Bach, Brahms, and Wagner.

[38.3] Nicolaisen, Wilhelm F. H. (1976). Name aesthetics. Midwest Journal
of Language and Folklore, 2, 56-63.
Development of the position that euphony is of major importance in
selection of a name, ex., Diana Fluck to Diana Dors, Frances Gumm to Judy
Garland. Makes the point that esthetic considerations are important and
have been neglected by scholars and those interested in the lexical meaning
of names. 11 refs.

39. SPELLING OF NAMES

[39.1] Garfield, Eugene. (1981, Feb. 16). What's in a surname? Current
Contents, No. 7, 5-9.
How surnames are spelled uniformly in the Citation Indexes.   Surnames
involving particles (Dos Passos, von Braun), those showing clan or father
relationships (McCarthy, O'Brien), Oriental, Muslim, Spanish, and
Portugese names are a special concern. 7 refs.

40. STATISTICS AND NAMES

[40.1] Ellegard, Alvar. (1958). Notes on the use of statistical methods in
the study of name vocabularies. Studia Neophilologica, 30, 214-231.
Description and evaluation of statistical procedures in study of first
names. 8 refs.

[40.2]   Stan, Aurelia & Stan, Ioan. (1966).   Concerning the relation
between first name (Christian name) and person. Proceedings of the Eighth
International Congress of Onomastic Sciences, Amsterdam, pp. 500-504.
Using 3 types of   community in Romania, reports development   of a
mathematical equation to demonstrate how the number of first names
increases with the population. 3 refs.

[40.3] Weitman, Sasha. (1981). Some methodological issues in quantitative
onomastics. Names, 29, 181-196.
An evaluation of 2 million first names in Israel from data in the
Population Ministry files from 1882 to 1980.   Concludes that F (simple

frequencies) is inappropriate, R (rank of the name in relation to all names of that year) is the most appropriate measure of change for an individual name, and that P (percentage of the total number of births that year) is best for evaluation of social groups. Discussion of useful information possibilities of data on a population. 1 ref.

[40.4] Weitman, Sasha. (1982). Cohort size and onomasticon size. Onoma, 26, 78-95.
Analysis of names data from the Israeli Population Registry for the years 1882-1980 confirms Jacques Maitre's theory concerning the differential popularity of first names. 5 refs.

41. STEREOTYPES OF NAMES

[41.1] Albott, William L. (1972). Given names and person perception. Dissertation Abstracts International, 32, 6667-B (University Microfilms No. 72-13,674)
Experimental investigation of stereotypes and impression formation. Results indicate consistent ratings from one condition to another.

[41.2] Andersen, Christopher P. (1977). The name game. New York: Harcourt Brace Jovanovich, 254 p.
Explains the effects of name stereotypes in social perception. Gives a brief stereotype comment on about 900 first names, ex., Eric = a big winner--very strong, Heidi = cute. Brief entries on 2500 additional names, and a state-by-state guide to laws on names. 32 refs.

[41.3] Arthaud, R. L., Hohneck, A. N., Ramsey, C. H., & Pratt, K. C. (1948). The relation of family name preferences to their frequency in the culture. Journal of Social Psychology, 28, 19-37.
College students evaluated monosyllabic vs. dissyllabic surnames such as Reeves vs. Scovill. A 2nd study compared names in the original language vs. the anglicized version, the German Bauer vs. Bower. Among the results and conclusions: there is a number of stereotypes on which men and women agree, the frequency of the name is not a factor in preference, and women are more satisfied with their surnames. 10 refs.

[41.4] Ashley, Leonard R. N. (1979). "Medallion or millstone, plume or plummet": Results of research by questionnaire of one hundred New York City college students on given names. ANS Bulletin, No. 56, 23-30.
A 15-item questionnaire (included) dealing with name stereotypes was administered. Among several results, it was determined that Brad was rated as active, Marvin was weak, Craig was strong. 2 refs.

[41.5] Bruning, James L. & Albott, W. (1974, March). Funny, you don't look Cecil. Human Behavior, 3(3), 56-57.
A popular article on first name stereotypes. Refers to work by Buchanan, Harari, and McDavid.

[41.6] Bruning, James L., & Husa, Frederick T. (1972). Given names and stereotyping. Developmental Psychology, 7, 91.
Elementary schoolchildren were tested with a variation of the Guess Who technique which employed pairs of stickmen with different names which were

rated in terms of Like-Dislike and Active-Passive dimensions. Results appear to indicate development of stereotypes of first names as early as the 3rd grade. 2 refs.

[41.7] Bruning, James L. & Liebert, Dale M. (1973). Name and facial feature stereotyping. Perceptual and Motor Skills, 37, 889-890.
First, judges rated slides (presumably of both men and women on masculinity-femininity. Then the 28 men and women respondents were asked to assign one of 25 names (both male and female) to each of the photographs. Results indicate that college students associated masculinity-femininity of photographs with names given similar ratings of masculinity-femininity. 2 refs.

[41.8] Buchanan, Barbara & Bruning, James L. (1971). Connotative meanings of first names and nicknames on three dimensions. Journal of Social Psychology, 85, 143-144.
Ratings were made along 3 dimensions, Active-Passive, Male-Female, and Like-Dislike on 618 male and 442 female first names by 1380 students at Ohio University. Results indicate: (1) women are more extreme in ratings than men, (2) men and women had a high level of agreement on male names, much less for female names, (3) the names did show variation of ratings on the 3 dimensions.

[41.9] Busse, Thomas V., & Love, Craig. (1973). The effect of first names on conflicted decisions: An experimental study. Journal of Psychology, 84, 253-256.
Ten stories were presented to 40 male and 40 female schoolchildren. In each story, the main character had to choose between 2 courses of action. The first name of the main character was randomly varied with liked and disliked first names. The expected name effect, that children who possessed liked names would be judged as right more frequently than those with disliked first names, was not found. 9 refs.

[41.10] Darden, Donna K. (1983). Symbolic interactionist sociology and onomastics. Names, 31, 288-299.
To apply social interaction theory of meaning, 10 men's names were evaluated using multi-dimensional scaling. There were 2 solutions, a 3-dimensional and a 4-dimensional. For the 3-dimensional solution, the dimensions are Activity, Evaluation, and Potency; for the 4-dimensional, Character, Maturity, Sociability, and Virility. Both solutions are acceptable using standard criteria. Nicknames are shown to be a composite of the other dimensions rather than a separate dimension. 32 refs. fig. French abstract.

[41.11] Darden, Donna K., & Robinson, Ira E. (1976). Multidimensional scaling of men's first names: A sociolinguistic approach. Sociometry, 39, 422-431.
Drawing from the approach of social interactionism, a multidimensional mapping process was employed to evaluate men's names using the semantic differential. Results indicate that a 4-dimensional solution is best although a 3-dimensional is acceptable. Concludes that the measurement of the meaning of names may be an indicator of social change. 48 refs.

[41.12] Duffy, James C. & Ridinger, Bruce. (1981). Stereotyped connotations of masculine and feminine names. Sex Roles, 7, 25-33.
College students rated male and female names on 20 semantic differential

scales imagining "real" or "ideal" persons. The semantic dimension of Potency was associated more with masculine than with feminine names. 13 refs.

[41.13] Dulin, Ken L., & Duran, Ramona. (1977). Ninth graders' responses to story characters with pun-producing surnames. Journal of Reading, 21, 205-207.
Story passages were created where fictional characters had connoting and contrasting surnames such as Goodman and Kindlie vs. Baddman and Week. Responses from students indicates that the choice of surname is important in the affective response of the reader.

[41.14] Ellington, Jane A., Marsh, Luther A., & Critelli, Joseph. (1980). Personality characteristics of women with masculine names. Journal of Social Psychology, 111, 211-218.
On 13 dimensions of personality including femininity, women with more masculine names did not differ from feminine-named controls. However, women known by more masculine names were less anxious, less neurotic, higher on family dependence, cultural sophistication, and leadership potential. 28 refs.

[41.15] Erwin, P. G. & Calev, A. (1984). The influence of christian name stereotypes on the marking of children's essays. British Journal of Educational Psychology, 54, 223-227.
Demonstrates in a complex experiment using college students as participants, that those who were attractively-named themselves, gave essays higher grades than raters not attractively-named. 21 refs.

[41.16] Evans, Cleveland Kent. (1983). Two studies in the psychology of names. Papers of the North Central Names Institute, 4, 16-42.
Study 1 used the semantic differential to show how stereotypes of male and female names to explain how frequency is related to evaluation. Study 2 used the names Chauncy and Jason to study impression formation. Results of Study 2 were negative. 31 refs.

[41.17] Ford, Martin E., Masters, John C., & Miura, Irene. (1984). Effects of social stimulus value on academic achievement and social competence: A reconsideration of children's first name characteristics. Journal of Educational Psychology, 76, 1149-1158.
One sample of 23,878 children, grades 2-11, and a 2nd sample of 479 high school students were used to conclude that when appropriate methodological procedures are followed children's academic and social competence are unrelated to the frequency or desirability of their names. 40 refs.

[41.18] Garwood, S. Gray. (1976). First-name stereotypes as a factor in self-concept and school achievement. Journal of Educational Psychology, 68, 482-487.
Using the Tennessee Self Concept Scale, the Children's Self-Concept of Achievement Test, and the Iowa Test of Basic Skills, 47 boys were evaluated in 2 groups: those with desirable first names and those with undesirable first names as determined by a teacher sample. Results indicate that the desirable names group differed significantly from the other group on variability, flexibility of self-description, conflict, personality integration, and aspirations about achievement. Discussion of implications for teachers. 19 refs.

[41.19] Garwood, S. Gray; Baer, Susan; Levine, Douglas; Carroll, Sudie; & O'Neal, Ed. (1981). Sex-role expectations of socially desirable first names. Sex Roles, 7, 257-262.
The research tested whether desirable male and female first names would be rated as more sex-typed the more frequently they occurred in the culture. Results with undergraduates confirm this. No effect was found with undesirable first names.

[41.20] Garwood, S. Gray; Cox, Lewis; Kaplan, Valerie; Wasserman, Neal, & Sulzer, Jefferson L. (1980). Beauty is only "Name" deep: The effect of first-name on ratings of physical attraction. Journal of Applied Social Psychology, 10, 431-435.
Investigated selection of a beauty queen by college students. In the condition where the photograph was assigned a desirable first name, the vote was overwhelmingly larger. 8 refs.

[41.21] Garwood, S. Gray, & McDavid, John W. (1974). Ethnic factors in stereotypes of given names. Paper presented at the meeting of the American Psychological Association, New Orleans, 1974. (ERIC Document Reproduction Service No. ED 097 994)
White, black, and Spanish teachers at locations in Miami and Atlanta (N = 147) rated 14 male and 14 female names on 9 semantic differential scales. Male names such as David, Steven, and Ralph; for females, Karen, Hilda, and Lisa. For the Spanish groups, there were some substitutions such as Miguel and Maria. Results indicate differences in quality and content among the teacher groups. The differences are clearer for female names and male names regarded as undesirable. Some evidence of a chauvinistic masculinity-femininity set was seen in the Florida groups. 6 refs.

[41.22] Garwood, S. Gray., Sulzer, Jefferson L., Levine, Douglas L., Cox, Lewis, & Kaplan, Valerie. (1983). Should Henrietta be punished or rewarded? The effects of name desirability on responsibility attribution and sanction assignment. Names, 31, 318-333.
Men and women college students evaluated stories with differing types of outcome to evaluate first name desirability and relationship to sanction assignment. For male actors with undesirable names there was more punishment and less reward; for female actors with undesirable names there was less punishment. 26 refs. 4 figs. French abstract.

[41.23] Gilbreth, Frank, Jr. (1972, July 29). Bunkers, Claghorns, and other name-droppers. Saturday Review, pp. 71-72.
A writer whose middle name is Bunker ponders on how radio and TV shows have influenced perception of surnames such as Bunker and Claghorn and first names such as Kim and Mortimer.

[41.24] Goldberg, Philip. (1968). Are women prejudiced against women? Trans-Action, 5(5), 28-30.
Male and female students read articles in 6 fields fictitiously attributed to authors in a John T. McKay or Joan T. McKay style. Both sexes rated the article more valuable and the author more competent with a masculine name. 3 refs.

[41.25] Harari, Herbert, & McDavid, John W. (1973). Name stereotypes and teacher expectations. Journal of Educational Psychology, 65, 222-225.
Evaluated the reactions of 80 women elementary teachers and 80 women college students to essays purportedly written by 10-yr-old pupils

identified only by first names on the topic "What I did last Sunday." Authorship was attributed in 2 categories: (1) desirable and popular names such as David or Karen, (2) rare and undesirable names such as Elmer or Bertha. The hypothesis was confirmed that attributed quality of each essay was higher when attributed authorship was linked with a desirable name. This bias was more pronounced for experienced teachers than for college sophomores and more for male names than female. Widely-cited investigation. 13 refs.

[41.26] Hensley, Wayne & Spencer, Barbara. (1985). The effect of first names on perceptions of female attractiveness. Sex Roles, 12, 723-729.
Using 4 pictures and 4 names (2 attractive, 2 unattractive), investigators failed to confirm the results of Garwood et al. [41.20] that names affect perception of beauty. 10 refs.

[41.27] Johnson, Peter A., & Staffieri, J. Robert. (1971). Stereotypic affective properties of personal names and somatotypes in children. Developmental Psychology, 5, 176.
Results with 120 boys indicate that common names are more favorably associated with favorable stereotypes. 1 ref.

[41.28] King, Jocelyn., Davis, L. D., & Gary, A. L. (1978). Rating of repeated first names: a function of halo or fixed response? Journal of Social Psychology, 104, 307-308.
Twenty women teachers familiar with at least 2 women students bearing that name rated 20 names on 3 semantic differential scales. Raters seemed to associate first names with well-defined impressions of memories of various people.

[41.29] Lawson, Edwin D. (1971). Semantic differential analysis of men's first names. Journal of Psychology, 78, 229-240.
In 2 investigations, male and female undergraduates did semantic differential ratings on male first names. The 1st study dealt with common first names; the 2nd with a random sample of first names. Three-dimensional models were constructed and compared for men and women under the 4 conditions. Results show significant correlations between frequency (popularity) of a name and its position on the Osgood factors of Evaluation, Potency, and Activity. Ratings of men and women show correlation. 17 refs. 4 figs.

[41.30] Lawson, Edwin D. (1973). Men's first names, nicknames, and short names: A semantic differential analysis. Names, 21, 22-27.
Using the same technique as Lawson [41.29], this investigation focused on men's first names (William, Richard), nicknames or affectionate names (Danny, Tommy), and short or hypocoristic names (Dan, Tom) for 10 triads of names in random order. For both men and women short names were preferred over full first and nicknames. Semantic differential figures show the relationships. 5 refs. 2 figs.

[41.31] Lawson, Edwin D. (1974). Women's first names: A semantic differential analysis. Names, 22, 52-58.
Using the technique of Lawson [41.29], the 20 most common women's names on the campus at SUNY, Fredonia were evaluated by 50 men and 50 women. Men and women showed a high level of agreement on the Evaluative dimension. 9 refs. 2 figs.

[41.32] Lawson, Edwin D. (1980). First names on the campus: A semantic differential analysis. Names, 28, 69-83.
Using the technique of earlier Lawson studies, the 100 most common male names and the 103 most common female names on the campus at SUNY, Fredonia were evaluated on the 3 Osgood factors of Evaluation, Potency, and Activity. Results with male names confirm that frequency of a name (popularity) is associated by both sexes with the Osgood factors and demonstrates the existence of stereotypes. Results with women's names are less clear-cut. 11 refs.

[41.33] Lawson, Edwin D. (1985). Psychological dimensions of men's names: A semantic differential analysis. XV, Internationaler Kongress fuer Namenforschung, 1984, Leipzig, 3, 143-148.
The Osgood semantic differential was used to measure 453 common men's names on 6 dimensions, Good-Bad, Strong-Weak, Active-Passive, Sincere-Insincere, Intelligent-Dumb, and Calm-Emotional. 15 refs.

[41.34] Marcus, Mary G. (1976, Oct.). The power of a name. Psychology Today, pp. 75-76, 108.
Discussion of names and their stereotypes drawn from the work of a number of investigators including, Buchanan & Bruning, Lawson, Savage & Wells, Harari & McDavid, Garwood, and Jahoda.

[41.35] McDavid, John W., & Harari, Herbert. (1966). Stereotyping of names and popularity in grade school children. Child Development, 37, 453-459.
This research investigated the relationship between social desirability of first names and sociometric popularity status in elementary schoolchildren (28 boys, 31 girls). Popularity was found to be highly correlated with the social desirability score of the child's first name as rated by members of the individual's own group. It was also found that popularity correlated with name scores of children in other groups unfamiliar with the individual bearing that name. This last result raises questions on the methodology of sociometric research with children which might be contaminated by reactions to a socially undesirable name. 20 refs.

[41.36] Meeker, Frederick B., & Kleinke, Chris. (1972). Knowledge of names for in- and outgroup members of different sex and ethnic groups. Psychological Reports, 31, 832-834.
This research was done with black, white, and Chicano students of both sexes at a California State College. Using the listing method, it was found that names such as "Whitey" or "Gringo" were used by both in- and outgroups. However, some names were used exclusively by one group. 2 refs.

[41.37] Nelson, Susan D. (1977). First name stereotypes and expected academic achievement of students. Psychological Reports, 41, 1343-1344.
Tested Garwood's hypothesis [46.18] that the expected academic achievement is influenced by the student's name. Names of students from upper and lower 10% of a college population were randomly selected and shown for categorization. Female names in the honor group were given more favorable than unfavorable ratings. But this was not true for male names. The sample was composed of 45 students and 30 teachers. Results show some confirmation for Garwood. 8 refs.

[41.38] Paludi, Michele A. & Bauer, William D. (1983). Goldberg revisited: What's in an author's name. Sex Roles, 9, 387-390.

A follow-up and extension of Goldberg [41.24]. Appears to show general confirmation that articles perceived as written by a male are evaluated higher. 6 refs.

[41.39]   Paludi, Michele A. & Strayer, Lisa A. (1985). What's in an author's name? Differential evaluations of performance as a function of author's name. Sex Roles, 12, 353-361.
Gives results of an experiment in which "masculine," "feminine," and "neutral" academic articles (from politics, psychology of women, and education) were attributed to John T., Joan T., J. T., Chris T., and no author in various combinations. There was a positive bias for a masculine name or an ambiguous name perceived as masculine. 20 refs.

[41.40]   Peters, Douglas P., & Ceci, Stephen J. (1982). Peer review practices of psychological journals: The fate of published articles, submitted again. Behavioral and Brain Sciences, 5, 187-255.
An investigation of bias in evaluation of mss. submitted to professional journals. resubmitted to the journals that had originally accepted them but with alterations: the name of the author, the title, the beginning paragraphs, and some other minor changes. Only 3 of the articles were detected. Of the remaining 9, 8 were rejected. Discussion of the impact of interviewer bias. 28 refs. See also review--Adams, Virginia. (1980, July). What's in a name? Maybe everything. Psychology Today, pp. 42.

[41.41]   Razran, Gregory. (1950). Ethnic dislikes and stereotypes: A laboratory study. Journal of Abnormal and Social Psychology, 45, 7-27.
Samples of 50 Columbia students, 50 Barnard College students, and 50 older men rated photographs of 30 college women on characteristics such as general liking, beauty, and intelligence. Two months later, fictitious first names and surnames representing 3 ethnic groups (Irish, Italian, and Jewish) were attached to the photographs which were then rerated. Results indicate that the addition of the names significantly changed the ratings of the photographs in the direction of ethnic stereotypes. 25 refs.

[41.42]   Schoenfeld, Nathan. (1942). An experimental study of some problems related to stereotypes. Archives of Psychology, 38 (270), (Monograph), pp. 37-55.
Experimental investigation of trait stereotypes associated with 8 common male and 8 common female first names. Evidence that stereotypes do exist. Widely cited investigation. 38 refs.

[41.43]   Seits, Laurence E. (1981). The grading of community college English essays: A study of the effects of student name stereotypes, 115 p. Dissertation Abstracts International, 42, 1618A-1619A. (University Microfilms No. 81-22,248)
Used community college students in a follow-up study of Harari and McDavid [41.25]. No significant relationships were found between first names and measures of English writing. On miscellaneous negative comments, the name George received the highest number; Daniel, the least. With surnames, Mendez received the highest number of miscellaneous positive comments.

[41.44]   Seraydarian, Louisa & Busse, Thomas V. (1981). First-name stereotypes and essay grading. Journal of Psychology, 108, 253-257.
In a follow-up to Harari and McDavid [41.25], women in education courses rated an essay with a purported first name. Results failed to confirm that name desirability affects grades on essay papers. 11 refs.

[41.45] Sheppard, David. (1963). Characteristics associated with Christian names. British Journal of Psychology, 54, 167-174.
In a British follow-up study of Schoenfeld [41.41], respondents rated personality traits associated with 7 male and 10 female names. Evidence obtained for the halo effect--a name thought desirable on one characteristic is so perceived on other characteristics. Results seem to indicate confirmation for Schoenfeld. 3 refs.

[41.46] Wober, Mallory. (1970, Sept.). Popular images of personal names. Science Journal, 39-43.
Discussion of naming. Describes an English study where schoolgirls matched adjectives with girls' names. 7 refs.

42. STYLE OF NAMES AND NAMING

[42.1] Boshier, Roger. (1973). Name style and conservatism. Journal of Social Psychology, 84, 45-53.
Name style may be a useful cue for predicting personality. Adult education students, most liberal of students studied, showed more tendency to use "John Smith" style. Respondents who used one name style across all situations were found to score higher on the Wilson and Patterson Conservatism scale.

[42.2] Farley, Jennie. (1970). Women going back to work: Preliminary problems. Journal of Employment Counseling, 7, 130-135.
Concludes that women who use their husbands' first names on job applications may be less likely to find work.

[42.3] Farley, Jennie. (1975). Married women's name styles and interest in continuing education. Journal of Employment Counseling, 12, 91-95.
The woman who uses an independent name style,i. e., her own first name vs. that of her husband is more likely to express an interest in furthering her education. 6 refs.

[42.4] Farley, Jennie. (1976). Women at work: Name styles and job level. Journal of Employment Counseling, 13, 174-181.
At a large university 3547 employees returned postcards which indicated their signature style. The differing patterns tell something about the social structure of a university setting. Results indicate that the less prestigious the job, the more often the title "Miss" or "Mrs." was used. The different variations are discussed. 18 refs.

[42.5] Garfield, Eugene. (1975, Aug. 11). Why initials instead of first names in ISI's indexes. Current Contents, No. 32, 5-6.
Explains that the Institute for Scientific Information uses initials for authors' first names because not all original journals give the first name. 2 refs.

[42.6] Hartman, A. Arthur. (1958). Name styles in relation to personality. Journal of General Psychology, 59, 289-294.
Description and psychological analysis of major name styles: John J. Brown, John Jacob Brown, J. J. Brown, J. Jacob Brown, John J. Brown III, Colonel John J. Brown as well as variations including Junior. 3 refs.

[42.7] Minton, Arthur. (1958). Some aspects of the form of personal names. American Speech, 33, Part 2, 35-45.
Comment on the pattern by individuals who sign their names as Robert Russell Bennett or W. Averell Harriman but are known as Russell Bennett or Averell Harriman. Further comment on those who use initials in place of first names. 65 refs.

[42.8] Newman, Edwin. (1975). Strictly speaking. New York, Warner Books, pp. 137-152.
Comment on British hyphenated names; practice of dropping the first name as, Foster Dulles; and names of a number of American college presidents who have "interchangeable" names, i. e., have first names which could be surnames and vice versa as, Dixon Ryan Fox.

[42.9] Osborn, George C. (1957). Woodrow Wilson: The evolution of a name. North Carolina Historical Review, 34, 507-516.
Shows forms Tommy, T. W., T. Wilson, Thomas W. Wilson, T. Woodrow Wilson, and Woodrow Wilson. Also reports a story that cousin Harriet's refusal to marry him and his vow to remember her always is the basis for the first name of Woodrow. 15 refs.

[42.10] Zweigenhaft, Richard L. (1975). Name styles in America and name styles in New Zealand. Journal of Social Psychology, 97, 289-290.
Californians chose the John Public style, 61%; John Q. Public, 30%; other forms, 9%. Older people preferred the John Q. Public style. New Zealanders chose J. Q. Public, 56%; J. Public, 61%; John Q. Public, 30%; and other forms, 9%. No relationship was found between scores on a personality test and name style. 2 refs.

43. SURNAMES
(includes Family Names, Last Name, and Patronyms)

43.1. Surnames: General

[43.1.1] Brown, Samuel L. (1967). Surnames are the fossils of speech Published by author, 350 p.
Lists about 7500 common American surnames with their derivations. Name list was derived from vital statistics records in 5 daily newspapers.

[43.1.2] Carroll, Kenneth Lane. (1962). Joseph Nichols and the Nicholites. Easton, MD: Easton Publ, 116 p.
Describes a 19th Century religious sect (sometimes called the New Quakers) centered on the Eastern Shore of Maryland. Contains 5 lists of names (surnames & first names) from birth, marriage, legal, and church records. 50 refs.

[43.1.3] Gingerich, Melvin. (1974). Mennonite family names in Iowa. Annals of Iowa, 42, 397-403.
General historical description of the Mennonites followed by a description of their communities in Iowa. Included are a number of surnames in over a dozen counties. 4 refs.

[43.1.4] Gold, David (1971). Addenda et corrigenda: R. M. R. and Beatrice Hall's "Some apparent orthographic inconsistencies in American family names of Yiddish origin." Names, 19, 223-228.
Response on 10 points to the article by R. M. R. and Hall [43.1.13].

[43.1.5] Harris, Marvin. (1972). A trip through Ma Bell's zoo. Natural History, 81, pp. 6, 8, 12.
Lists a number of zoonyms (animal names) used as surnames such as Fox, Wolf, and Tiger from the Manhattan telephone directory. Goes on to question why other names such as Owl, Penguin, or Bison do not appear.

[43.1.6] Hook, J. N. (1982). Family names. New York: Macmillan, 388 p.
Gives a world of information on 2800 surnames of the many cultural groups that came to the United States. 30+ ethnic groups represented. 30 refs.

[43.1.7] Howell, George Rogers. (1894?) The origin and meaning of English and Dutch surnames of New York State families. Paper read before the Albany Institute, May 15, 1894. Albany, 13 p. (In collection of Drake Library, State University of New York College at Brockport)
Background material on origin and meaning of surnames. Listings of about 100 names of Dutch origin; 100 of British.

[43.1.8]   Johnson, E. D. (1955). Family names in Louisiana. Names, 3, 165-168.
While French surnames have persisted well, there have been pressures to simplify (Americanize?) French names as Geaux > Joe, Rousseau > Russo.

[43.1.9] Kolb, Avery E. (1974). The grand-families of America, 1776-1976. Baltimore: Gateway Pr., 103 p.
Discussion of the cultural background and geographic distribution of the top 50 names in frequency in 1776 and the most common names in each state. Comparisons made with 1976. Results indicate that of the top 50 names in 1776, 44 are still in the top group. Tables of names for leading cities. Maps. 27 refs.

[43.1.10] McWhiney, Grady and McDonald, Forrest. (1983). Celtic names in the antebellum United States. Names, 31, 89-102.
After evaluation of a great deal of material and application of statistics involving surname analysis, concludes that the Celts were about 60% of the pre-Civil War Southern population of British extraction and the English, 40%. In New York and New England, this ratio was reversed. 95 refs.

[43.1.11] Mockler, William E. (1956). Surnames of Trans-Allegheny Virginia: 1750-1800 I. Names, 4, 1-17.
Analysis of documents from the Monongalia region of West Virginia, Ohio, and Pennsylvania. Evaluation serves several purposes: helps to identify modern surnames, indicates the regions in England the families came from, philology, lexicography, and the value of surnames in placename study. Tables. Map. 32 refs.

[43.1.12] Mockler, William E. (1956). Surnames of Trans-Allegheny Virginia 1750-1800 II. Names, 4, 96-118.
Comprehensive description of how surnames changed. Some changed in pronunciation and spelling, others were changed due to religious, political, or social reasons. Some discussion of middle names.   About 150 refs. See Mockler above.

[43.1.13]   R., R. M.,   & Hall, Beatrice L. (1969).   Some apparent
orthographic inconsistencies   in American family names of Yiddish origin.
Names, 17, 250-262.
Using Greater New York telephone directories as sources, a system has been
set up to explain variations in spelling of many Jewish surnames by
reference to Old High German, Modern Standard German, Central Yiddish,
North-East Yiddish, and Standard Literary Yiddish. Thus, a name could be
spelled as Schwartz, Swartz, Swarts, and Svarts. Examples. 8 refs.

[43.1.14]   Read, William A. (1963). Louisiana-French (rev. ed.). Baton
Rouge: Louisiana State University Pr., 263 p.
Pp. 202-219 contains a section on about 100 Louisiana names of Southern
French origin. Among these are: Loustalot ("little house") and Sartre
("tailor"). 22 refs.

[43.1.15] Rogers, P. Burwell. (1956). Changes in Virgina names. American
Speech, 31, 21-24.
Analysis of a number of old Virginia surnames that have changed their
pronunciation.   Thus, Woodward has changed from WOOD-ard to WOOD-WARD;
Meahger, MAHR to MEAGER; Monroe, Mon-ROE to MON-roe. Concludes that
Virginia is just catching up with the 20th century. 1 ref.

[43.1.16] Social Security Administration. (1974, Sept. 1). Report of the
distribution of surnames in the Social Security Number File. Washington,
DC: Social Security Administration, 80 p.
Used over 239 million records to identify those surnames with a frequency
of 10,000 or more. A 2nd listing is given in alphabetical order.

[43.1.17]   Smith, Elsdon C. (1969). American surnames. Philadelphia:
Chilton, 370 p.
Introduction to surnames followed by treatment of names developed as
patronyms, from occupations, from nicknames, and from other sources.
Listing of the 2000 most common surnames from records of the Social
Security Administration. Approx 7500 names covered. 47 refs.

[43.1.18]   Smith, Elsdon C. (1972).   New dictionary of American family
names. New York: Harper, 570 p.
Introduction. A comprehensive alphabetical listing of approximately 25,000
surnames with information on nationality of origin and meaning. 2 specific
refs.

[43.1.19] Weyl, Nathaniel. (1961). Ethnic and national characteristics of
the US elite. Mankind Quarterly, 1, 242-247.
Surnames were used to categorize 13 ethnic groups. Scores were then
derived for each group based upon performance scores of eminence based upon
number of listings in Who's Who in America and other sources.   There are
also 2 special groups: English clerical and special English occupations. 1
ref.

[43.1.20]   Weyl, Nathaniel. (1961). Dynamics of the American elite.
Mankind Quarterly, 2, 48-55.
Used surname representation in Who's Who in America to derive a performance
score of eminence for different ethnic groups which are compared to scores
in the National Social Directory. Among the groups compared are those from
the British Isles, Dutch, French, German, Scandinavians, Jews,
Spanish-speaking, and Italians. 3 refs.

[43.1.21] Weyl, Nathaniel. (1962). Class origin of surnames and
achievement. Mankind Quarterly, 2, 159-164.
Using Who's Who in America as a source, concludes that Irish American
bearers of "royal" names such as O'Brien and McNeil had a higher rate of
performance than those with "non-royal" names, such as Maloney and
Sullivan. English names derived from personality characteristics such as
Quick and Darling ranked highest followed by occupational names such as
Harper and Burgess and those with patronymics such as Thomas and William.
2 refs.

[43.1.22] Weyl, Nathaniel. (1964). National origins of the Phi Beta Kappa
membership. Names, 12, 119-122.
Selected names assumed to be representative of 15 ethnic groups were used
to measure the ethnic composition of Phi Beta Kappa. 4 refs.

[43.1.23] Yoder, Robert M. (1958, Aug. 9). You're on this list. Saturday
Evening Post, pp. 37, 83-84.
Description and comment about the most common and also most unusual
surnames from a list of 1,100,000 different names published by the Social
Security Administration. Among the most common, there are 304,468
individuals named Nelson; 207,898 Rogers; and 404,070, Young. Unusual
names include McZeal, Damn, and God.

43.2. Surnames: Specific

[43.2.1] Bye, Arthur Edwin. (1968). The surname Bye. Names, 16, 111-118.
After examining a number of possible explanations, concludes that the
surname Bye is a contraction of Bayeux, the city in Normandy. 18 refs.

[43.2.2] Deliquant, Don. (1971, September 20). Call him Willy--or Carlos
or Lee. Everybody does. Sports Illustrated, p. 68.
Comment on all the major league baseball players with the surname
May(e)/Mays/Maze, 8, at the time article was written.

[43.2.3] Lamberts, J. J. (1956). Knickerbocker. Names, 4, 70-74.
After evaluation of a number of possibilities, concludes that the name
Knickerbocker ("marble baker") may be derived from a nickname of an earlier
era similar to our calling a person a "feather merchant" today. 4 refs.

[43.2.4] Magoun, Francis P., Jr. (1980). The surname Peabody.
Neuphilologischer Verein, 81, 65.
Brief comment on the name with the explanation that the root is the "proud
one" but there are still questions. 5 refs.

[43.2.5] McDavid, Raven I., Jr., & Levin, Samuel R. (1964). The Levys of
New Orleans: An old myth and a new problem. Names, 12, 82-88.
Mencken once stated that Levy was one of the most common names in New
Orleans. This is not true. The error is traced to Mencken's source Howard
F. Barker. Tables. 10 refs.

[43.2.6] Pfaller, Benedict. (1969). The family name Pfaller. Names, 17,
244.
Traces the name to Der Pfahl (post), a placename for Roman fortifications
in the Jura mountains of Bavaria. 6 refs.

[43.2.7]   Smith, Elsdon C. (1956). West North Versus East South. Names, 4, 166-167.
Explains that the names West and North are more common than East and South because migration in England was more likely to be toward the more heavily populated areas in the South and East. 1 ref.

[43.2.8]   Smith, Elsdon C. (1978). The book of Smith (Stephen C.   Bice, Ed.). New York: Nellen, 218 p.
Incidence of Smith in various forms world-wide.   Glossary of Smith surnames.

[43.2.9]   Smith, H. Allen. (1950). People named Smith. Garden City, NY: Doubleday, 255 p.
Description in a light vein of numerous Smiths from Capt. John Smith to Governor Al Smith to Standfast Smith (he devised a method of extracting salt from sea water). Illustrations.

[43.2.10] Tibon, Gutierre. (1953). Names in brief: The name Dante. Names, 1, 208.
The origin of the name is Thor's raven. 2 refs.

[43.2.11] Your name. (1954). Names, 2, 210-213.
Gives derivation of the following surnames: Ackerman, Beeler, Gudde, Saroyan, Stewart; first and last names for Assar Janzen and Elsdon Smith.

[43.2.12] Your name. (1955). Names, 3, 132-134.
Background material on the following surnames: Allan, Bryant, Droege, Greet, Moffit, Seely, and Taube.

[43.2.13] Your name. (1956). Names, 4, 187-189.
Analysis of the meaning of these surnames: Childers, Hammon, Pearce, Rudnyckyj, Wolfeschlegelsteinhausenbergerdorff, and Woods.

44. TEKNONYMS

[44.1]   Geertz, Hildred & Geertz, Clifford. (1964). Teknonymy in Bali: Parenthood, age-grading and genealogical amnesia. Journal of the Royal Anthropological Institute of Great Britain, 94(2), 94-108.
A teknonym is a name given to a parent through identification with a child, ex., Abou Daoud means "father of Daoud (David)." In American culture an example would be "Shirley Temple's mother." Systematic discussion of teknonyms. 15 refs. diagrams, notes.

45. TWINS AND NAMES

[45.1]   Plank, Robert. (1964). Names of twins. Names, 12, 1-5. The pattern of twins' personal names is different from that of the general population. In a survey of 187 pairs of twins 62% of the pairs had the same initial. Identical twins were more similarly named than fraternals. A large percentage of twins has first names beginning with the letter J. 5 refs.

46. UNIQUE NAMES
(includes Low Frequency, Peculiar, Singular, Uncommon, and Unusual Names)

[46.1] Algeo, John & Algeo, Adele. (1983). Bible   Belt onomastics
revisited. Names, 31, 103-116.
Reexamination of Bible Belt onomastics 24 years after the original study of
Pyles [25.3.21]. Few names of the exotic type remain.   Among several
conclusions: women favor double names (Amy Beth); male "good ol' boy" and
commemorative names are disappearing. Extensive listing of current Bible
Belt names in appendix. 5 refs.

[46.2] Ames, Jay. (1984). Odd names. Bulletin of the Illinois Name
Society, 2, 30-32.
Listing of a number of unusual names taken from the Toronto (Ontario) Star
and the Toronto telephone directory. Among the unusual names are Jennifer
Anne Peese, Toots Belz, May Day, June Knight. Among the surnames are: Aye,
Bee, Cee, Dee etc, Brnc, Cyz, and others.

[46.3] Buxbaum. Katherine. (1933). Christian names. American Speech,
8(3), 72-73.
Comments on about 50 unusual names encountered by the author mostly at a
college.   Male names include Oriel, Lathal, and Koith; female, Marvel,
Fairy, and Dimple.

[46.4] Byrd, James W. (1980). White names: Strange, passing strange. In
Lawrence E. Seits (Ed.), What's in a name (pp. 38-45), Vol. 1, Papers of
the North Central Names Institute.   Sugar Grove, IL: Waubansee Community
College,
In response to a statement by Arthur P. Hudson that blacks give their
children "oddest, gaudiest, most humorous (names)...", Byrd presents a
collection of white unusual names. Included are: Juan Loveluck, Nancy
Anguish, Studs Terkle, Mary Butts, and Harry Screws. 2 refs.

[46.5] Ellis, Albert & Beechley, Robert M. (1954). Emotional disturbance
in children with peculiar given names. Journal of Genetic Psychology, 85,
337-339.
An investigation of the case histories of 1147 children in a guidance
clinic showed that a number had "peculiar" (unique) names.   A "peculiar"
name was defined as one that occurred twice or less in the sample; with
boys it was 9%, with girls, 7%. The authors conclude that there is a
relationship between disturbance and boys whose names are unique, but not
with girls. 2 refs.

[46.6] Crowell, Thomas L. (1948). Opinions on onomastic individualism.
American Speech, 23, 265-272.
A rejoinder to Pyles' (1947) article (see Smith--[6.16], No. 579) on
onomastic individualism in Oklahoma. Speaks in favor of having an unusual
name to distinguish oneself from others. Shows lengthy lists of unusual
names from Oklahoma and Washington, D. C. 4 refs.

[46.7] Duckert, Audrey R. (1975). A cabinet of curiosities, along with
diverse speculations. Names, 23, 190-193.
Discussion and comment on unusual names. 2 refs.

[46.8] Fletcher, Barbara. (1981). Don't blame the stork: The cyclopedia of unusual names. Seattle, WA: Rainbow Publications, 294 p.
A collection, in a humorous vein, of thousands of unusual names arranged with comments in over 100 categories, ex., No. 55, Strike Up the Band, has Camille Fife, Steve Tuba, and Larry Sax. No. 78, In the Pub, has Keith Mead, Johnny Steele Casebeer, and May I. Drinkwater. 55 refs.

[46.9] Gladding, Samuel T., & Farrar, Merry Kathleen. (1982). Perceptions of common and unusual names of therapists. Psychological Reports, 50, 595-601.
Psychology students (N = 97) evaluated 18 common and unique names on liking and for being appropriate for mental health professions. Significant differences were found between the ratings of men and women. Women, in general, liked the names less but did show a greater preference for unusual names. Some names, Mason, Meyer, Edgar, and Jerilyn were at the top for marriage and family therapists, psychologists, and psychiatrists. 9 refs.

[46.10] Hartman, A. Arthur; Nicolay, Robert C.; & Hurley, Jesse. (1968). Unique personal names as a social adjustment factor. Journal of Social Psychology, 75, 107-110.
In a study of court psychiatric clinic cases, 88 white men who had unique names were compared to a matched group with popular names. Results indicate a significantly higher rate of psychosis in the unique name group. No other significant findings were found in other diagnostic classifications or in comparisons on type of offense, work record, marital history, and arrests. Discussion of implications. 5 refs.

[46.11] Hughes, James Pennethorne. (1965). Is thy name Wart? London: Phoenix House, 128 p.
Interprets 1200 names which for one reason or another present a curious sound or written appearance. Includes such names as Bugg, Death, Daft, Sillyman, and Snodgrass. Index.

[46.12] Joubert, Charles E. (1983). Unusual names and academic achievement. Psychological Reports, 53, 266.
Results with 580 men and 810 women indicate that men with unique names suffer no handicap in graduating with honors, but that women with unique names are less likely to graduate with honors. 5 refs.

[46.13] Remington, Frank. (1969, November). The names people play. Today's Health, 50-51, 70-71.
Describes some unusual names (Welcome John Weaver, Tonsillitis Jackson, Orange Marmalade Lemon) and their origins. General discussion of naming and nicknaming practices.

[46.14] Rennick, Robert M. (1966). The folklore of curious and unusual names. New York Folklore Quarterly, 22, 5-14.
Discussion of some reasons for name change based on records of New York County Supreme Court. Primary was that the name (surname) was considered to be offensive, undignified, causing ridicule or having unfortunate economic or social consequences. Second was that the name was considered obscene. Many examples with discussion, a Dr. Coffin, a soldier named Goldbrick. Unusual names listed are Wesley Howl, director of a glee club and Dr. Minor Payne. Also traces to Pepys's diary the story of Dr. Sullivan, ne Levy, who wished to change his name to Kilpatrick so that when asked what his previous name was could say Sullivan. 4 refs.

[46.15] Rennick, Robert M. (1982). The alleged "Hogg sisters," or simple ground rules for collectors of "odd" names. _Names_, _30_, 193-197.
While Ima Hogg, daughter of Governor Hogg, did exist, Ura Hogg, her alleged sister, did not, and was only mythological. Ima Hogg was named after a heroine in a story of the Civil War written by the governor's older brother. Rennick states that proper documentation of unusual names is a necessity. 9 refs.

[46.16] Sadowski, Cyril; Wheeler, Karen J., & Cash, Michele. (1983). Unusual first names and achievement among male psychologists. _Journal of Social Psychology_, _119_, 181-185.
Four studies were done with unique names. Holders of unique names were overrepresented in Division 10 (Arts) of the American Psychological Association, among writers of social psychology textbooks, and among journal reviewers. Membership ratio in the Division of Personality and Social Psychology was not different. 9 refs.

[46.17] Schonberg, William B., & Murphy, D. Michael. (1974). _Journal of Social Psychology_, _93_, 147-148.
The Edwards Personal Preference Schedule (15 variables) was administered to men and women who had high frequency names (those in the top third of a frequency distribution of the college names) or low frequency names (the lower third) in a test for personality differences. Results with the low frequency men (those with more unique names) had a lower score on the Abasement scale indicating less guilt, inferiority, and timidity, than their more commonly named peers. With women, there were no differences. There were 57 cases in the men's samples; 83, in the women's. 2 refs.

[46.18] Skinner, Nicholas F. (1984). Unusual given names and university grades: A rose by any other name does smell as sweet. _Psychological Reports_, _54_, 546.
Contrary to Joubert [46.12], this Canadian study concludes that unique names do not lead to poorer academic performance. 2 refs.

[46.19] Smith, Elsdon C. (1962). Common American surnames and their relation to eminence. _Names_, _10_, 38-44.
Based upon data from _Who's Who in America_ concludes that unusual surnames are more associated with eminence. 2 refs.

[46.20] Train, John. (1977). Remarkable names of real people. New York Clarkson N. Potter, 64 p.
Introduction by S. J. Perelman. Lists approximately 200 unusual names such as Fanny Finger, Hugh Pugh, and Justin Tune. Most items are referenced. Index.

[46.21] Train, John. (1979). _Even more remarkable names_. New York: Clarkson N. Potter, 64 p.
Forward by Brendan Gill. Lists approximately 155 unusual names. These include Betty Burp, Christ T. Seraphin (a judge), Crystal Toot, and Evan Keel. A number of related names are also included. Index. Many items referenced. Dedication of the book is to the Egyptian god Ptah whom Train feels is the patron of onomastics.

[46.22] Wells, F. L., & Palwick, Helen R. (1950). Notes on usage of male personal names. _Journal of Social Psychology_, _31_, 291-294.
Common male first names were compared with unique names among those

considered eminent in Who's Who and other directories. Most preferred style is first name, middle initial, surname, except by members of the US House of Representatives who preferred the short first name form. 3 refs.

[46.23] Willis, Frank N., Willis, Lois A., & Gier, Joseph A. (1982). Given names, social class, and professional achievement. Psychological Reports, 51, 543-549.
Analyzing a sample of 6300 residents of Kansas City, concludes that unique first names are more frequent for women, the poor, and blacks. Unique first are found most among black poor. 8 refs.

[46.24] Zweigenhaft, Richard L. (1977). The other side of unusual first names. Journal of Social Psychology, 103, 291-302.
Three studies were done on unusual names. Those with unusual names in the Social Register had a better chance of appearing in Who's Who, those in high school had higher IQ scores. Naming of a hypothetical child gave differing evaluations. 16 refs.

[46.25] Zweigenhaft, Richard L. (1981). Unusual names and uniqueness. Journal of Social Psychology, 114, 297-298.
At Guilford College, unusually named women scored higher on the Uniqueness Scale than those with common names; unusually named men scored higher than commonly named men but not significantly so. No significant differences were found with unusual surnames. 1 ref.

[46.26] Zweigenhaft, Richard L. (1983). Unusual first names: A positive outlook. Names, 31, 258-270.
Reviews the literature on unusual names. Integrates work which offers evidence that unusual names thoughtfully chosen can be an advantage. 30 refs. German abstract.

[46.27] Zweigenhaft, Richard L., Hayes, Karen N., & Haagen, C. Hess. (1980). The psychological impact of names. Journal of Social Psychology, 110, 203-210
Results with the California Personality Inventory and unusual names show that: unusually named men and women are no lower; some women score higher; no differences occurred for those with androgynous names; Jrs. did score lower than those with number suffixes. 12 refs.

47. WOMEN AND NAMES

[47.1] Embleton, Sheila M., & King, Ruth. (1984). Attitudes toward maiden name retention. Onomastica Canadiana, No. 66 (December), 11-22.
Brief historical review of the practice of the woman changing her surname at marriage to that of the husband. Results of a Canadian survey at 2 bars. Among other findings, the results indicate that the woman who maintains her maiden name is perceived as being assertive and oriented to the job. 11 refs.

[47.2] Miller, Casey & Swift, Kate. (1976). Words and women. Garden City, NY: Anchor Press/Doubleday, pp. 1-17.
This chapter describes a number of ways in which women are subject to inferior status in the naming process and use of names. For example, women

give up their names at marriage; women are referred to more often by first
name than men. 23 refs.

[47.3] Stannard, Una. (1977). **Mrs. Man.** San Francisco: Germainbooks, 386
p.
Most of the chapters deal with some aspect of women and names, from
pseudonyms to use of maiden name or married name. Describes how name usage
reflects the changing status of women; attention to Lucy Stone and her
importance. Over 350 refs, many relating to some aspect of women and
names.

48. WORDS FROM NAMES

[48.1] Ashley, Leonard R. N.'(1980).   "There be of them that have left a
name behind them": Names from the Bible and common English words.
Christianity and Literature, 30(1), 88-95.
Discussion and explanation behind a number of names from the Bible that
have become words. Examples include: philistine, lucifer, veronica, and
babel. 4 refs.

[48.2] Boycott, Rosie. (1982). **Batty, bloomers and boycott.** New York:
Peter Bedrick Books, 128 p.
Listing of 250-300 words derived from personal names. Thus, batty comes
from Fitzherbert Batty, a Jamaican lawyer who was certified as insane;
bloomers from Amelia Jenks Bloomer who introduced a type of garment; and
boycott from events regarding rent collection by a man with that name in
Ireland.

[48.3] Bryant, Margaret W. (1957). Names in everyday speech. Names, 5,
47-58.
Explanation of how about 100 names of people, gods, literary figures, and
cartoons have come into language. Examples include ampere, Adonis,
doubting Thomas, and Dennis the Menace. 15 refs.

[48.4] Cannon, Garland. (1972). New proper-noun derivatives in American
English. Names, 25, 213-220.
Assesses Webster's 6,000 words (1976) for additions and deletions of words
associated with names included in Webster's Third new international
dictionary (1961) and the 1966 and 1971 Addenda. Other dictionaries also
consulted.   Among items added are: Jesus freak, tesla, Rorschach, and
Chomskian. The dropped names seem to be placename related. 6 refs.

[48.5] Gerus-Tarnawecka, Iraida. (1981). Appellativization of proper names
as a stylistic function. Proceedings of the 13th Congress of Onomastic
Sciences, 1978, Cracow, 1, 425-435.
Surnames can take the function of a lexico-semantical appellative as, a
sandwich, a pullman, a Don Juan, or a Lutheran; or a grammatical one, as
Volta to voltage, Freud to Freudian. In Ukrainian, appellativized names
appear in 5 types of functional style: scientific, official-business,
social-political, belles-lettres, and colloquial. 5 refs.

[48.6] Glaser, Rosemarie. (1985). Proper names in the formation of terms
and nomenclature in the natural and social sciences. XV, Internationaler

Kongress fuer Namenforschung, 1984, Leipzig, 3, 74-80.
Gives a number of categories of words from names. Examples are from
English and German including: Newton's law, kelvin, cardigan, and macadam.
4 refs

[48.7] Hendrickson, Robert. (1972). Human words, Philadelphia: Chilton,
342 p.
Background stories of 3500+ individuals of all types whose name have become
words. Included are: Gallup Poll (George Gallup), marmalade ("Marie est
malade"), and salmonella (Daniel Elmer Salmon). 130+ refs.

[48.8] Highet, Gilbert. (n. d.). Name into word, Audio-Forum No. 23324.
New York: Jeffrey Norton. (Cassette recording)
Entertaining discussion of how words such as nicotine, tawdry, sandwich,
boycott, lynch, and cardigan came into language from the names of people.

[48.9] Nestmann, Ralf. (1984). Motivation and structure of names in
medical language. XV, Internationaler Kongress fuer Namenforschung, 1984,
Leipzig, 3, 164-169.
Discussion and listing of 40+ medical terms derived from names of
individuals. Included are: Graves' disease, Begbie syndrome, Reed cells,
organ of Corti and freudism. 2 refs.

[48.10] Pizer, Vernon. (1981). Take my word for it. New York: Dodd, Mead,
124 p.
Explanation of words such as derrick, candy, booze, shrapnel, praline,
bowdlerize, graham cracker, mesmerize, and others which are derived from
the names of people.

[48.11] Sorel, Nancy Caldwell. (1970). Word people. New York: American
Heritage, 304 p.
Gives the background stories of about 80 words that are derived from the
names of people. Included are: bloomer, braille, dahlia, doily, dunce,
nicotine, and watt.

[48.12] Strix. (1959, March 6). The striggle naught availeth. The
Spectator, 202, p. 326.
Brief witty comment on names such as Quisling, Ohm, and Shrapnel which have
become words. 1 ref.

[48.13] U., L. (1981, August). Onomastic nervosa. Verbatim, 8, p. 6.
Gives the meaning of about 50 common slang names, Molly = a screw for
plaster walls, Virgin Mary = a Bloody Mary without vodka.

[48.14] Urdang, Laurence & Ruffner, Frederick G., Jr. (Eds.). (1982).
Allusions: Cultural, literary, Biblical, and historical: A thematic
dictionary. Detroit, MI: Gale,487 p.
Contains more than 7000 references in 628 thematic categories. Many of the
references are from personal names, ex., in the Curiosity theme, there are
Lot's wife and Nosy Parker (from a meddlesome Elizabethan archbishop).
Other entries include Calamity Jane, Captain Bligh, and Lucullus whose
names have become words. Over 1100 refs. but this is for all entries.

[48.15]   Wolk, Allan. (1980). <u>Everyday words from names of people and
places</u>. New York: Elsevier/Nelson, 315 p.
Lists approximately 1500 words that come from literature, people, places,
ethnic, and religious group names. Among the words are zeppelin, Baedeker,
ohm, and pasteurization.

AUTHOR INDEX

Scheetz, George H. 1.11,
8.23.2.38
Schmidt, Herbert, Mrs. 26.1.23
Schmidt, Jacob E. 10.3.9
Schoen, Robert & Nelson, Verne E.
35.3
Schoenfeld, Nathan. 41.42
Schonberg, William B., & Murphy, D.
Michael. 46.17
Schwartz, David S. 22.15
Schwartz, Stephen P. 8.28.10,
25.1.16
Searle, John R. 22.16
Seary, E. R., & Lynch, Sheila M. P.
8.12.10
Seeman, Mary V. 25.2.13, 34.1.5,
34.2.23, 34.2.24, 34.5.18
Segal, Mady Wechsler. 4.5
Seits, Laurence E. 41.43
Selby, Maija L.; Lee, Eun Sul;
Tuttle, Dorothy M., & Loe, Hardy
D., Jr. 35.4
Selishchev, A. M. 8.55.16
Selten, Bo. 8.23.1.23, 8.23.1.24,
8.23.1.25, 8.23.1.26
Senn, Alfred. 8.43.2, 8.63.4
Seraydarian, Louisa & Busse, Thomas
V. 41.44
Shah, Sayed Idries. 17.10
Shankle, George E. 26.1.24
Shanta, M. A. 8.33.10
Sharma, Mohan Lal. 8.33.11,
8.33.12
Sharp, Harold S. 33.9
Shaul, David L. 8.3.15
Sheby, David. 8.40.28
Sheppard, David. 8.23.1.27, 41.45
Sherif, Muzafer & Cantril, Hadley.
1.10
Shevoroskin, V. 8.5.14
Shin, Eui-Hang & Yu, Eui-Young.
8.41.1
Sholola, Bandele. 8.2.40, 8.2.41
Sibata, Takesi. 8.39.5
Sifakis, Carl. 26.1.25
Silverman, Michael Henry. 8.5.15,
8.40.29
Singerman, Robert. 6.14
Skinner, Alanson. 8.3.16
Skinner, Nicholas F. 46.18
Skipper, James K., Jr. 26.1.26,
26.1.27, 26.1.28, 26.1.29,
26.1.30, 26.1.31
Slavutych, Yar. 8.65.6, 8.65.7,
8.65.8
Sleigh, Linwood & Johnson, Charles.

10.3.10, 10.3.11
Slobin, Dan I., Miller, Stephen H.,
& Porter, Lyman W. 2.9
Slovenko, Ralph. 1.12, 20.11,
20.12, 20.13
Smallman, Mary H. 24.14
Smart, Veronica. 8.23.1.28
Smith, Daniel Scott. 25.3.24,
25.3.25, 25.3.26
Smith, Elmer Lewis. 8.4.3
Smith, Elmer Lewis; Stewart, John
G., & Kyger, M. Ellsworth.
25.3.27
Smith, Elsdon C. 1.13, 1.14,
1.15, 6.15, 6.16, 7.22, 10.3.12,
12.11, 43.1.17, 43.1.18, 43.2.7,
43.2.8, 46.19
Smith, F. Porter 8.16.6
Smith, H. Allen. 26.1.32, 43.2.9
Smith, William Carlson. 7.23
Snyder, C. R., & Fromkin, Howard L.
34.5.19, 36.3
Social Security Administration.
43.1.16
Sondergaard, George. 8.21.5
Sorel, Nancy Caldwell. 48.11
Sorensen, Holger Steen. 22.17
Sosnowski, Jan. 8.55.19
Sotiroff, George. 8.28.11,
8.58.7, 12.12
Spears, James E. 26.1.33
Speer, David G. 8.26.7
Spencer, Robert F. 8.64.1
Spier, Leslie & Sapir, Edward.
8.3.17
St. Clair-Sobell, James. 8.55.17
St. Clair-Sobell, James & Carlsen,
8.55.18
St. Mary's College Symposium.
8.52.10
Staats, Arthur W., Higa, William
R., & Reid, Ian. 34.6.20
Staff. 1.16, 7.24
Stamm, Johann Jakob. 5.1.12
Stampfer, Judah. 34.5.20
Stan, Aurelia & Stan, Ioan. 40.2
Stankiewicz, Edward. 8.55.20
Stannard, Una. 20.14, 20.15,
47.3
Stark, Jurgen Kurt. 8.5.16
Starnes, D. T. 25.2.14
Stekel, Wilhelm. 34.2.25
Stephens, J. C. 29.16
Stevenson, Noel C. 20.16
Stewart, George R. 1.17, 10.1.7,
24.15

SUBJECT INDEX

Note: The term <u>Name</u> (or <u>Names</u>) is assumed to follow many of the categories such as Change, Ethnic, or Unique.

The following abbreviations have been used:

anc.   ancient.
isl.   island.
lang.   language or dialect.
reg.   region or area.
tri.   tribe, refers to any culture, people, or society

Major sections are in capitals and the entries in those sections have been placed first.

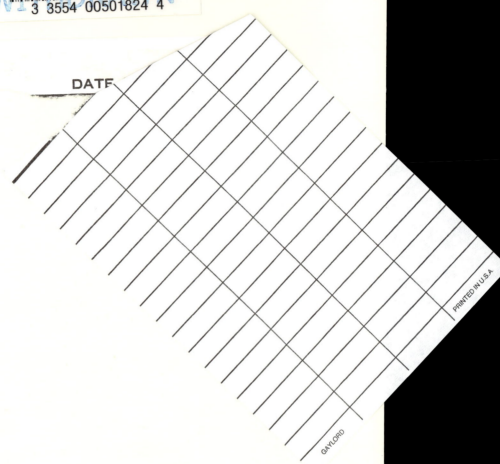